Controlling und Rechnungslegung – Managerial and Financial Accounting

Reihe herausgegeben von
M. Lachmann, Berlin, Deutschland

In dieser Reihe werden aktuelle Forschungserkenntnisse im Bereich Controlling und Rechnungslegung publiziert. Methodisch liegt der Schwerpunkt auf empirischen und experimentellen Studien, die den Erkenntnisstand für Wissenschaft und Praxis erweitern und vertiefen. Forschungsarbeiten, die in dieser Reihe veröffentlicht werden, nehmen eine innovative Sichtweise auf aktuelle Themenstellungen im Bereich Controlling oder Rechnungslegung ein und generieren auf Basis anspruchsvoller Forschungsmethoden neuartige wissenschaftliche Erkenntnisse. Ein Fokus wird dabei auf verhaltensorientierte Aspekte von Controlling und Rechnungslegung gelegt.

This series aims to provide an outlet for recent research in the areas of managerial and financial accounting. It includes empirical and experimental studies that contribute to a deeper understanding of accounting theory and practice. Research published in this series takes an innovative view on current topics in managerial and financial accounting to provide novel insights based on rigorous research design. A focus of this series are behavioral aspects of managerial and financial accounting.

Weitere Bände in der Reihe http://www.springer.com/series/16139

Theresa Herrmann

The Decision Usefulness of Additional Fair Value Disclosures

One Disclosure Type Does Not Fit All Nonprofessional Investors' Needs

With a foreword by Prof. Dr. Maik Lachmann

Springer Gabler

Theresa Herrmann
Berlin, Germany

Dissertation Technische Universität Berlin, 2018

u. d. T. The decision usefulness of additional disclosures on fair value estimates for nonprofessional investors: One disclosure type does not fit all

ISSN 2524-5686 ISSN 2524-5694 (electronic)
Controlling und Rechnungslegung – Managerial and Financial Accounting
ISBN 978-3-658-24831-4 ISBN 978-3-658-24832-1 (eBook)
https://doi.org/10.1007/978-3-658-24832-1

Library of Congress Control Number: 2018965238

Springer Gabler

This Springer Gabler imprint is published by the registered company Springer Fachmedien Wiesbaden GmbH part of Springer Nature
The registered company address is: Abraham-Lincoln-Str. 46, 65189 Wiesbaden, Germany

Foreword

In recent years, there has been an ongoing and controversial discussion on the decision usefulness and reliability of fair value estimates. Additional disclosures are often considered as a pathway to increase the decision usefulness of fair values, but may also result in information overload for investors. In this context, this research investigates why some disclosures on fair value estimates are not incorporated into nonprofessional investors' investment decisions. Further, it is explored if the aim of the standard setter to mandate disclosures on assets measured at fair value can be met. Conducting an experiment, this study analyzes whether the exclusion of information is caused by the *presentation format* or the *content*, and whether this depends on the development of the fair value of a firm's key asset (gain vs. loss). The results of this experimental study indicate first, that the decision usefulness at the financial statement level is significantly determined by the reliability of both the fair value of a firm's key asset and the reliability of the financial statement. Second, the presentation format affects the acquisition and correct evaluation of information, but these findings are not independent of the development of the firm's key asset measured at fair value. Nonprofessional investors are more likely to acquire and evaluate fair value information correctly when the information is presented salient with a gain compared to a loss. Third, with a fair value gain, none of the disclosure information significantly increases decision usefulness, irrespective of the presentation format. When a fair value loss occurs, fair value disclosures presented in a salient presentation format significantly decrease decision usefulness. Thus, investors become aware of the low reliability of fair values only when disclosure information is presented saliently. The standard setter originally mandated disclosures to make the corresponding financial statement items more decision-useful for investors. It seems that this aim cannot be met for saliently displayed disclosures with a fair value loss. Overall, the results indicate that investors have varying needs regarding the presentation format, depending on the development of the company's key assets.

Against the background of the ongoing discussion on information overload in the context of fair values, this research considerably contributes to a deeper understanding of the decision making-processes of nonprofessional investors and thereby addresses a timely and innovative topic. I am therefore convinced that this book will find an interested and broad readership.

Prof. Dr. Maik Lachmann

v

Acknowledgement

This dissertation was submitted for obtaining the degree of Doctor of Philosophy (in German: Dr. rer. oec.) at the Technical University of Berlin. The research described herein was conducted under the supervision of Prof. Maik Lachmann at the department of financial accounting and management control, Technical University of Berlin, between January 2015 and April 2018.

First, I would like to thank Prof. Maik Lachmann. I am very grateful for his supervision, support, enthusiasm and knowledge concerning my research project. With his sincere and genuine manner, he greatly contributed to the success of this project. Further, I would like to thank Prof. Hans Hirth for being the second assessor of my dissertation.

A big thank you goes to Daniel Lutter and Thorben Ehrlich for enabling the collection of my data as well as Prof. James R. Moon. He gave me valuable feedback on my project during my stay as a visiting researcher at Georgia State University in Atlanta (USA). I want to thank my colleagues Anna Faust and Hanna Schachel for their review of several presentations and manuscripts as well as their guidance, tireless support and motivation. Besides, I would like to thank Lisa-Marie Wibbeke for her organizational help with my experiment.

For all the positive memories I created during my time as a research assistant at the Technical University of Berlin, I would like to thank our secretary Susan Mehr as well as my colleagues Dr. Karola Bastini, David Dang, Fares Getzin, Christoph Groth-Tonberge, Franziska Spallek and Sophia Stark.

A very special thank you goes out to my family and friends who have supported me in every possible way throughout all different stages in my life. Specifically, I am very grateful for my husband's tolerance, never-ending support and affectionate optimism through all ups and downs of my dissertation. I dedicate this work to him.

Dr. Theresa Herrmann

Acknowledgement

This [illegible] for obtaining the degree of Doctor of Philosophy in [illegible] [illegible] [illegible] was conducted [illegible] University of Stirling between January 201[illegible] and [illegible] 2018.

First, I would like to thank [illegible] [illegible]

[illegible]

[illegible]

[illegible]

Table of content

List of abbreviations

AMEX	American Stock Exchange
AG	Aktiengesellschaft *(Public limited company)*
APV	Adjusted Present Value
BC	Basis for conclusion
BCIN	Basis for conclusion (on the conceptual framework for financial reporting)
cf.	confer *(compare)*
DCF	Discounted cash flow
EBIT	Earnings before interest, tax
EBT	Earnings before tax
ED	Exposure Draft
EFRAG	European Financial Reporting Advisory Group
e.g.	exempli gratia *(for example)*
EPS	Earnings per share
EU	European Union
EY	Ernst and Young Global Limited
FASB	Financial Accounting Standards Board
FD	Fair disclosure
FTE	Flow-to-equity
US-GAAP	United States Generally accepted accounting principles
H	Hypothesis
IASB	International Accounting Standards Board
ICAS	Institute of Chartered Accountants of Scotland
IDW	Institut der Wirtschaftsprüfer (e.V.) *(Institute of Auditors in Germany)*
i.e.	id est *(this is/this means)*

IFRS	International Financial Reporting Standards
IVS	International Valuation Standards
IVSC	International Valuation Standards Committee
kEUR	Thousand Euro
N/A	Not applicable
NASDAQ	National Association of Securities Dealers Automated Quotations
NPI	Nonprofessional investor
NYSE	New York Stock Exchange
OCI	Other comprehensive income
OECD	Organization for Economic Co-operation and Development
P/E	Price/Earnings
PPE	Property, plant and equipment
pwc	PricewaterhouseCoopers GmbH Wirtschaftsprüfungsgesellschaft
RICS	Royal Institution of Chartered Surveyors
RQ	Research question
S	Supporting information
SEC	Securities and Exchange Comission
SFAS	Statement of Financial Accounting Standards
SOX	Sarbanes-Oxley-Act
TCF	Total cash flow
TEGoVA	European Group of Valuers Association
UK	United Kingdom
US	United States (of America)
vs.	versus
WACC	Weighted average cost of capital

List of figures

List of tables

List of equations

1 Introduction

1.1 Motivation and scope

As a structured medium, financial statements intend to provide decision-useful financial accounting information for investors (Guay et al., 2016). Due to the growing complexity of accounting rules, the requirements for these financial statement information have strongly increased over the past 15 years, resulting in a potential disclosure overload for investors (Guay et al., 2016; Siegel, 2018). Consequently, the Financial Accounting Standards Board (FASB) made the improvement of disclosure effectiveness one of their main goals and initiated the disclosure framework project (Siegel, 2018). Financial statement information is considered effective when the presented information is reliable and decision-useful (IASB, 2015).

The disclosure overload problem especially applies to assets and liabilities measured at fair value (Landsman, 2007). Fair values are often not measured in a reliable manner, which is why their disclosure information is of high importance to provide further and more detailed information to investors. Despite these disclosures, financial statement users, particularly nonprofessional investors (NPIs), often fail to incorporate these disclosures into their investment decision processes (Clor-Proell et al., 2014).

In this thesis, I will draw on prior work that calls for researchers to examine the variation of reliability and to better understand the role of fair value disclosures (McDonough & Shakespeare, 2015). I will address this call and explore the effects of a change in the fair value development (gain vs. loss) on the reliability and decision usefulness of fair value disclosures. Further, prior research suggests that additional information in the notes of financial statements can increase reliability for financial statement users (Hodge et al., 2004; Pitt, 2001). This approach concludes that enclosing additional information does not (always) lead to a higher perceived reliability of accounting data and might result in disclosure overload (Beerbaum, 2016). By introducing different types of disclosure categorization (qualitative vs. quantitative), I will assess what type of disclosure delivers the greatest benefits in terms of decision usefulness for its users. Specifically, I will test the qualitative disclosure on the fair value hierarchy, the quantitative disclosure on the sensitivity analysis, and the quantitative disclosure on the reconciliation between carrying amounts. By using these three different types of disclosures, my study will differentiate between a qualitative disclosure, a range value (sensitivity analysis), and change value (reconciliation between carrying amounts). My results point out new ways to design and organize disclosures to be more decision-useful for NPIs. By adjusting fair value disclosures more precisely to the key asset specifics, less disclosures may be necessary and decision usefulness can be improved compared to the current disclosure policy.

To evaluate the effects of my manipulations, I have utilized the widely used framework by Maines and McDaniel (2000) (Clor-Proell et al., 2014; Lachmann et al., 2015; Müller et al., 2015; Reimsbach et al., 2017). The framework divides information processing into three steps: the acquisition, evaluation and weighting of information, followed by a performance assessment judgement. To acquire information, a person stores and recalls previously read

T. Herrmann, *The Decision Usefulness of Additional Fair Value Disclosures*, Controlling und Rechnungslegung – Managerial and Financial Accounting,
https://doi.org/10.1007/978-3-658-24832-1_1

information from memory. Information acquisition is necessary for an individual to be able to evaluate the stored and recalled information correctly. By weighting the previously acquired and correctly evaluated information, the individual considers the importance of the information for the assessment of the firm's performance (Maines & McDaniel, 2000).

Using this framework will also allow me to distinguish between the salient presentation of disclosure information and the current presentation format required by the International Financial Reporting Standards (IFRS). My design will allow me to evaluate the degree of reliability and decision usefulness based on the format or content of the disclosure information. I predict that the acquisition of information is more likely if fair value related information is presented more saliently. To increase the level of salience, I have applied a novel approach and presented fair value related information in an additional column in the balance sheet. I further predict that information acquisition is more likely when the salient information is presented with a fair value gain compared to a fair value loss, as a fair value gain represents a non-extreme level of earnings for investors (Erickson et al., 2017; Hayn, 1995).

As a result, I expect that investors who acquire the information from a more salient presentation will also more likely evaluate the information correctly and place higher weight on the information (Maines & McDaniel, 2000), and thus can more ably judge the reliability and decision usefulness of the accounting figures. In addition, I predict that information evaluation is more likely to be correct when the related fair value information is presented in a salient manner with a fair value gain compared to a fair value loss. This prediction will remain unchanged for the weights investors place on related fair value information as I predict that the weighting of fair value information will be higher if the related fair value information is presented in a salient manner with a fair value gain compared to a fair value loss.

To extend prior research on format effects that exclusively examines (fair value) gains (Clor-Proell et al., 2014; Hodge et al., 2010; Maines & McDaniel, 2000), I will analyze both fair value gains and losses. Following earlier research contributions on fair value gains, I predict that the salient presentation of fair value disclosure information will lead to an increase in the perceived reliability and decision usefulness for NPIs with a fair value gain. Still, the probability of a fair value varying is high (Barth et al., 1995; Song, 2015) and almost all firms face (fair value) gains and losses over time (Hayn, 1995; Manchiraju et al., 2015). These gains and losses are perceived differently by investors (Hou et al., 2014) since investors perceive losses as extreme levels of earnings, which makes them less informative than gains (Hayn, 1995; Kahneman & Tversky, 1979). The investor's perception of risk is lower when earnings are smooth relative to extreme levels of earnings (e.g., losses) (Erickson et al., 2017).

For a fair value loss, I predict that a salient presentation of a fair value disclosure will emphasize the underlying measurement subjectivity of an asset measured at fair value. This would lead to a decrease in reliability and decision usefulness for NPIs. The result would suggest that the intention of the International Accounting Standards Board (IASB) to mandate fair value disclosures to make fair values more reliable would not be attained. I further suggest that the perceived reliability and decision usefulness for NPIs is lower when fair value information is presented saliently with a fair value loss compared to a fair value gain. My results based on this suggestion would emphasize the importance of distinguishing between gains and losses. Moreover, these research questions examine, first, the causes of the struggle of NPIs to incorporate fair value disclosures into their decision-making process and, second, the type of disclosure (quantitative or qualitative) that leads to the highest and lowest reliability and decision usefulness with either a fair value gain or loss. The results would help to better understand NPIs' disclosure information needs.

The framework by Maines and McDaniel (2000) that I use in this thesis does not only divide information processing into three steps but also researches on how format effects influence performance assessment judgements. These assessments are important for making an investment decision or when buying shares. I thus further predict that if decision usefulness of information is high, NPIs will feel more capable of making an investment decision compared to when the decision usefulness of financial statements is low. Besides, I predict that when the level of decision usefulness is high, NPIs will rather decide to purchase shares of a firm.

To test my predictions, I have used a 4 x 2 between-subjects design that manipulates the presentation format of fair value related information (current format, fair value hierarchy, sensitivity analysis, reconciliation between carrying amounts between prior year to current year) as well as the fair value development of investment properties compared to the previous year (gain vs. loss). In the current format, disclosures are presented according to the IFRS, while the other experimental treatments present the respective disclosure information salient in the balance sheet in an additional column to facilitate information acquisition. While presenting disclosure information in the additional column next to the fair value in the balance sheet, I have referred to this related fair value disclosure information as *additional disclosure*. By doing so, I have made the disclosure information salient to the financial statement user. This presentation format does not apply to disclosures in the current format mandated under the IFRS, where disclosures are displayed in the footnotes only. The participants were assigned randomly to one of the eight treatments and had limited time to read the financial statements. The questions they answered throughout this experiment allowed me to observe how the manipulations affect the NPIs' information processing and judgements on reliability and decision usefulness. I conducted this experiment with 190 career starters at a Big Four accounting firm, who serve as proxies for NPIs with a decent accounting knowledge. I utilized career starters as participants because they have the requisite academic degrees, essential accounting knowledge, and professional experience to qualify as proxies for the NPIs in tasks characterized with high integrative complexity (Elliott et al., 2007).

With my research, I will first provide evidence that decision usefulness is determined by the reliability of a firm's key asset. This indicates that a firm can increase the decision usefulness of the financial statement by providing reliable information on fair values. Further, and consistent with my expectations, I find that the information acquisition of fair value information is more likely with salient fair value disclosures. When salient disclosures are presented with a fair value gain compared to a fair value loss, information acquisition is more likely. The format of the disclosure information does not affect the correct evaluation of information in general but NPIs seem to be more likely to evaluate information correctly with a fair value gain compared to a fair value loss. The weighting of fair value information is not significantly higher when the related information is presented in a salient disclosure format. Contrary to what I predict, the weight NPIs place on the value of a firm's key asset are higher with a fair value loss compared to a fair value gain.

I also examine the differences in reliability and decision usefulness between a fair value gain and loss. With a fair value gain, the reliability and decision usefulness of the NPIs increase most with the additional disclosure on sensitivity analysis data compared to the current format; still, the result is not significant. When NPIs face a fair value loss, all types of salient disclosure information cause a decrease in both the reliability and decision usefulness of the information. The decrease is strongest when the sensitivity analysis is presented saliently. Therefore, NPIs become aware of the low reliability only when additional disclosures are presented with a fair value loss. In my additional analysis, I find that the higher NPIs rate decision usefulness, the more they feel capable of making an investment decision. Moreover, with a higher reliability, NPIs are more likely to invest in a company.

Collectively, my results indicate that the information needs of NPIs differ depending on the development of the firm's key asset. Furthermore, the current format of disclosures is a curse and blessing at the same time; it is most reliable and decision-useful for NPIs with a fair value loss but the least reliable and decision-useful with a fair value gain. Even though format changes affect reliability and decision usefulness, I find that with a constant format, reliability and decision usefulness vary. With a fair value loss, additional disclosures highlight the uncertainty of fair values and thus decrease reliability and decision usefulness. Consequently, and opposite to what was intended by the standard setter, disclosures decrease reliability and decision usefulness with a fair value loss. Finally, to improve decision usefulness for NPIs, disclosures should be tailored to the development of a firm's key asset instead of pursuing a "one-fits-all approach."

My findings contribute to the growing literature stream on how format changes facilitate the information processing of investors (Clor-Proell et al., 2014; Hodge et al., 2004; Hodge et al., 2010; Maines & McDaniel, 2000; Reimsbach et al., 2017). Format changes affect reliability and decision usefulness when the content is held constant. But even after varying the content, I find that format changes could no longer facilitate the information processing of investors. Thus, NPIs struggle to incorporate fair value disclosures into their decision-making process due to the content and not the format of the information.

In addition, I provide practical advice and contribute to the literature stream on disclosure overload (Beerbaum, 2016; Eppler & Mengis, 2004). The FASB and the IASB aim to develop a disclosure framework to address complaints by investors on disclosure overload (IASB, 2013). My results point out new ways to design and organize disclosures to be more decision-useful for NPIs. By tailoring fair value disclosures to the key asset and presenting them in the balance sheet, less mandatory disclosures are necessary and decision usefulness can be improved compared to the current disclosure policy.

1.2 General structure

This thesis first concentrates on the financial reporting for capital market participants (chapter 2: Financial reporting for capital market participants). This topic is divided into subtopics starting with the theoretical background of the accounting principles and their design. Further, the development of the IFRS Framework will be described as this work focuses on these international accounting principles. By doing so, the main objectives of the standards will be pointed out and the latest changes to the framework will be outlined. As the decision usefulness of the accounting information is one of the main purposes of financial reporting, qualitative and quantitative characteristics of decision useful information, with a focus on the qualitative characteristics, will be explained. In the next step, the concept of fair value measurement will be evaluated, as this is driven by the fact that the standard setter aims to provide highly decision useful information to the financial statement users. When explaining the concept of fair value in general, I considered the valuation of investment properties specifically as this is the context where this experiment was set into. Besides, the different types of disclosures that are mandated by the standard setter for these kinds of assets are also discussed. The fair value followed by the evaluation of specific characteristics of real estate valuation is also pointed out.

The next chapter (chapter 3: Differences in information needs and usage by capital providers) deals with the differences in information needs and usage by capital providers. The characteristics of the different types of capital providers will be explained: equity investors, which is further distinguished between outside professional, private, and retail as well as inside and family ownership equity providers; debt investors and trade creditors. Subsequently, the differences in information usage and information claims of these different types of capital providers are pointed out. In this context, the stewardship roles of financial decision-making as well as the importance of decision usefulness in the context are focused on. The second part of this chapter deals with the information processing of capital market participants. The key aspect of information processing as well as ways of problem solving using decision heuristics are illustrated. Distinction between professional and NPIs (professional vs. NPI) is shown with focus on NPIs as this thesis focuses on knowledgeable but nonprofessional equity providers.
In chapter 4: Theoretical background and predictions on facilitating the usage of disclosures for investors, the research questions and hypotheses are provided. First, the ways to facilitate the usage of disclosure information is looked at. Then, the mandated disclosures for investment properties measured at fair value will be categorized into three different categories. Further, how these fair value disclosures are incorporated into the decision-making process of the NPIs will also be explained in this chapter. Second, for my hypotheses, I have chosen four different subtopics. The first subtopic affiliates the relationship between the perceived reliability and decision usefulness of accounting information. The second subtopic deals with the information processing of NPIs. I use the framework introduced by Maines and McDaniel (2000) to make predictions on disclosure presentation and information processing. The third subtopic deals with my mediating effect, which is the development of the fair value compared to the prior period (gain vs. loss) and makes predictions on the perceived reliability and decision usefulness of accounting information when disclosure information is presented in different ways with both a fair value gain and loss compared to the previous period. The last subtopic makes predictions

on the investment decision of investors and how information processing may influence them. This chapter closes with a presentation of an overview of all hypotheses and pointing out of the connections between the hypotheses topics.

The research question and hypotheses chapter is followed by the chapter on the method (chapter 5) used for my research. The experimental setting as well as the participants and design will be described. This chapter will close with the materials and procedures used for the experiment. Next, the results of the experiment (chapter 6) will be presented. It will start with the manipulation check results before pointing out the results for the hypotheses in the same order it was originally deduced and presented. Some additional analysis is performed and the results for the research questions are stated. This thesis closes with a discussion of the results (chapter 7).

2 Financial reporting for capital market participants

This chapter will deal with the theoretical background of the accounting principles. I will shed light on the design of the principles and point out their main objectives. This includes information on the general purpose and objectives of financial reporting, which include providing decision-useful accounting information. Further, I will point out the qualitative characteristics of decision-useful accounting information and ultimately link the decision usefulness of accounting information to the fair value approach introduced by the standard setter. By doing so, I will clarify the concept of fair value for investment properties as I chose this type of assets as my research context.

2.1 Theoretical principles of accounting

Entrepreneurs have been trying to make their economic actions transparent for themselves and others by reporting business numbers or figures. This process is called accounting (Pellens et al., 2014). Accounting is defined as the process of identifying, as well as measuring, recording, and classifying economic information (American Accounting Association, 1966; Sterling, 1967). Furthermore, this information is interpreted by information users and communicated by entrepreneurs. The aim of the process of accounting is to facilitate the decision-making of users by utilizing accounting data (Belkaoui, 1991). Unlike cost accounting (management accounting), where the main objective is self-information, financial accounting primarily serves the objective of informing parties outside a company on the financial status of a company and is subject to national and international accounting standards. Even though accounting principles have developed differently in various countries in the past, the basic components of accounting are the same worldwide, consisting of a balance sheet, a profit and loss statement or an (internal) income statement, and, depending on the size of a company, a cash-flow statement. While the balance sheet accounts for inventories on a reporting date, the profit and loss statement is a periodical calculation that accounts for changes in the inventories (Pellens et al., 2014; Watts & Zimmerman, 1978).

Generally, accounting is based on an individual or a group of individuals, who know(s) more about the/an accounting entity than other individuals, particularly the recipients of financial reporting. This "more" on knowledge about the accounting entity entitles the information asymmetry in the economic sense (Diamond & Verrecchia, 1991; Evans, 2016; Lambert et al., 2011). This asymmetry is addressed by financial reporting with the aim to decrease it (Evans, 2016). Due to this, the basic purpose of financial accounting is the reduction of information asymmetry between the accounting entity and the recipients of financial reporting (Akerlof, 1970; Pellens et al., 2014; Stiglitz, 2000). Financial accounting is generally public and, thus, available to an unlimited number of recipients. Still, contractual partners usually show the greatest interest in the financial accounting figures of a firm. This is because, primarily, individuals who have a direct contractual relationship with an entity take the time to evaluate accounting publications in detail. Thus, people or institutions that fulfill these mentioned requirements are the primary user group of financial reports according to the IFRS. This group consists of potential and existing investors, creditors, and other lenders. These individuals are

T. Herrmann, *The Decision Usefulness of Additional Fair Value Disclosures*,
Controlling und Rechnungslegung – Managerial and Financial Accounting,
https://doi.org/10.1007/978-3-658-24832-1_2

not in a position to require information to be provided to them directly according to Exposure Draft (ED) /2015/4 as defined by the IASB (2015-Basis for Conclusion (BC) 1.11).

The meta-purpose of the financial reporting to be informative addresses two more specific information needs: to account for past actions and to provide information with which the future development of a company and, ultimately, the enterprise value can be estimated. The process of accounting past actions is also known as *coordination function*. This is because the accountability primarily serves the contract coordination and, thus, consequently the direct and indirect behavioral control of the corporate players. The other mentioned information need is also known as *valuation function* because future information serves the primary purpose of valuation needs (IASB, 2015). The coordination and the valuation function are not identical. There are future financial information that has no implications on the information of the firm's past actions. Such information can be useful for the valuation of shares but potentially not for manager compensation contracts. On the other hand, coordination information can enhance an effective firm coordination, even though it might be irrelevant for valuation purposes. Consequently, the communication of a firm always must depend on the respective situation (Pellens et al., 2014).

2.2 Design of accounting principles

There is an ongoing debate about which type of accounting standard is better suited to meet the objectives of financial reposting (FASB, 2016): *principles-based* or *rules-based accounting standards*. While too many abstract principles can lead to problems in terms of comparability, too many rules can lead to high complexity and, thus, cause difficulties in applying them correctly (Kaburek, 2016). This debate reached its heights after the accounting scandals of Enron and Worldcom and, consequently, the demise of Arthur Anderson, a former auditing firm known as a part of the Big Five. Especially with regard to the Enron fiasco, rules-based accounting principles such as the United States Generally Accepted Accounting Principles (US-GAAP) were held responsible (Braun et al., 2015). With the detailed guidance and bright-line tests provided by the US-GAAP, research claims that earnings manipulation was enabled. This was done by not following the economic substance of transactions but rather the "letter of law" (Schipper, 2003). Addressing the failure of Enron and, consequently, the misleading result of the accounting procedures revealed during the investigations were directly addressed by the Sarbanes-Oxley-Act (SOX) in 2002 (Benston et al., 2006). This act included a provision for the Securities and Exchange Commission (SEC) to investigate whether the adoption of a principles-based accounting system could be an option to prevent such scandals in the future (SOX 2002, Section 108(d)). The SEC, specifically the chief accountant office of economic analysis, fulfilled this obligation and issued a 68-page long report (SEC, 2003). The FASB responded to this report in July 2004 and agreed with the SEC on nearly all matters (FASB, 2004).

As a member of the FASB, Schipper (2003) investigates to what extent principles-based accounting already exists in the United States (US). The author argues that a rules-based approach fosters a "check-box" mentality. Some researchers claim that this mentality could undermine high quality financial accounting. A principles-based approach like the IFRS (IFRS

Foundation, 2016)[1] on the other hand allows and requires an appropriate amount of professional judgement (Peytcheva et al., 2014). While the rules-based approach has a lot of scope and treatment exceptions, the principles-based approach does not. Also, detailed implementation guidance is usually necessary for the rules-based approach. Consequently, the US-GAAP are seen as a rules-based approach as they require a high amount of implementation guidance even though they are based on recognizable principles (Schipper, 2003) and ultimately on the FASB (2004). Possible effects regarding the implementation of a principles-based approach over a rules-based approach affect the preparer and auditor expertise, inconsistencies in financial reporting, transition, the interaction between the reporting standards and corporate governance, as well as the volatility of reported income. The latter is one of the main subjects to initiate research on the debate of principles- vs. rules-based standards (Braun et al., 2015).

Early research in this field indicates that preparers of financial statements are less likely to classify operating leases as operating when relying on the principles-based standards compared to when relying on the more precise rules-based standard (Psaros & Trotman, 2004). Agoglia et al. (2011) find that CFOs are more likely to report aggressively when applying a rules-based approach compared to the less precise principles-based approach. The reporting is not only influenced by the applied approach but also by the presence of a strong audit committee. While using a rules-based standard, the type of auditor (principles oriented, rules-oriented, or client-oriented) does not influence the tendency of managers to report transactions off-balance sheet. This is different when a principles-based approach is applied. In fact, the tendency to report off-balance sheet is lowest when the auditor is principles-oriented. These findings indicate that a further movement toward a principles-based approach and, thus, the application of IFRS (IFRS Foundation, 2016) may improve the quality of financial reporting, when there is also a change in the mind-set of the auditor toward a more principle-oriented approach (Jamal & Tan, 2010). The principles-based approach of accounting standards further increases the process accountability of auditors, which is defined as the expectation of having to justify their decision process to others independent of the decision outcome (Libby et al., 2004; Markman & Tetlock, 2000; Peytcheva et al., 2014).

Besides research that supports the development of a principles-based approach for financial reporting, there are also contributions that provide somewhat conflicting findings in the debate of principles- vs. rules-based approach (Niemeier, 2008; Schipper, 2003). One big disadvantage in the principles-based approach is the space for interpretation, which will ultimately lead to lower quality financial reports and a decrease in audit quality. In addition, as the approach calls for significant judgement, manipulation of the management and pressure on the management to judge situations in a certain way could be an objective. Keeping this in mind, the approach could decrease perceived reliability for financial statement readers as the provided information is less objective when significant judgements are necessary. Nevertheless, latest research

[1] According to Pellens et al. (2014), the principles-based approach of the IFRS becomes clearer in the most recently released IFRS standards. Especially with regard to older IFRS and IAS standards, the view of IFRS being strongly principles-based is seen critically (Heuser (2012)).

contributions in this field argue that the principle-based approach is more advantageous for financial statement preparers and users (Peytcheva et al., 2014).

Consequently, the FASB seeks to improve the benefits of financial reporting for investors and other users of financial information. The board does so by setting high standards like the US-GAAP. Besides the standards on a US-level, the FASB seeks to provide internationally comparable information for which more comparable global accounting standards are necessary. This comparability is aimed to be achieved by a closer alignment of the standards on the US- and European-level. Standards that are easier to compare will further reduce costs for preparers and users. Thus, the SEC requires the FASB to consider comparability when the board develops new standards. This comparability is supposed to increase the bilateral convergence program that was started in 2002 by the FASB and the IASB. In the three-part strategy with the aim to increase convergence, the FASB plans to develop GAAP standards of high quality, participate actively in the development of IFRS standards, and enhance relations with other national standards setters (FASB, 2017). The IFRS, in their current form, are principles-based standards and the setting I choose for my research.

The principles-based IFRS consists of the IFRS itself, the International Accounting Standards (IAS) set by the International Accounting Standards Committee (IASC), and completed by the interpretation of the standards by the International Financial Reporting Interpretation Committee (IFRIC) (Pellens et al., 2014). The standards as well as the interpretations are enclosed by the conceptual framework. The core piece of the set of rules according to the IFRS are the accounting standards in a broader sense. The standards, together with the IAS that were developed prior to 2002 but are still applicable, are subsumed under the term IFRS in practice. This also includes the corresponding interpretations by the Standards Interpretations Committee (SIC) as well as the IFRIC (IASB, 2015).

The IFRS standards follow a uniform structure and start with an introduction followed by their objective as well as their scope. This rather general information is followed by specific information in terms of recognition, measurement, and disclosure requirements. The standards close with the transitional provisions and effective date. Any standard may be supplemented by additional guidance regarding the definition of the key terms of the standard. Moreover, implementation guidance, illustrative examples, basis for conclusion, or dissenting opinions of certain board members may be provided along with the standards itself (Pellens et al., 2014). Before the individual principles-based standards relevant for my research will be explained in more detail, it is first necessary to understand the main objectives of the standard setting framework.

2.3 Accounting framework according to IFRS

A central reference for the conceptual basis and main objectives of the IFRS is the conceptual framework for financial reporting. In 2004, in the US, the FASB and IASB decided to develop a new common conceptual framework. This framework was built upon the existing IASB Framework and the FASB Conceptual Framework and led to a framework that both boards could use as an accounting standards basis (Deloitte, 2017a; IASB, 2015). This led to the result of two new sections regarding the main objectives and qualitative requirements of financial statements, which were integrated into the already existing framework for the preparation and presentation of the financial statements of the IASB in 2010 (IASB, 2010). Subsequently, the further development of a joint framework was ceased in potential favor of (more) important convergence projects. Toward the end of 2012, the IASB decided to continue the work on the revision of the conceptual framework independent of the FASB. As a result, the discussion paper DP/2013/1 "A Review of the Conceptual Framework for Financial Reporting" was released in 2013. The framework showed the following main objectives: helping the IASB with the development and revision of new and already existing standards, help other parties (e.g. auditors) with the preparation of financial statements and interpretation of the IFRS and further, enable them to solve financial reporting issues in the sense of the IFRS, if the issue is not explicitly regulated by a certain standard. The scope of the framework's application were all financial statements that are accounted for under the IFRS. With regard to the framework, a financial statement is defined as a company publication, which is done and released at least once a year. This publication further had to meet the joint requirements of a wide target audience. The scope implied that the framework is relevant for both individual and consolidated financial statements (IASB, 2015; Pellens et al., 2014).

On May 28th, 2015, the Exposure Drafts (ED) ED/2015/3 "Conceptual Framework for Financial Reporting" and ED/2015/4 "Updating References to the Conceptual Framework" were published (Deloitte, 2017a; IASB, 2015). The main aim of both proposals is to improve financial reporting by providing a clearer and updated set of concepts and to be more complete than previous frameworks. The IASB (2015) argues that the ED can be used by itself when it comes to developing new and existing IFRS along with other standards to help apply them in a different context. Compared to previous concepts, the IASB (2015) states that the ED is more complete. This is because the ED covers areas that are either not covered or covered in less detail in the previous frameworks. Specifically, these areas are the measurement, financial performance (including the use of comprehensive income), presentation and disclosure, derecognition, and the reporting entity. Besides, the ED clarifies aspects with regard to the existing framework:

- The information needed to meet the objective of financial reporting includes information that can be used to help assess management's stewardship of the entity's resources;
- Explains the roles of prudence and substance over form in financial reporting;
- Clarifies that a high level of measurement uncertainty can make financial information less relevant;

- Clarifies further that important decisions on, for example, recognition and measurement, are driven by considering the nature of the resulting information about both financial performance and financial position;
- Provides clearer definitions of assets and liabilities and more extensive guidance to support those definitions; and
- Updates the parts of the existing Conceptual Framework that are out of date. For example, this ED clarifies the role of probability in the definitions of assets and liabilities (Deloitte, 2017a; IASB, 2015)

The original comment deadline set by the IASB was 26th October 2015 but was then rescheduled to 25th November 2015. Since then, there have been several sessions in which aspects of the framework have been discussed amongst the board of the IASB. The latest discussion was held on the 27th February 2017 (Deloitte, 2017a). This might be because many responders to the Discussion Paper wanted the IASB to spend more time to develop a robust concept (IASB, 2015). In the context of this dissertation, the main point of attention is set to the general purpose of financial reporting in a principles-based accounting approach. Further, the qualitative characteristics of the financial reporting information will be evaluated. As an element of the financial statement, the assets measured at fair value and their role in the current framework will be discussed.

2.3.1 Objective and general purpose of financial reporting

"The objective of general purpose financial reporting forms the foundation of the Conceptual Framework" (IASB, 2010). Other aspects of the conceptual framework flow logically from this objective, like a reporting entity concept, qualitative characteristics of useful financial information, elements of financial statements, and other contents of financial accounting standards like recognition, measurement, presentation, and disclosure (IASB, 2010). The board of the IASB states that the main objective of financial reporting is to provide financial information to investors, lenders, and other creditors that is (decision-) useful for making investment decisions as capital providers (IFRS Foundation, 2016). These decisions include the buying, selling, and holding of debt and equity instruments (IASB, 2010). Figure 1 below depicts the objective and general purpose of financial reporting along with the main and enhancing qualitative characteristics of decision-useful financial reporting information. The boxes with standard lettering are in accordance with the conceptual framework 2010 (IASB, 2010), while the boxes with italic lettering represent the topics (re-) introduced in the ED for a new conceptual framework (IASB, 2015). Further, the round-shaped boxes present concretization of the faithful representation/reliability as one of the main characteristics of decision-useful information. The conceptual framework of 2010 as well as proposed changes in the frame of the ED 2015 are presented in more detail hereafter.

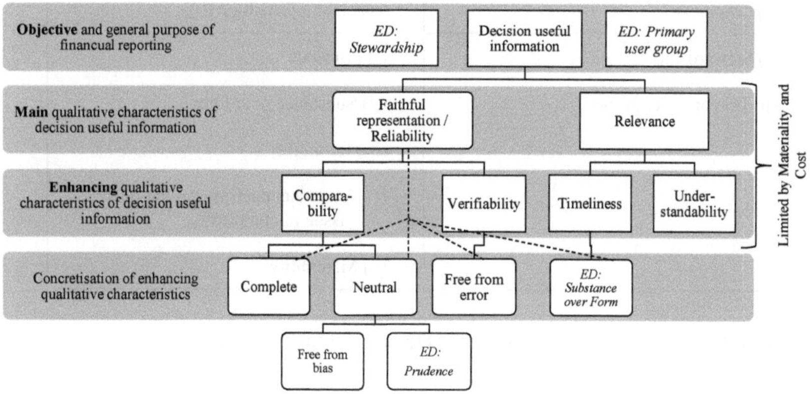

Figure 1: Objective and qualitative characteristics of financial reporting information according to the conceptual framework 2010 with changes proposed in the ED of the conceptual framework 2015[2]

Furthermore, the conceptual framework is mentioned as the foundation of financial reporting. Besides financial reporting, the conceptual framework contains other aspects such as qualitative characteristics, elements of financial statements, and measurements. These aspects aim to ensure that the objectives of financial reporting can be met (IASB, 2008b). After restarting its conceptual framework project in 2012, the IASB received several comments on a wide range of topics. The comments received on the earlier framework relate to the two main areas of the objective and general purpose of financial reporting (a) and the qualitative characteristics of useful financial information (b). The comments addressed especially the following points, which is why the IASB considered making changes especially to the following areas accordingly (IASB, 2015):

[2] Author's own illustration according to IASB (2010) and IASB (2015).

Objective and general purpose of financial reporting (a)	Qualitative characteristics of useful financial information (b)
(i) Stewardship	(i) Prudence
(ii) Primary user group	(ii) Substance over form
	(iii) Reliability
	(iv) Understandability and the related issue of complexity
	(v) Materiality

Table 1: Objective and qualitative characteristics of financial reporting information[3]

To be able to evaluate the prospects of future cash flows for an entity, potential investors need information about the entity. The earlier version of the conceptual framework stated that a part of the information required by investors focus on the management of the entity and its usage of the entities' resources with regard to efficiency and effectiveness. This is supposed to provide information to financial statement users on how the management of an entity contributes toward meeting the objectives of financial reporting. Doing so, the objectives of financial reporting can be met - amongst others - by providing information to financial statement users helping them assess the management's stewardship. As translation difficulties were feared by the IASB, they decided to give a detailed description on stewardship in chapter 1 of the conceptual framework (IASB, 2015). This change was feared by discussants, because making the concept of stewardship more prominent could lead to prioritizing this over the other objectives of financial reporting. Consequently, this could lead to a management bias when it comes to measurement and recognition decisions (IASB, 2015). The IASB noted that even though stewardship is an important topic to many financial statement readers, as they aim to gain information about future cash inflows to the entity, this is not always the case as related party information is of subordinate importance to assess the prospects of future cash inflows. Taking this into account, the IASB decided to reintroduce the term stewardship in the ED of the conceptual framework of 2015. According to them, the positive aspects of clarity that are reached by reintroducing the term outweigh the (potential) negative aspects like translation differences identified in 2010 (IASB, 2015). Still, the stewardship role of financial accounting is not seen as an equivalent to the prominent objective of financial reporting as mentioned in the beginning of this paragraph. This is due to two main reasons: firstly, information concerning the stewardship role of the management is also part of information that helps investors make an investment decision (buy, sell, or hold an equity investment) and secondly, the IASB argues that the introduction of another primary objective could be confusing for financial reporting users (IASB, 2015).

[3] Own table based on IASB (2015) BC 1.2.

Primary users of financial statements are existing and potential investors, lenders, and creditors who use financial reports as they do not have another source that provides information directly to them (IASB, 2015). These users are considered the primary user group of financial reporting. This is viewed skeptically by respondents to the ED as they argue that there are also other users that apply financial statements for various reasons even though they do not intend to provide resources to the entity. Consequently, the respondents demand to eliminate the term "primary user group" and support a broader group of users instead. Some argue that the information needs of the management are not considered sufficiently. The IASB does not meet this demand as it fears that a broader group of users and the absence of a primary user group could lead to a conceptual framework that is unduly abstract or vague (IASB, 2015 BC 1.14). With regard to the management's information needs, the board argues that they, compared to the primary user group, have other means to access financial reporting information and, thus, do not need to be part of the primary user group. Other respondents demand an even smaller primary user group. According to them, the group should be limited to existing shareholders and, thus, potential investors should be excluded from the primary user group. Also, there are claims that the current user group results in too much information in the financial statements due to the varying needs of the different types of investors in terms of financial statement information.

Even though the growing financial statement information supply is seen as a major topic by standard setters (e.g. disclosure overload) (Beerbaum, 2016), the IASB decided to keep its earlier definition of the primary user group with potential and already existing investors, lenders, and creditors due to three main reasons (IASB, 2015 BC 1.15). First, the current primary user group has an immediate and most critical need for financial reporting information. They need the standard setter to ensure that they are provided with the financial statement information as they would not have a claim to make the entity provide this information to them otherwise. Second, the board and the FASB stated that their responsibilities comprise of serving the capital market participants. This does not only include already existing lenders but also potential lenders and other creditors. Third, the IASB claimed that, with the current primary user group, the information needs of users are met, independent of the corporate governance model (shareholder value vs. stakeholder value) (IASB, 2015). Thus, the board tries to meet the information needs for a maximum of the primary users in cost-beneficial ways by providing common information to them. This also addresses the claim by some respondents who supported the composition of the primary user group as confirmed by the standard setter. In addition, they claim a hierarchy within the primary user group, which is not tracked further by the IASB.

2.3.2 Qualitative characteristics of decision-useful financial statement information

Qualitative characteristics contribute to the usefulness of financial statements. These are the *faithful representation* (reliability) of accounting figures and the *relevance* of these. According to the IASB (2010), these two criteria are seen as fundamental qualitative characteristics of decision-useful financial information. Moreover, the qualitative characteristics of *comparability, verifiability, timeliness*, and *understandability* are crucial are seen as criteria that may enhance the usefulness of financial information (IASB, 2010). These two main characteristics, supported by the enhancing characteristics, help financial statement users to distinguish between less and more useful financial information. All the mentioned financial statement information aspects are limited by materiality and cost. Consequently, the IASB takes these qualitative characteristics into account when developing reporting standards. Thus, financial reporting is supposed to meet the general purpose and objectives of financial reporting, for which the information that is reported must be both relevant and faithful (IASB, 2008b).

2.3.2.1 Main characteristics of decision-useful financial statement information

The standard defines that *relevant* financial information can change a decision made by a financial statement user. By doing so, this relevant information has a confirmatory or/and predictive value. While the predictive value is defined as information that can be used to predict future outcomes for users, a confirmatory value provides feedback to a user on previous evaluations. Both types of values are interrelated as predictive value often also has a confirmative value e.g., the revenues of a current financial year that are used as a basis to predict future revenues. For information to be relevant, it needs to be material. The standard setter considers information to be material if misstating or omitting it could influence the decision of a financial statement user. Besides, materiality is an entity-specific aspect of relevance. Due to this entity-specification, the standard setter is not able to specify a quantitative threshold for materiality (IASB, 2010).

As the concept is already clearly described in the existing framework, they did not suggest making any changes. Due to the recent topic of disclosure overload, however, the IASB considered to provide additional guidance to apply the concept of materiality in connection with the discussion paper. This approach was favored by many respondents. Still, the IASB decided not to make any changes to the concept of materiality in the conceptual framework but clarified the user group that was referred to in the concept. This user group consists of the primary users of financial statements as described earlier. Nevertheless, the IASB announced to consider providing additional guidance for the concept of materiality along with the disclosure initiative (IASB, 2015). While some scholars in this field (Clor-Proell et al., 2014) introduce the term faithfulness, other and later contributions to this research stream continue using the word reliability (Müller et al., 2015).

For financial statement information to be completely and faithfully represented, the *faithful representation (reliability)*[4] would need to be complete, free from error, and neutral. Consequently, the standard setter aims so maximize these qualities. For a complete depiction, all necessary information must be provided to enhance the user's understanding of the depicted

[4] The IASB introduced the term faithful representation in their Conceptual Framework of 2010 and intended to keep this term in the draft of the latest Conceptual framework of 2015. I decided to use the term reliability instead of faithful representation as I cannot ensure that all participants in this experiment are aware of the latest changes to the conceptual framework. This approach is in line with several correspondents on the Exposure Draft of the new Conceptual framework, who claim that the term reliability should be reintroduced as the term is clearer and better understood among the primary user group (IASB, 2015). This reasoning is consistent with Müller et al. (2015).

phenomenon. In terms of assets (e.g., investment properties), a complete depiction would include at least a numerical depiction of all assets in the group and the nature of the asset group complemented by a description of what the numerical depiction represents (e.g., in terms of investment properties that they are measured at fair value). A neutral depiction is defined as being free from bias in terms of selection or presentation of financial information. Free from error in the context of faithful representation does not mean accurate. The definition by the standard setter rather emphasizes that there can be no errors or omission in terms of the description of the phenomenon as well as the process that is used to produce the reported information. Again, in terms of investment properties where prices and values are often unobservable, the determined value of price cannot be determined as inaccurate or accurate (IASB, 2010). Neutral would indicate that the fair value of investment properties as well as the underlying valuation is free of earnings management. Hence, earnings management can be a threat to neutrality and, thus, reliability of financial statement information (van Tendeloo & Vanstraelen, 2005). Earnings management implies that earnings are managed with the intention to misdirect stakeholders in terms of a firm's performance on reported financial statement numbers (Healy & Wahlen, 1999). Still, the presentation can be faithful if it is described clearly and accurate as being an estimated value or price (IASB, 2010).

The pre-2010 framework names three characteristics of reliability: completeness, neutrality, and prudence (IASB, 2015, 2010). Instead of using the term reliability, the term faithful representation was introduced by the conceptual framework in 2010. Hence, faithful financial information represents what it intends to present, when it is useful and relevant. The IASB stated that the main reason for the introduction of the term faithful representation in 2010 was that there was no common understanding with regard to the term reliability among the user groups. Rather than the understanding of the term reliability, as supported by the IASB, intending to describe more than just being free from material error and being verifiable, the user group would equate reliability with information being free from material error or the information being verifiable.

Many respondents commented on the use of the new term faithful representation and argued that the term reliability should be reintroduced due to four main reasons: First, the term reliability is better understood and clearer than the new term that was introduced. Second, if sufficient disclosures are provided, anything can be presented faithfully. Thus, faithfulness does not fulfill its role as an effective filter to distinguish between information that should be included in the financial statement and information that should not. It would even allow the recognition of items in the financial statement that have a lack of reliability. Third, the pre-2010 framework contained the trade-off relationship between reliability and relevance of qualitative information. Information that is less reliable may be more relevant and information that is less relevant may be more reliable. Some respondents argue that this view that was expressed in the pre-2010 framework is missing in the new proposed conceptual framework. Last, financial statements should provide information that users can depend on and, thus, information should be reliable. Consequently, financial statements should be credible. Respondents claim that this key concept should be acknowledged in the conceptual framework (IASB, 2015).

Considering the comments of the respondents, the IASB decided to keep the label faithful representation for the former qualitative characteristic of reliability. The IASB justified this decision among other things with the misunderstanding of the term of reliability that became clear when looking at the respondent's comments. Some comments of respondents, to the discussion paper, pointed out that reliability is equated with a tolerable level of measurement uncertainty and not the broader definition that was introduced in the pre-2010 framework. Further, the existing conceptual framework already points out that relevant information may not be relevant if it faces a high level of uncertainty, though many readers seem to overlook this idea. Thus, changes are proposed by the IASB to make this concept more visible, they clarify that uncertainty affects the relevance of an estimate and that there is a trade-off between the two. In the changes proposed, the IASB points out that judgement is needed to determine relevant pieces of information. Also, the framework provides factors that enable users to rely on financial information. By implementing these changes, the IASB found it unnecessary to reintroduce the term reliability or add any further reference to the term (IASB, 2015).

The 2010 framework stated that faithfully represented financial statement information should be complete, neutral, and free from error. The pre-2010 framework also stated that financial statements should be neutral. In this context, the word neutral is defined as free from bias. The IASB also provides a negative delamination of the word, by stating that financial statements are not neutral, when the presentation or selection of information affects the decision-making or judgement of the information, and this is done intentionally to achieve a predestined results or outcome. This judgement is needed when uncertainties occur, and they are considered by exercising prudence when it comes to the preparation of financial statements. Such uncertainties can occur with doubtful receivables or when estimating the useful life of property, plant, and equipment (PPE). Prudence does not imply the creation of excessive provisions or hidden reserves due to a deliberate understatement of assets. Thus, prudence does take uncertainties into account but, with its exercise, the financial statements still remain neutral in order to contain accounting figures that are reliable (IASB, 2015).

In an earlier version of the ED, the reference to *prudence* was removed as the IASB feared an interpretation amongst users that would not be in line with the neutrality of financial statements. Many comments were received on that issue, and respondents argued that prudence should be reinstated. Still, the board was concerned, because prudence is a term that can be understood differently by different users, e.g. they could use the term to refer to a need of asymmetry, namely losses being recognized at an earlier stage than gains (IASB, 2015). Thus, the understanding of prudence is linked to neutrality as proposed by the IASB, which can be identified by means of the following two aspects: the selection and application of neutral accounting policies. Selecting neutral accounting policies ensures the faithful representation of the items that it purports to depict, while the application of neutral accounting policies ensures that the selected policy is unbiased and, thus, neutral (IASB, 2015). Due to this mutual dependency between prudence and neutrality, the IASB introduced the term cautious prudence.

Caution is needed when judgements must be made in uncertain conditions as part of the prudence term defined by the IASB. Prudence and, thus, caution can help in achieving accounting policies that are neutral in their application. Consequently, cautious prudence is one of the factors to ensure a faithful representation of financial statement items on both the asset and liability side. By introducing cautious prudence, the conceptual framework is expected to help auditors, regulators, and financial statement preparers to counteract a natural bias toward optimism they may have (IASB, 2015). Caution prudence could, thus, call attention when selecting inputs for estimating a measure that is not directly observable, e.g., the fair value of investment properties that is often measured with unobservable inputs. Due to this reasoning, the IASB proposed to reintroduce the term prudence, now more precisely defined as cautious prudence (IASB, 2015). By doing so, the IASB tried to make auditors, regulators, and financial statement preparers aware of the fact that cautious prudence works in the overstatement and understatement direction and is, thus, different from the principle of prudence known, e.g., in the German GAAP Context.

Substance is a widespread term in the IFRS. Even though it appears fairly often, it is a term that is seen differently by individuals and, thus, the primary user group. This could cause differences in the application of the IFRS among companies, industries, and territories (PWC, 2006). Besides cautious prudence, substance over form is one of the qualitative characteristics of useful financial information (IASB, 2015). For some respondents, substance over form refers to the concept that the accounting outcome should not be influenced by the legal form of a transaction. Thus, transactions or balances should have the same accounting result when they have the same economic outcome, even though the legal structures of the transactions or balances may differ from each other. Other respondents may define reliability as an economic outcome is reflected in profit and loss as substance. Consequently, a gain should only be accounted for if the economic changes are in line with this development. Otherwise, if economic changes give rise to a loss and the entity still reports a gain, the report would violate the core principle of substance. Again, there are other groups of people who state that substance is something that can be called upon when being unsure of the treatment of a certain transaction or balance. This however is a rare case, as most of these cases are resisted by auditors (PWC, 2006). So far, the conceptual framework does not contain an explicit reference to substance over form. Still, the IASB is aware of the different understandings of substance mentioned above, which is why the basis for the conclusion of the framework makes clear that priority is given to compliance with the legal form prior to the compliance with economic substance. Furthermore, the standard setter emphasizes its choice by stating that making the compliance with economic substance a priority could lead to a non-faithful representation of transactions and balances. As noted by many respondents, an explicit reference to substance over form was added to the ED of the new conceptual framework 2015 with the aim of adding clarity. This treatment of substance over form as part of reliability was already introduced in a pre-2010 framework, which is why the latest changes concerning this topic can be seen as a re-introduction (IASB, 2015).

2.3.2.2 Enhancing qualitative characteristics of decision-useful financial statement information

To enhance the decision usefulness of relevant and faithfully represented information, the *comparability, verifiability, timeliness*, and *understandability* of financial accounting information enhances the qualitative characteristics of financial information. Since the decision of financial statement users to buy, hold, or sell an investment in one reporting entity or another includes a choice between alternatives, financial statement information is considered to be more useful when it is *comparable* with similar information from another entity or other information from the same entity but from a different period. Hence, comparability helps financial statement users to identify similarities and differences among information. To some degree, the enhancing qualitative characteristic of comparability is already met by the main qualitative characteristics of faithful representation and relevance since a relevant and faithfully represented phenomenon would naturally possess a certain degree of comparability with another economic phenomenon (IASB, 2010).

Along with the criterion of faithful representation, *verifiability* assures financial statement users that the information faithfully represents the economic phenomena it is supposed to present. Verifiability describes an agreement on the faithfully depicted representation of information by independent and different knowledgeable observers who reach a certain consensus. Hence, this consensus does not necessarily need to be a complete agreement. Verification can be both direct and indirect. A direct verification would be, for example, the counting of cash using a direct observation. An indirect verification can mean verifying the input parameters for a formula or model that is being used in the financial reporting information. This is the case for fair values classified at level 3 with unobservable input parameters. Even though the standard setter requires the entity to disclose the underlying assumptions for formulas or models, the verifiability of information will usually only be possible to a certain extent (IASB, 2010).
To have information ready for decision makers in time so as to influence their decision to buy, hold, or sell an investment is gathered under the term *timeliness*. Timeliness is important for information users as old information is generally considered to be less useful. Though, some information can be timeliness for investors even if it is old information. This type of information can be useful in helping them identify future trends or assess past information long after the initial reporting period (IASB, 2010).

When information is characterized, classified, and clear, it is called *understandable*. Some accounting information can be very complex and, thus, harm the general understandability of these information. Hence, the conceptual framework points out that the exclusion of such information could be misleading for investors and would further lead to incomplete financial reporting. Also, financial reports are prepared for knowledgeable financial statement users. Knowledgeable, in this context, is defined as having knowledge of the economic and business activities and being able to analyze and review financial information. At times, even knowledgeable investors may seek the help of advisers to understand certain accounting phenomena (IASB, 2010).

In the light of the ED on the new conceptual framework by the IASB, changes to the qualitative characteristics were considered for *understandability* and the related issue of *complexity*. A qualitative characteristic of useful financial information (IASB, 2015) is *understandability* and the related issue of *complexity*. It is defined as a characteristic of useful financial information as its application is supposed to make financial information less complex and, thus, more understandable and ultimately useful. Respondents claimed that understandability should be raised to being one of the main qualitative characteristics. Some even requested understandability to become one of the main objectives of financial reporting. As the term understandability is linked to the term of complexity, the IASB decided not to change the role of understandability to a main objective or qualitative characteristic as this could result in an exclusion of complex information, which may still be useful for financial statement users (IASB, 2015). Some respondents requested that the conceptual framework should try to avoid too much complexity in the standards and, thus, discuss sources of complexity in terms of financial reporting. Referring to the existing material on the cost of constraints and understandability, the IASB argued that there is already adequate guidance (IASB, 2015).

The conceptual framework emphasized that the enhancing criteria of qualitative decision-useful financial information should be maximized but pointed out that this goal cannot be met when the information is irrelevant or is not faithfully represented. Besides, the application of this criteria does not follow a certain prescribed order but is rather an iterative process. This iterative process may include a temporary reduction of one of these enhancing characteristics. If, for example, a new accounting standard or valuation model needs to be considered (e.g. cost model vs. fair value model), the comparability of the corresponding accounting figures may temporarily be reduced while an improvement of faithful representation and relevance can be achieved. By mandating disclosures for such situations, the conceptual framework tries to partly compensate for this current non-comparability (IASB, 2010).

While the cost and materiality constraints are applicable for all main and enhancing qualitative characteristics of decision-useful financial statement information, materiality is assigned primarily to the topic of relevance (IASB, 2010). Cost, on the other hand, is assigned primarily to the enhancing qualitative characteristics. According to the conceptual framework, different types of cost are to be considered. On the one hand, financial statement providers face the costs by collecting, processing, verifying, and disseminating financial information for financial statement users. Yet, these users also bear these costs through reduced return due to the expenditures. Still, if the required information is not provided in a sufficient way, financial statement users face costs to obtain the required information form another source. The board applies this cost constraint as well (e.g. when working on accounting standards and the conceptual framework). By doing so, the board aims to evaluate if the benefit of a particular accounting information justifies the costs to provide and use this information. Due to the inherent subjectivity of the cost of information, the board deems differences in firm size, ways of raising capital (publicly or privately), and other factors appropriate (IASB, 2010).

As shortly mentioned in the chapters above, fair value plays an important role when it comes to the objective as well as the main and enhancing qualitative characteristics of decision-useful information. Hence, the concept of fair value accounting is described in more detail hereafter.

2.4 Concept of fair value measurement as an attribute in financial reporting

Over the past decade, fair value accounting has been amongst the most controversial discussed accounting topics (Bens et al., 2016). According to IFRS 13, fair value accounting can be applied to assets and reliabilities.[5] To understand how assets, especially investment properties, are accounted for at fair value according to the IFRS, three standards have to be taken into account: IAS 1, IAS 40, and IFRS 13. The fair value of an asset is defined as "[...] the price that would be received to sell an asset or paid to transfer a liability in an orderly transaction between market participants at the measurement date" (IFRS 13.9). IAS 1 describes the general requirements for the presentation of financial statements. Specifically, it is a guideline for the structure of the financial statement of a firm and states the minimum requirements in terms on content. This means that a complete set of financial statements is to be presented by a firm at least annually. In addition, comparative amounts of the previous year need to be presented. The financial statement comprises of a statement of financial position[6] at the end of the period, a statement of profit and loss, a statement of changes in equity if applicable, and a statement of cash flow. Moreover, the statement comprises of notes that contain information on significant explanatory information and accounting policies. All items of the financial statement are valued according to a positive going concern premise unless there is other indication. The application of IAS 1 has the ultimate aim to achieve a fair presentation of accounting figures like investment properties classified under IAS 40.

2.4.1 Valuation of investment properties

For the accounting of property held to earn rentals or for the appreciation of capital, or both, the standard IAS 40 Investment Property applies. The property referred to by the standard can be either land and/or buildings. While, generally, investment properties are measured at cost when initially recognized in the balance sheet, the standard states two different models for the subsequent measurement: the cost model and the fair value model. The latter recognizes changes in the fair value through profit and loss (Deloitte, 2017b; IAS 40). The ED for this standard was published in October 1984 with the title E26 Accounting for Investments. In March 1995, IAS 25 with the same title was issued. The effective date of IAS 25 was 01/01/1987 for financial statements beginning on or after that date. More than 10 years later, in July 1999, the ED E64, with the title Investment Property, was issued and the comment deadline was set to the end of October 1999. IAS 40 (2000) was then issued in April 2000 to supersede the IAS 25 with respect to investment property with an effective date for financial statements beginning on or after 01/01/2001. Two years later, in May 2002, Improvements to International Accounting Standards (2000) in the form of another ED was published with a comment deadline until September 2002. Consequently, the IAS 40 was issued in 2003 with an effective date for financial statements for periods beginning on or after 01/01/2005. In May 2008, changes to the standard were made by amendments in the Annual Improvement to IFRS 2007 that included property under construction or the development of property for future use within scope with an

[5] The further explanations of this work focus on assets measured at fair value as the research subject of this work is investment properties that are accounted for as assets in the balance sheet.

[6] In this work, the term balance sheet is used as a synonym for statement of financial position.

effective date for financial statements for periods beginning on or after 01/01/2009. Again, the IAS 40 was subject to amendments by the Annual Improvements of IFRS 2011-2013 cycle that especially addressed the interrelationship between the IFRS 3 Business Combinations and IAS 40. The amendments to the IAS 40 were forwarded by the transfer of investment property in December 2016. Changes resulting from these amendments, especially clarifying when there is a transfer to or from investment properties, have an effective date for financial statements for periods beginning on or after 01/01/2018 and will, thus, not be considered further in this thesis. Besides, the latest changes are of no relevance to the research topic of this work (Deloitte, 2017b; IFRS Foundation, 2017). As of 2017, there are no further amendments under consideration by the IASB.

The IAS 40 defines investment property as the land or a building or even a part of a building or both that is held by the owner to either earn rentals or to appreciate capital or both. The standard further specifies that the owner who accounts for the investment property can be the owner but also a lessee under a finance lease (IAS 40). Examples for investment property according to the IAS 40 are land held for long-term capital appreciation, land held for a currently undetermined future use, building leased out under an operating lease, vacant building held to be leased out under an operating lease, and property that is being constructed or developed for future use as an investment property. The latter expands the scope of IAS 40 as of May 2008. Before 2008, this type of property fell within the scope of the IAS 16. The standard refers to several types of property that are out of the scope of the IAS 40. There are some other classification issued within the IAS 40, especially referring to property held under an operating lease (IAS 40.6), partial own use of the property (IAS 40.10), ancillary services (IAS 40.13), and intercompany rentals (IAS 40.13). The named classification issues are not of importance for the scope of this work.

When it is probable that future economic benefits can be assigned to the property, the property is to be recognized as an investment property. Further, the costs of the property need to be measured reliably and the economic benefits assigned to the property need to flow to the entity that holds the property (IAS 40.16). When recognizing the investment property, the initial measurement is at cost model, including the transaction costs of the property (IAS 40.20). These transaction costs are directly attributable expenditures, such as professional fees for legal services, property transfer taxes, and transaction costs (IAS 40.21). For the subsequent measurement of the property, the standard permits the entity to choose between two different models: the fair value model and the cost model. The chosen method needs to be adopted for all investment properties of the entity (IAS 40.30). A change is possible but permitted only if the change leads to a more appropriate presentation of the investment property value. This is according to the standard highly unlikely for a change from the fair value to the cost model (IAS 40.48 and IAS 40.53). The main aspects of the two are summarized in the table below.

	An entity may choose between the fair value model and the cost model (IAS 40.32A) *General consistency requirement*	
	Cost model	Fair value model
Measurement after recognition	Cost less accumulated depreciation less accumulated impairment losses (IAS 40.56 and IAS 16.30)	Fair value valuation if reliable determination is possible on a continuing basis (IAS 40.53)
Frequency of an impairment test	Annual examination of the useful life, depreciation method and residual value of the asset (IAS 16.51)	No explicit guideline on the frequency to determine the fair value
Recognition of impairment losses	IAS 36 impairment test and recognized impairment losses if applicable (IAS 40.2f and IAS 36)	Changes in fair value are recognized through profit and loss

Table 2: Measurement of investment properties subsequent to initial recognition according to IAS 40[7]

The IAS 40 does not prescribe a specific order to determine the fair value of an investment property. The market value according to the legal guidelines of the IVSC and the European Group of Valuers Association (TEGoVA) was adopted by the Royal Institution of Chartered Surveyors (RICS). The definition of market value as stated by the RICS only differs in some choices of words from the definition of fair value according to the standard setter (RICS, 2017). Still, an order that is common especially among German practitioners comprises of two steps. In the first step, the entity evaluates if either a reliable fair value determination is possible on the basis of an independent expert market reports or if current market prices on an active market for similar property in a similar location and condition are available (IAS 40.45). If neither of them is accessible or available to the entity, the fair value can be determined in a second step by using additional information sources. These sources can be transaction prices from earlier transactions that are amended to current conditions or by using valuation models, e.g. the discounted cash flow (DCF) model that discounts future cash flows of the property to the reporting date or period. If both options pointed out in step two cannot be applied, a fair value determination is not possible because it would not be reliable enough. If the property classified as investment property according to the IAS 40 is initially recognized in this period, it is measured at the cost model, even though the measurement takes place after recognition is possible.

[7] Own illustration in accordance with IAS 40, IAS 26 and IAS 16 and Hans Böckler Stiftung (2014).

The DCF model can be used to calculate property as well as enterprise values and, thus, help to assess investment decisions. It is based on the idea of the dynamic calculation of development costs (Rottke & Thomas, 2011). The model was originally used to determine the enterprise value in the Anglo-Saxon area but is now used widely across Europe (Fest et al., 2006). Especially German firms with international investors use this globally accepted valuation method. According to the Institut der Wirtschaftsprüfer (IDW) Standard 1,[8] the value of a firm is determined by the financial goal of creating a net value out of the cash flows to the entity owners (Rottke & Thomas, 2011). Besides the IDW Standard 1, the IDW Standard 10 provides a framework for the valuation of properties. Contrary to firm values determined using a DCF model, the fair value of a property determined by a DCF model is assessed before taxes and financing considerations (IDW Standard 10). Consequently, the value of the firm is exclusively driven by the cash flow itself. When it comes to the valuation of firms, the DCF method is mainly used within the methods of the weighted average cost of capital (WACC), the adjusted present value (APV), the total cash flow (TCF) and the flow-to-equity (FTE) (Ballwieser & Hachmeister, 2016; Rottke & Thomas, 2011). In the context of this thesis the DCF is used to calculate the (market) value of a property which is why the model will be described in this context. The calculation of the market value for properties using the DCF method according to the European Standards is stated below (RICS, 2017):

$$\text{Market value} = \sum_{1}^{n} \left(\frac{FCF_i}{(1 + i_{equated})^n} \right) + \left(\frac{RV}{(1 + i_{equivalent})^n} \right)$$

$FCF_i = Free\ cash\ flow$

$\boldsymbol{i = discount\ rate}$

$n = years$

$RV = Residual\ value$

Equation 1: DCF method to calculate the market value of a property[9]

Typically, the DCF method, when used to determine the value of a property, is divided into two phases (Rottke & Thomas, 2011). The forecast phase covers a period of 10 to 15 years (Simon, 2000). A longer period is not appropriate as an accurate forecast of the income and expenses becomes more difficult with an increasing time horizon. This could create a spurious accuracy but still not improve the informative value of the calculation (Fest et al., 2006). The future income and all factors associated to this period are forecasted and then discounted to the valuation date using a discount rate that is determined up front. This rate will typically derive from matching risk property investments. The residual value is then determined in the second phase using a multiplier for the estimated remaining useful life of the property. Usually, the

[8] IDW is the Institute of Auditors in Germany. This reference is used in this context as the conducted experiment uses a fictional public real estate firm that is subject to the standards set by the IDW.

[9] Cf. Rottke & Thomas (2011), p. 810-811.

multiplier used is derived from forecast period discount rate and is reduced by the expected growth rate in rent. Since Wagenhofer and Ewert (2007) state that market value and, thus, the income approach using DCF is basically the same as the fair value approach introduced by the IASB, the following chapter provides more detail on the fair value approach and fair value hierarchy.

2.4.2 Fair value measurement of investment properties

The IASB provides a principles-based framework to measure fair values in accordance with the IFRS 13, which was introduced in May 2012 (EY, 2012). As mentioned in the previous chapter, "[t]he IFRS defines fair value as the price that would be received to sell an asset or paid to transfer a liability in an orderly transaction between market participants at the measurement date" (IFRS 13.9). According to the IFRS 13.BC31, the fair value is a market-based measurement and, thus, is, in the meaning, similar to the determination of the market value by the RICS (2017). This objective of the standard to determine a market value persists with different levels of market activities that may influence the exit price or valuation techniques. Consequently, even if a significant decrease in the level of activity or the volume for asset or liability arises, the fair value remains a market-based exit price considering the measurement date's market conditions (EY, 2012). Besides providing a definition of fair value, the IFRS 13 provides a framework to apply the definition to a financial reporting context. Several components of the fair value framework interact and are interrelated and, thus, should be considered in the context of the entire approach (EY, 2012). The figure below shows the various components that need to be adapted for the context of investment properties:

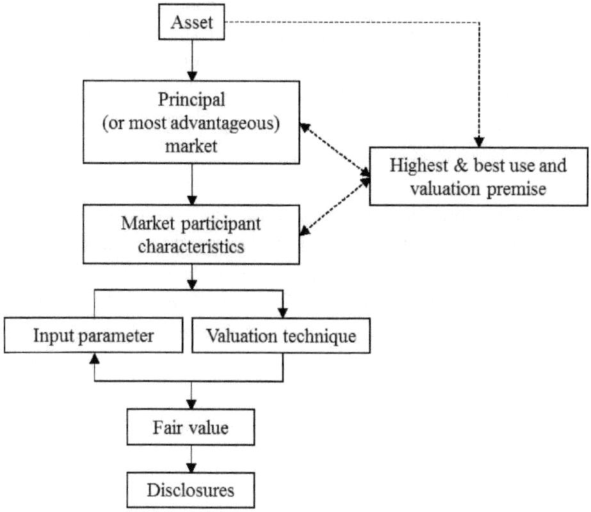

Figure 2: Fair value measurement framework for investment properties[10]

As the figure shows, the IFRS 13.11 indicates that the fair value measurement is for a certain asset and that characteristics of the asset, such as location and condition, need to be considered as well as possible restrictions on the use of the asset. The IFRS 13.13 extends the definition of a single asset and points out that the framework may as well apply to a group of assets. The standard then assumes that the asset is exchanged in an orderly transaction between market participants (IFRS 13.15). The standards specify this by stating that transfer either happens on a principal market or, if a principal market is absence, on the most advantageous market (IFRS 13.16). A principal market, in this context, does not mean that prices need to be directly observable (IFRS 13.18), which would not be the case with real estate assets since they are highly heterogeneous. Moreover, real estate markets are characterized by a high lack of transparency. The price of the asset on a principal market can be estimated using a valuation technique (IFRS 13.18). Furthermore, the standard makes clear that the entity needs access to the market, but this does not mean that the entity needs to be able to sell the asset on the measurement date. The market participants in the model introduced by the standard setter are assumed to act in their best economic interest when they price assets (IFRS 13.22). Both the participants and the market on which the asset is priced are influenced by the usage of the asset and the valuation premise. The standard requires the fair value measurement to consider that market participants want to generate economic benefit by having the highest and best in use asset (IFRS 13.27). Generally taken, highest and best use of non-financial assets takes into account that the use needs to be physically possible, legally permissible, and financially feasible for the firm (IFRS 13.28). Special requirements apply when the management determines that

[10] Author's own illustration based on EY (2012).

the asset is not the highest and best in use. Hence, in my context, the properties are highest and best in use, which is why these aspects are not further discussed. When the management of a firm determines the highest and best use for assets, the standard differentiates between a single asset or a group of assets (IFRS 13.31). If the highest and best use of an asset is in combination with other assets, the fair value is determined assuming that the asset will be sold along with the other assets for the use of market participants.

With mixed-use property portfolio (office vs. residential), which is the case in the context chosen for this experiment, in most cases, the fair value would be maximized as a group. Still, entities should only assume that the fair value of an asset is maximized through the use with other assets if there is sufficient support for this assertion (EY, 2013). Specifically, if a real estate firm owns a portfolio of assets which includes several buildings with similar use in different cities and all of them are classified as investment properties according to the IAS 40, then, each building counts as a separate unit of account. This is the case with the setting of this experiment as the firm holds several investment properties with the same use (office and residential) in different German cities.

In terms of valuation techniques, the IFRS does not prescribe anything in particular, which is why there is guidance regarding this topic by the IVS. Using the IVSC, especially the IVS 230 C12-24, three approaches emerge: market approach, income approach, and cost approach. The market approach uses market prices of comparable assets and is seen as a comparison approach. As mentioned earlier, properties are heterogeneous and, thus, problems, when comparing transactions, may arise. Still, firms use this approach to value their properties (EY, 2013). This might be due to the reason that some properties are less heterogeneous than others, and it further depends on the location of the property. In this experimental setting, however, the market approach is not applicable, which is why the income approach was used. This approach converts future cash-inflows to a current amount (e.g. using the DCF method). EY (2013) point out that the DCF approach is still reliable when the income stream is likely to change in the future compared to the current period. This is the case in this setting as future rent cash-inflows for the mixed-used portfolio cannot be predicted with high certainty. The last approach is the cost approach that reflects the amount of money that would be required to replace the asset. According to the IVSC, this method should only be applied in exceptional cases (IVS 230).

The inputs to the valuation techniques that determine the fair value are arranged in a fair value hierarchy, where quoted prices qualify as level 1 input parameters, inputs other than quoted prices but still observable (direct or indirect) as level 2, and unobservable input parameters as level 3 (IFRS 13.72-90). In this hierarchy, the highest priority is given to quoted prices (level 1), while unobservable inputs (level 3) have the lowest priority (IFRS 13.72). For real estate assets, level 1 has no relevance as this level of the fair value hierarchy applies for unadjusted quotes prices in active markets for identical assets at the measurement date (IFRS 13.76-80). Thus, real estate assets from a theoretical point of view can either be classified as level 2 or level 3. The IFRS 13 level 2 allows the adjustment of observable inputs in a non-significant way to reflect differences between the assets that have been in an observable transaction. Real estate that categorizes at level 2 would be, for instance, condominium apartments. Also, the recent sales volume of transactions for which prices could be observed would need to be available. Practitioners claim that, in many cases, the adjustments that need to be made to observable prices would be significant and, consequently, the fair value should be classified at level 3. They state that the real estate market is often inactive and not transparent compared to other markets and it is, thus, unlikely that real estate assets will be classified at level 2 (EY, 2013). This will be especially the case when the market liquidity is low. When specific assets are classified at one level and others at another level (e.g., level 2 and level 3), the fair value measurement is classified entirely at the lowest input level (level 3) that is significant to the entire measurement (IFRS 13.73). Keeping this in mind, the properties in this setting have been classified as level 3 fair value measurement input parameters. The management has to state the level of the fair value measurement of a property in the disclosure and also state how the property groups into classes of assets. For level 3, a description of the valuation process is necessary.

The IFRS 13 requires disclosures of all different types: qualitative disclosure information as well as a value range, the change of a value compared to the prior period, and a point value. Qualitative disclosure information according to the IFRS 13.93 is the level of the fair value hierarchy that needs to be enclosed as well as the description of valuation techniques and inputs that were used for the measurement of the fair value and changes made to the value including the reasons for such changes. A range value in accordance with the IFRS 13.93 is, for example, the amount of transfers into or out of level 3 fair value hierarchy, including reasons for the transfer as well as policies that determine the transfer between the different levels of the fair value hierarchy. Another example is the description of the sensitivity of the fair value to changes in unobservable inputs. The fair value measurement at the end of the reporting date can be classified as a point value. Point value, in this context, defines an exact value for a given point in time such as the fair value of an investment property (IFRS 13.93).

In the context of investment properties, the IAS 40 requires the disclosure of a change value for changes in the fair value compared to the prior period. Specifically, the cumulative change in fair value that is recognized in profit and loss needs to be disclosed (IAS 40.75). In addition, the reconciliation between carrying amounts of the investment property at the beginning and end of the period needs to be disclosed in the financial statement (IAS 40.76). A complete list of all disclosures for investment properties measured at fair value and their categorization according to the one proposed above and used throughout this thesis (IAS 40 and IFRS 13) is provided in Appendix S1.

3 Differences in information needs and usage by capital providers

The following chapter will define the different types of investors. First, equity investors are further distinguished into outside professional, private, and retail as well as inside and family ownership equity investors, followed by debt investors, and trade creditors. The chapter then evaluates the differences in information claim and usage among the different types of investors and presents the stewardship role and financial decision-making along with the concept of decision usefulness. The processing of information by capital market participants (professional vs. NPIs) is evaluated thereafter. I will further shed light into decision heuristics investors' use when they make an investment decision and point out their information processing strategies.

3.1 Types of capital providers

The growing complexity of financial products, the changes to international reporting standards, and the internationalization of capital markets changed the information environment for capital providers in the recent years. This change to their environment affects not only the sources by which the information is provided but also the way it is used by them. The most common form of capital for firms in the European Union (EU) is debt (Cascino et al., 2013). Nevertheless, research on capital providers focuses on equity (Armstrong et al., 2010; Fields et al., 2001; Kothari, 2001). In practical terms, the average European country has an equity market that is just half the size of its debt market, even though there are significant differences on an international level. When considering specific European markets, the different sizes of debt and equity markets become even more extreme, e.g., Austria and Portugal have equity markets that mark just one quarter of its debt markets[11] showing that there are large differences across Europe (Cascino et al., 2013). Firms in the US have more equity, lower liabilities, and, in particular, less current liabilities than European firms. When it comes to the total liabilities of European firms, only 30% are denoted to other liabilities, while 70% are liabilities due to bank or other creditors. Consequently, the debt market is assessed more often by European firms than the equity market. Still, studies of credit markets are not adequately represented in the accounting literature (Armstrong et al., 2010). This underrepresentation of research on the debt market may lead to an insufficient understanding of information usage among capital providers[12], for both academics and standard setters.

[11] This statement is indicated by data available at the ORBIS database. It refers to the capital structure of 15 publicly listed EU firms that present consolidated accounts and have data available for the year ending December 2011. Firms where the total assets do not equal the sum of shareholders' equity plus current and non-current liabilities are not included. The same applies for firms with a negative shareholders' equity.

[12] The terms "providers", "investors" and "holders" will be used as synonyms hereafter.

T. Herrmann, *The Decision Usefulness of Additional Fair Value Disclosures*, Controlling und Rechnungslegung – Managerial and Financial Accounting, https://doi.org/10.1007/978-3-658-24832-1_3

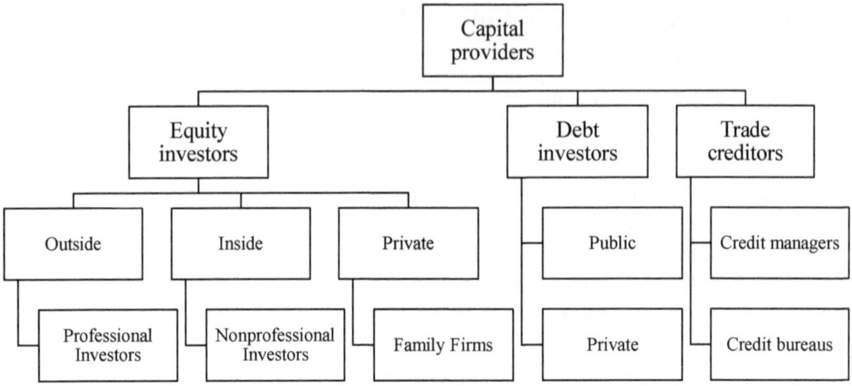

Figure 3: Overview of different capital providers[13]

Most literature agrees that equity and debtholders have varying needs when it comes to the provided financial information. Moreover, they agree that different information is needed but also that it is used in different ways (Ball et al., 2008; Brown, 2016; Kothari et al., 2010). The literature further argues that financial accounting developed this way due to the separation of managers and investors. Since managers have the most complete information about the development and profitability of the firm but are not the most reliable information source for investors, auditors mark the third party in this triangle. The need for auditors arises from the need for an independent verification of reliable information demanded by the investors (Geiger & Epstein, 1994; Gold et al., 2012). Not only due to the differences between managers and investors, but also due to the pointed out differences between debt and equity, are capital providers refined further as follows: equity investors, debt providers, and trade creditors. Additionally, both equity and debt providers are split into "insiders" and "outsiders" following the classification approach by Cascino et al. (2013). In this context, "insiders" are equity or debt providers who are able to directly negotiate within the company for their (investment) decision, while "outsiders" are equity and debt providers who need to rely on information that is publicly available. Since this thesis focuses on the information needs of NPIs and, thus, private and non-professional equity investors, the focus in the following chapters will be set on this user group. Though, the other user groups, especially the one of professional equity investors, will be described hereafter as the literature distinguishes between the different information needs of professional and nonprofessional equity investors.[14] Debt investors and trade creditors will be neglected as part of this thesis.

[13] Own illustration based on the classification of capital providers used by Cascino et al. (2014).

[14] See chapter 3.4. and 3.6 for more detail.

3.2 Equity investors

As shown in the section above, financial users have different information needs. The following section structures the different types of capital providers. Even though studies show that debt plays a greater role than equity when it comes to the financing of European firms (European Central Bank, 2012), the majority of the literature on information processing needs of investors focusses on equity (Cascino et al., 2014). In this dissertation, the focus will be on equity providers; nevertheless, information needs of debt providers and trade creditors will also be pointed out shortly. In the case of equity providers, this research will distinguish between "outside" and "inside" equity providers. Inside equity investors are eligible to access the firm's internal price-sensitive information (e.g., as family owners) while outside equity investors do not have that access and, thus, have to rely on generally publicly available information. Besides, a differentiation between institutional/professional equity investors and retail/private equity investors as well as inside equity investors is made. Consequently, the information needs of equity providers will be described in more detail compared to debt providers and trade creditors, even though debt plays a more important role when looking at companies' financing structures. When looking at equity investors, the different information needs for NPIs and professional investors are described in detail. For the theoretical framework used in this research, it is important to understand the differences in the information needs of both professional investors and NPIs.

3.2.1 Outside professional equity investors

Over the past years, there has been a growth in institutional equity investments in the geographical area of the Organization for Economic Co-operation and Development (OECD) (Cascino et al., 2013).[15] This trend also applies to Germany, a country that is traditionally dominated by bank financing. The main aim of professional private equity investors is to value and invest in firms. By doing so, they take into account information that can affect the firm valuation in the long run (e.g., the quality of the management) (Wright et al., 2009). Further, they try to maximize risk-adjusted-stock return relating to an index or benchmark and evaluate if the shares are under or overvalued taking into account the uncertainty of future cash flows and earnings (Barker, 1999; Crifo et al., 2015). Thus, professional private equity investors demand information about both future cash flows and/or earnings as well as about the associated risk (Cascino et al., 2014). Also, they try to make managers take account for their (past) actions in the frame of stewardship. Thus, accounting information that is not future but past orientated can be useful for them in terms of management appointment and remuneration claims of the management (Bushman et al., 2006).

Professional equity investors use valuation models for their investment decisions (Imam et al., 2008) but also rely heavily on financial statements (Chambost, 2008; Gassen & Schwedler, 2010; Vergoossen, 1993). This was recently complemented by intellectual capital in analyst reports (Abhayawansa & Guthrie, 2016). Furthermore, direct contact with employees of the

[15] For a list of all OECD member countries (e.g., Australia, European Countries and the US), see OECD (2016).

firm is highly relevant for professional equity investors and can even be more important than financial reporting itself (Barker et al., 2012; Barker, 1998).[16]

3.2.1.1 Information sources used by professional equity investors

European surveys (e.g., Gassen & Schwedler, 2010) indicate that professional equity investors especially use financial statements. Within the financial statements, they consider the income statement most useful. Nevertheless, they also consider the contact to the management of a firm important (Pellens & Schmidt, 2014). Most European surveys deal with limitations due to the assumption that the sources of information are used independently by investors. Nevertheless, research contributions find that information sources are not used independently (Barker et al., 2012; Barker & Imam, 2008; Glaum & Friedrich, 2006). Manager meetings are, for example, used by investors to build a context around hard accounting data provided by the companies and analysts (Barker et al., 2012). Thus, management information adds meaning to accounting data and can make it more verifiable, which is why it is an important source of information for professional equity investors even though it is not reflected in prices (Barker & Imam, 2008).

Besides the management information, notes on financial statements are also important to professional equity investors (Gassen & Schwedler, 2010; Olbert, 1994). Another problem that professional investors face when analyzing financial accounting information is the complexity of the provided information. Thus, the interpretation of the accounting information can be wrong, e.g., with regard to fair value accounting for liabilities (Lachmann et al., 2011). Gassen and Schwedler (2010) provide empirical evidence that professional investors prefer assets measured at fair value if the operating asset is liquid and, thus, measured on mark-to-market basis. However, their preference of the fair values is not the same when it comes to illiquid operating assets. Their findings are in line with the results of Hitz (2007), who concludes that the validity of assets measured at fair value is especially a problem when model-based valuations are necessary. Nelson and Tayler (2007) find that recognized figures are more important to investors than disclosures in notes. Thus, the question of where to present a financial information should be highly relevant to standard setters.

For professional equity investors, financial statements are an important reference document that helps to resolve uncertainty about the recent past and present. Thus, the financial statement is seen as a basis to forecast future earnings (Marton, 1998). Additionally, financial statement information can serve as a benchmark to assess relevant and timely disclosures (Beyer et al., 2010).

3.2.2 Private and retail equity investors

Compared to professional investors, private investors use publicly available media information, information provided by financial institutions, information provided to them by friends and family, as well as financial statement information as sources of information when it comes to their investment decision (Cascino et al., 2014). Early research contribution in this field

[16] Abhayawansa and Guthrie (2016) also point out alternative information sources. Hence, there is little consensus on their relative importance in the literature (Cascino et al., 2014).

provides evidence that private investors rely on information provided to them by financial institutions and brokers for their decisions as capital providers (Lee & Tweedie, 1975). More recent research contributions indicate that publicly available media information plays a major role (Pellens & Schmidt, 2014). This publicly available data includes presenting financial accounting information on a web-based interface. The drilldown capability of the interface can reduce the cognitive load for investors. This means that investors can navigate from a more general view of the data (e.g., the balance sheet of an entity) to a more specific one (e.g., a certain disclosure of an asset that is part of the balance sheet) by just one click. In addition, NPIs are less accessible for earnings fixation when the drilldown function is available compared to when there is no drilldown function provided. Thus, the usefulness of web-based financial reports can be enhanced by disaggregating the financial statements (Kelton & Murthy, 2016). What both sources of information have in common is that they provide "filtered" or "aggregated" financial statement information to NPIs. Filtered or aggregated, in this context, means that parts of the underlying financial statement information have been selected by financial institutions, brokers, or the media before being compressed and interpreted by these sources (Cascino et al., 2014). The usage of "raw" financial statement information by NPIs, meaning financial statement information that is neither filtered nor aggregated, is linked to lower returns on investment (Elliott et al., 2008). These results occur especially for less experienced NPIs. Thus, NPIs who have investment experience and are well-educated tend to rely more on raw financial statement information, because the usage for them is not linked to lower returns, compared to NPIs with less experience and education (Elliott et al., 2008; Rosen, 2009). When NPIs use raw financial statement information, they mainly focus on the balance sheet and the income statement. Additionally, they use the cash flow statement for their investment decision, but only to a small extent. The footnote disclosures are hardly incorporated into NPIs' investment decisions (Rosen, 2009). If the choice between audited and non-audited financial statement information is an option for NPIs, they prefer audited information (Hodge et al., 2010; Rosen, 2009). NPIs' believe that managers engage in earnings management about 50% of the time (Hodge, 2003). Moreover, NPIs are afraid that they could be exploited by other stakeholders, specifically 40% of the NPIs assess the possibility of this exploitation as "high" and "very high" (Rosen, 2009).

Bhattacharya et al. (2012) provide experimental evidence by carrying out a large field study with around 8.000 NPIs and find that most of them would need financial advice for their investment decision. Still, the NPIs who receive the requested advice hardly follow it and, consequently, are not able to improve the efficiency of their portfolio. They argue that it is necessary to have unbiased financial statement information available for NPIs, but providing this information is not a sufficient condition to favor all NPIs. When using the financial statement information, NPIs are often deceived by pro-forma earnings disclosures. Besides, they tend to use very simple valuation models that may lead to differing results compared to more detailed valuation models (Elliott, 2006; Frederickson & Miller, 2004). Presentation of the provided information within the financial statement matters for NPIs as well as for professional equity investors. Depending on where the information in the financial statement is provided, different weights are assigned by NPIs (Hodge et al., 2010; Lachmann et al., 2011; Maines & McDaniel, 2000).

NPIs are not able to adjust for biases in the recommendation of analysts. Specifically, they follow both buy and hold recommendations by security analysts who tend to bias stock recommendations upwards. Still, they feel no pressure to follow hold recommendations (Malmendier & Shanthikumar, 2007). Further, the power of extreme earnings surprises to predict future abnormal returns is not subsumed by the NPIs. They are net buyers regardless of whether the extreme earnings surprise is positive or negative (Hirshleifer et al., 2008). Liquidity can be improved, and information asymmetry can be decreased by Regulation Fair Disclosure (FD). This decline in information asymmetry is associated with a lower participation rate in the period prior to the announcement and more active trading of NPIs compared to professional investors after the current period earnings are released (Chiyachantana et al., 2004). NPIs, on average, rather invest in firms that show precise and clear financial disclosures. This relation between disclosure information and investment behavior is less pronounced for professional investors, who have a high frequency of trading and are familiar with financial statements. The results imply that the disadvantage NPIs have in incorporating financial statement information into their investment decision may be reduced by providing clear and concise financial disclosures. Ultimately, both NPIs and professional investors can benefit from improved corporate disclosure (Lawrence, 2013). Moreover, NPIs use financial accounting information for stewardship purposes. When shareholders, especially NPIs, feel remote from the company, annual general meetings can help them understand the complex accounting data through verbal explanation and visual aids. Therefore, the stewardship function of the accounting data is enabled by annual general meetings. While financial statements inform investors about the past, annual general meetings offer them the opportunity to ask the management further questions about certain topics and, thus, gain the most recent and, possibly, also future information (Carrington & Johed, 2007).

To sum up, NPIs prefer using the aggregated information provided to them by information intermediaries, like the media or financial advisors, compared to raw and unfiltered information, for their investment process. This demand for information can be explained by their limited cognitive capacity and, thus, limited processing of information. The demand for aggregated information can lead to a behavioral bias that explains the sub-optimal demand for information being linked to the level of liquidity. Thus, if information asymmetry is high and NPIs are consequently poorly informed, it leads to lower liquidity. When the information asymmetry between the different investor types is reduced, it leads to higher trading activity by NPIs (Kelly & Ljungqvist, 2012).

3.3 Debt investors

Debt investors are understood to be advanced readers and users of financial statement information in existing research literature. Compared to equity providers, debt contractors usually have multiple contract terms, e.g., collateral, interest, and maturity (Bharath et al., 2008). They use accounting data with the main objectives of finding out financial distress of the firm and debt contracting. These main objectives apply to all debt providers (Cascino et al., 2014).

Evaluating potential financial distress is one of the main objectives of debt providers. This evaluation affects their decision if they lend money, how much, and on what terms (e.g., interest rate). The research field of the usefulness of accounting data to predict financial distress is well developed. Still, with regard to the question of how financial distress can be predicted most effectively, researchers propose different solutions: the use of ratios, models, and the recommendation of bond/credit analysts (Cascino et al., 2014). The use of ratios is proposed by Beaver (1966) in one of the earliest research contributions in this field. The usefulness of ratios in predicting financial distress of firms is later confirmed by other researchers (e.g., Shumway, 2001).

Besides ratios to predict financial distress, the usage of models plays an important role. The most known is probably the model by Black and Scholes (1973). After that, several other models that use market value-based variables were published (e.g., Bharath & Shumway, 2008; Campbell et al., 2008). Still, it remains unclear which model serves best in predicting financial distress (Campbell et al., 2008), and several models are proposed depending on surroundings (e.g., the type of market) (Charalambakis & Garrett, 2016). Besides the use of ratios and models, another literature stream brings analysts to the agenda when predicting financial distress. Analysts could be suitable as they collect information, including accounting information, from a variety of sources before providing recommendations (Chen & Lee, 1993). This data is generally suitable to predict credit ratings that ultimately are an indicator for financial distress, as a low credit rating brings attention to a potential financial distress. Credit ratings can be predicted reasonably well when using accounting data (Kaplan & Urwitz, 1979). This research shows that accounting data is a major input for credit analysts, however, there is also research that shows that other information also plays an important role for them (Jorion et al., 2005).

3.4 Information usage and differences in claims by capital providers

When it comes to information usage, there are differences in claims between debt providers, equity providers, namely shareholders, as well as the management of a firm on the other side. While the return of debt providers is limited upside and downside, the return of equity is only constrained downside. This is, in practical terms, the basic feature that distinguishes debt and equity (Cascino et al., 2013).

Bearing these differences in mind, the interest of shareholders and debtholders may conflict. This conflict arises, particularly, when the management of a firm and shareholders explicitly try to maximize the value of a firm's equity and not the firm value. As shareholders aim to maximize the value of equity, they may try to design the structure of a firm according to that goal (Zhong et al., 2017). This could lead to a financial structure and firms' operations that ultimately decrease the value of debt and the firm (Cascino et al., 2013). To address this conflict, debtholders require high interest rates. Furthermore, shareholders might incorporate certain covenants into their debt contracts, e.g., to restrict dividend payments, the distribution of assets, or the issuance of additional debt (Armstrong et al., 2010).

The value of debt claims is highly sensitive to a decrease in firm value, while an increase in firm value is treated asymmetrically. Thus, losses are more important to debtholders, resulting in covenants that secure potential losses but not increases in firm value. This asymmetry from debt providers leads to a stronger demand for accounting conservatism among them (Li, 2013). Due to this, financial statements can be especially important to debt providers. Besides differences between debt and equity providers, there are still differences in accounting standards amongst different countries (e.g., between IFRS and US-GAAP) (Barth et al., 2012). Even though international harmonization is at a high level, the legal and political institutions that are responsible for the enforcement of accounting standards remain mainly local. This leads to significant differences in international accounting as the accounting standards only set the boundaries on the outputs, but leave the enforcement to auditors, courts, and regulators, and the preparation to managers (Ball et al., 2003; Ball et al., 2000; Burgstahler et al., 2016, 2016). In fact, evidence suggests that there are large differences between common and civil law countries from 1950 to 2000 when it comes to procedural formalism. Thus, legal procedures may even have diverged or not converged (Balas et al., 2009).

The IFRS in Europe are a single set of accounting standards to be applied by large listed public entities. Still, the enforcement of these standards can be uneven and, thus, cause the remaining difference in financial reporting quality (Ball, 2006; van Tendeloo & Vanstraelen, 2005). Consequently, the same principles do not lead to equal quality of the financial statements, which makes a similar usage of financial accounting information among capital providers unlikely. After the introduction of the IFRS, the potential impact of international variation in financial reporting has been subject to research literature. This literature stream is mainly market-based research (Brüggemann et al., 2013). Direct evidence is still narrow when it comes to international differences in accounting standards and their effects on capital providers and stewardship (Cascino et al., 2013).

3.5 Financial decision-making and stewardship roles

The financial accounting information provided by a firm fulfils two roles: decision usefulness and stewardship. Stewardship describes the ex-post role of information. Ex-post information is used to control the management's use of capital since it was invested in a firm (Rashad Abdel-Khalik, 2010). This type of information mainly focuses on past actions and can imply key financial statement information (e.g., earnings per share (EPS)), especially when it comes to contractual agreements between lenders, investors, and managers (Cascino et al., 2013). The term "control" is a broad term that incorporates a wide range of activities. Even the narrower term "performance measurement" could imply valuation and, thus, function as a sub category of control. Though there is no agreed upon name for information that is not investment or valuation relevant, literature argues that the term "stewardship" is the one most commonly used by standard setters when discussing the objectives of accounting (Lambert, 2010). In contrast, decision usefulness fulfils the role of ex-ante information, as an investment decision takes into account the future development of a firm. According to the IASB (2015), information needs to be decision useful for investors to make investment decisions. Ex-ante information is future-oriented information that is required for investors to make an investment or valuation decision.

This is the case with investment properties measured at fair value. As these types of assets often have unobservable input parameters, the accounting figures rely on valuation models. These models are future orientated, and investors need this information to make investment decisions.

Compared to decision usefulness, the stewardship role of information plays a subordinate role in accounting research. Nevertheless, it did not only receive less information in the past but also faced decline as a topic in leading accounting journals[17] (O'Connell, 2007). Still, current research in leading journals focus on stewardship and distinguish between soft and hard managerial information (Şabac & Tian, 2015). In broader terms, when defining decision-useful information as valuation relevant information in line with the conceptual framework (IASB, 2010), there is more empirical evidence on this role of information compared to research on non-value-relevant information that is mostly based on theoretical analyses using agency models or focused on compensation. In general, research is divided, since some contributions argue that the role of stewardship and decision usefulness are aligned, others argue that they are not. Besides there were concerns about the future role of stewardship in accounting due to the effective demotion of stewardship in the IASB's Conceptual Framework of 2010 (IASB, 2010; Murphy et al., 2013) as described in chapter 2.3.1 and 2.3.2. Uncertainties about the future role of stewardship were not only created by the standard setters but also by accounting literature. While one literature contribution argues that performance measurement and stewardship are the primary focus of financial statements (Kothari et al., 2010), another contribution argues that the two roles are not always aligned, even though information for valuation could prove useful for stewardship (Lambert, 2010). Even though there are disagreements on the size of the sets, the extent of the intersection, and definition of terms, several authors agree that stewardship is not a subsection of decision usefulness (Beyer et al., 2010; Bushman et al., 2006; Kothari et al., 2010; Lambert, 2010; Şabac & Tian, 2015).

An early contribution to the role of decision usefulness and stewardship was made by Gjesdal (1981). For his research, he uses a generalized agency model and discusses the stewardship demand of information by the means of the model. Also, the model is extended, when fictional information is received. Based on this, he finds that there is a demand for stewardship function for accounting. In addition, his research indicates that the two objectives, decision usefulness and stewardship, are not always aligned. The distinction between the valuation role of earnings and the role of earnings to evaluate the performance of the management of a firm is also made in the literature contribution by Lambert (1993). The key point of the paper is that, for both managers and investors, financial statement information is useful as it is not affected by factors that are out of the control of managers, such as share prices. When it comes to stewardship, information about the effort of the management is valuable for capital providers. Still, to make financial decisions, investors need information to estimate future cash flows, while for stewardship purposes, past information affects the future cash flows (Holstrom, 1979). Even though information about the effort of the management is valuable to investors, a recent study finds that information on future cash flows is required by investors

[17] Number of articles citing "Stewardship" in The Accounting Review from 1960-1969: 42 articles; from 1990-1999: 13 articles.

regardless of whether the information is due to the effort of the management. The study reports differences between different types of corporate information (voluntary firm disclosures, mandatory firm disclosures, and analysts' reports), where voluntary management earnings forecasts explain the largest fraction of the quarterly stock return variation. The authors find that the major role for accounting-related information is firm valuation but could not examine if there are are other items that are are more important for the stewardship role (Beyer et al., 2010). Another contribution to this literature stream by Lambert (2010) finds that investors use information to estimate future cash flows to make financial decisions and information that would affect future cash flows for stewardship purposes. This contribution is in line with the finding of Kothari et al. (2010) that contribution packages influence the action of managers in a current period and are in line with the interests of shareholders.

Depending on the two proposed roles, the desirable attributes of financial reporting information may differ. When it comes to stewardship, accounting conservatism is often preferred, while for valuation purposes, accounting neutrality is favored (Kothari et al., 2010; Wu & Zhang, 2009). Further, the neutrality of accounting information is one of the characteristics of decision-useful accounting information (IASB, 2010). Hence, fair value accounting and, thus, fair value estimates (e.g., investment properties) that are value-relevant for investors should be accounted for neutrally. This is in line with the aspirations of the IASB (2015, 2010) as well as the IFRS 13. The standard introduced the fair value hierarchy to make the valuation of assets and liabilities measured at fair value more objective. This higher objectivity should also lead to an increase of neutrality of accounting figures measured at fair value. Dutta and Zhang (2002) find that, for managerial performance evaluation purposes, conservatism can be a preferable accounting ingredient as the manager has incentives that make him use his personal, sensitive information in a non-symmetrical way. Thus, from a stewardship perspective, mark-to-market accounting is not aspirational. This is caused by the fact that the mark-to-market accounting focuses on anticipated managerial performance and not necessarily delivered performance. To sum up, the theoretical research and the empirical market-based research show that there are intersections between stewardship and decision usefulness (Banker et al., 2009; Drymiotes & Hemmer, 2013).

3.6 Theories on information processing of capital market participants

This chapter will point out the different types of decision makers in psychological and economical context. Moreover, information processing concepts and methods will be reviewed, focusing on the information processing approach introduced by Payne et al. (1993) and building up on the initial work by Simon (1955). Besides, different capital market participants will be identified in terms of differentiating information needs with an explicit distinction between non-professional and professional investors.

3.6.1 Key aspects of information processing

Information processing is necessary for individuals, such as capital market participants[18], to make a decision. The term "information processing" stands for a theoretical and methodological framework paradigm that gave rise to innumerable research on human choice and judgement starting in the mid-twentieth century (Koehler & Harvey, 2004). This approach is attributed to the pioneering work of Simon (1978, 1956, 1955) in the field of psychology and part of the "cognitive revolution" in this field of research (Koehler & Harvey, 2004). In terms of the information processing approach to decision-making research, Simon (1955) introduces three relevant key aspects.

The first aspect is that decisions are made with procedural rationality but have to be seen in the context as substantive rationality. Consequently, he focuses his work on the process of choice and judgement. This distinguishes his research from the traditional economic research on decision-making as this literature stream focuses on what (type) of decisions are made. Subsuming, the first key aspect of Simon's work focuses on the question of how decisions are made (Simon, 1981). The second key aspect argues that the decision maker in the classical economic theory should be replaced with a decision maker that is closer to the actual decision needs of individuals. While the economic theory uses a rational decision maker, defined as an individual with complete knowledge, unlimited skill of computation (e.g., the skill of computing calculations that help the individual to weigh up different courses of action), as well as a stable system of preferences, Simon argues that the role of the decision maker in the field of psychology is closer to humans' actual computational capacities and memory systems (Simon, 1955).[19] He further argues that the computational capacity is limited. This is an important constraint when talking about the definition of rational choice, indicating that individuals may only exhibit a limited rationality. In the third aspect, Simon argues that the rational behavior of humans is shaped by structure of the information and the environment in which the task is performed as well as the computational capabilities (Simon, 1990a).

This aspect is in line with other research in this field arguing that judgements and choices are conditional to several tasks and context factors. This contingency is caused by the interaction between the decision environment and the human information processing system (Koehler & Harvey, 2004; Payne, 1982). Researchers find that the generation of a choice or response to a judgement is at least, in parts, caused by limitations in the capacity of information processing (Bettman, 1979; Payne et al., 1992; Slovic, 1995). In particular, individuals tend to not have well-defined and stable preferences but rather construct their beliefs and preferences on the spot, when needed. Further, these preferences are generated by using different decision heuristics as well as simplification mechanisms. The use of these multiple simplifying mechanisms (heuristics) when making a choice or judgement shows the labile beliefs and preferences of individuals that characterize a constructed response. This argumentation is again contrary to the economical approach, where preferences are generated by an invariant algorithm

[18] Further theoretical background on capital market participants is provided in chapter 3.6.5.
[19] In the course of time, the term computational capacity has been replaced by the term cognitive capacity in the field of psychology.

(Koehler & Harvey, 2004). These key aspects of information processing highly differ between the different types of information processors such as professional vs. NPIs (Hirst et al., 1995, Maines & Mc Daniel, 2000). These differences will be described in detail in chapter 3.6.5.

3.6.2 Concepts of information processing

The scarce resource for decision makers is conscious attention. This core idea of information processing was first introduced by Simon (1978). Consequently, individuals are highly selective about what information they draw their attention to and how it is used (Koehler & Harvey, 2004). Kahneman (1973) concertizes the term attention further and introduce two different types: voluntary and involuntary attention. When an individual devotes attention to achieve a goal they perceive is relevant, it is voluntary attention (Higgins, 2002). Involuntary attention can be seen in individuals who view unexpected potential as threatening as well as aspects that are new to the environment of the individual. Furthermore, the attention can be drawn related to an affect or by salient information. Consequently, examples for involuntary attention can be losses and changes relative to targets, reference levels, or aspiration (Koehler & Harvey, 2004). Besides the differentiation introduced by Kahneman (1973), attention is affected by emotions. They help individuals focus their attention and overcome limits of individuals' information processing that will usually follow a "one-at-a-time approach" (Simon, 1990b). Independent of attending information voluntary or involuntary, or favored by emotions, individuals will not necessarily realize that they focus their attention on certain aspects of the environment in which the task is performed. As they may be unaware of this fact, they will not realize that their decisions have been influenced.

Selective attention influences the decision-making and, thus, the way in which an individual performs a task (task effect). A task effect may result from making changes to the salience of the judgement and choice environment (Koehler & Harvey, 2004). Selective attention can affect aspects of a single (unique) alternative as well as multiple (common) alternatives but does not necessarily lead to a poor decision. Selective attention can be mapped onto relevant aspects of the decision environment and ignore aspects that are irrelevant for the decision-making. Thus, even choice mechanisms that are highly simplified may lead to satisfactory decisions (Johnson & Payne, 1985). Nevertheless, poor decisions can result from selective attention if relevant decision information is ignored and irrelevant information is paid attention. This could be the case if an individual only pays attention to the accounting figures of the current period but would not consider the development of these accounting figures compared to the prior period. Keeping in mind that when it comes to decision-making, attention is a scare resource, individuals can be supported in their decision-making by helping them manage their attention. Consequently, several decision aids are trying to ensure an evenly spread attention across different features of one or multiple decision options. Linked to the idea that attention is a scarce resource, a distinction between the cost to acquire information on the one hand and the cost to process information on the other hand needs to be made. Especially, the processing of information (deliberation) is costly (Conlisk, 1996). Thus, when modelling decision-making, both types of costs, processing, and acquisition should be considered as well as the relation between the two. When the cost of information acquisition increases, individuals will make greater use of simplification mechanisms to minimize the cost of information processing. The order in which an item of information is processed, if at all processed, is affected by the cost of acquisition and processing of information. Due to this and the finding that especially the processing of information is costly (Conlisk, 1996), individuals try to avoid spending cognitive effort on transforming provided information and rather accept the provided information in the given (presented) form (Slovic, 1972).

3.6.3 Problem solving and decision heuristics

According to Newell and Simon (1972), the solving of problems takes place in an external task environment. This external task environment is represented by an internal mental representation that is individually created by every problem solver. The internal presentation of a problem is reflected by a serial manipulation of choices, which represent a subset of behavioral alternatives. This manipulation of choices is involved in the decision-making process and, thus, an assumption of the information processing approach, even though this can be seen as a controversial claim (Simon, 1979). This process view is adopted by several researchers arguing that different types of processing happen parallelly (Gilovich et al., 2002; Sloman, 1996). This dual-process view distinguishes two different processing systems (Evans, 1984; Kahneman, 2003). System 1 is the associative system as it reflects the relations of temporal contiguity and similar structure; consequently, the type of processing in this system is associative, relatively automatic and parallel. System 2 is referred to in the literature as the rule-based system and operates on symbolic structures with variables and logical content. The label rule-based system arises from the fact that its computations have the properties that usually are designated to rules. The processing with system 2 is, therefore, serial and effortful (Koehler & Harvey, 2004; Sloman, 1996). As the systems serve complementary functions, the solutions generated by them may be different to a reasoning problem. System 2 may suppress system 1, still system 2 is unlikely to completely inhibit system 1 (Sloman, 1996). Consequently, most researchers in the decision processing literature focus on rule-based system (system 2) as the aspects of the decision processing, in this system, are attention demanding and serial (Gilovich et al., 2002; Koehler & Harvey, 2004). Also, system 2 may partly inhibit system 1 but not the other way around. The serial thinking of the rule-based system can be linked to the use of decision mechanisms, known as heuristics, as introduced by Simon (1955). The substance of his idea of bounded rationality is that the use of mechanisms is required due to the limited cognitive capacity of individuals. To solve decision problems, individuals need to select (using heuristics) and simply use them (Simon, 1955). Using heuristics to solve problems may lead to satisfactory outcomes (Tversky & Kahneman, 1973), but it can also lead to predictable and systematic errors commonly known under the term "cognitive bias." Even though many researchers adopted this view of Tversky and Kahneman (1973) on heuristics causing biases (Hilbert, 2012; Otuteye & Siddiquee, 2015), Gigerenzer (1996) claims that decision heuristics are suitable for most purposes.

Besides producing satisfactory outcomes, there are other reasons for individuals to use decision heuristics. First, individuals might not have another choice than using heuristics. This situation may arise when the time for information processing or the cognitive capacity is limited. This could be the case for NPIs who only have limited time and cognitive capacity to look at a financial statement to evaluate a potential investment in the firm. This problem is part of the current disclosure effectiveness debate that deals with the issue of too many (voluntary) disclosures on several accounting figures. This overload of disclosure information makes it impossible for investors to read through all financial statement information due to their limited cognitive capacity and consider them for their investment decision, which is why they regularly rely on heuristics. If the aspect of time and effort as a scarce resource of investors is introduced, the conflict of disclosure overload in an accounting context would aggravate. Second, individuals may use decision heuristics when the cost of effort and time are high, as they are scarce resources for them. Third, an individual may use decision heuristics because the individual has used them in the past and it had produced a satisfactory outcome. This could be the case with a functional fixation on a specific accounting figure like net income because such a fixation has worked well for the individual in the past in terms of a positive return on their investment. In addition, the heuristics are readily available in the memory of the individual if used previously (Koehler & Harvey, 2004).

There are different heuristic mechanisms with regard to problem solving. One heuristic proposed by Simon (1955) is to stop searching after finding the first satisfactory solution to a decision problem and, therefore, simplifying the process. Thus, the focus using this heuristic is to obtain a quick and satisfactory solution rather than spending resources on finding an optimal solution for the problem by researching exhaustively. This heuristic is linked to the idea that decision outcomes are either satisfactory or unsatisfactory and valued, therefore, by using a simple payoff scheme. By making changes in the reference point or aspiration level to which the outcome of the decision (satisfactory vs. unsatisfactory) is linked to, dynamic aspects of the decision behavior are captured. Still, when using these simple payoff schemes, choice biases may occur as individuals will typically not consider reasonable trade-offs among conflicting objectives (Koehler & Harvey, 2004). Gilovich et al. (2002) argue that decision heuristics may also involve problem redefinition. Thus, a difficult judgement problem may be solved by attribute substitution. The information processing approach in more general terms assumes that individuals possess a variety of heuristic strategies when it comes to solving decision problems (Payne et al., 1993). These strategies can be acquired by individuals through formal training and experience. Consequently, the use of heuristics, if the task demands it, is a way to intelligently adapt to complex decision environments for humans with limited cognitive capacity (Payne et al., 1988). To sum up, individuals use heuristics to produce satisfactory outcomes to make decisions in complex environments with limited capacity of resources (e.g. time, cognitive capacity). Decision errors (biases) may occur when using heuristics but will usually be systematic, which is why the errors are predictable. Thus, human error in decision-making does not necessarily arise from motivated irrationality but from limitations of the individual's information processor.

3.6.4 Information processing strategies and decision-making of investors

The prior psychological literature points out several different information processing strategies. These different strategies are used upon task demands to solve multi-attribute choice problems of individuals. While individuals tend to use different strategies, the strategies itself can also be distinguished. Generally, there are four strategies when it comes to information processing: first, strategies that involve the processing of all relevant information and consider trade-offs among values, which means that the strategies are compensatory. Second, heuristic strategies, where the use of information is limited and, thus, selected. When using heuristic strategies, trade-offs are avoided, and they are, consequently, non-compensatory. Third, strategies where the process of information is mainly driven by alternatives. Thus, several attributes of one option are considered and processed before another available option is considered and processed. Fourth, strategies with an attribute-focus concentrating on one single attribute for the values of several alternatives. Hence, another attribute is not considered before the (first) single attribute is fully examined. These strategies value several alternatives based on one single attribute before considering another or other attribute(s) for them (Koehler & Harvey, 2004). What remains critical when taking the different strategies into account is how and why a certain strategy is selected by a decision-maker instead of another for a specific task.

Beach and Mitchell (1978) and Payne (1976) predict that strategy selection depends on the goal of individuals of achieving a satisfactory level of decision accuracy, on the one hand, and to minimize cognitive effort on the other. Payne et al. (1993) emphasize that individuals are flexible in their approach to problems and, consequently, in their choice of strategy. They find that individuals further experience the upcoming decision as a tension that can only be released by making a decision. Thus, they will try to make the decision as easy and quickly as possible. Tversky and Kahneman (1973) argue that the process of information depends on several variables such as the task itself, the person trying to solve it - their cognitive ability and knowledge - and the context in which the task is performed (especially the social accountability). Making even just a minor change to any of these variables may change the way the decision is made by an individual as well as the solution the individual comes up with. An example for such a change could be a change to the way in which the information is presented (format change). Moreover, individuals will make a more intuitive rather than analytic and quicker decision if there are many cues, cues that are redundant, the decomposition of the task is low, environmental cues equally weighted, organizational principles not available, information is displayed simultaneously, and the period is brief. According to Payne et al. (1993), adaptivity failures occur when the situation is misunderstood by the decision maker or the cues are misread. Besides, failure can be caused if an individual does not know one's desired accuracy.

Using decision heuristics may reduce an individual's cognitive effort. When making even a slight change to the presentation format, the judgement related to the information is likely to change. This change can induce costs for individuals as they might make a suboptimal decision that leads to an unsatisfactory result (Payne et al., 1993). Thus, individuals may respond by a switch to a simpler and less accurate alternative when the overall number of alternatives increases (Kleinmuntz & Schkade, 1993). The change of format, however, can also have a positive effect on the decision-making process as making information salient can ease the strain on attention and memory (Einhorn & Hogarth, 1981; Kleinmuntz & Schkade, 1993). By easing the strain on the memory and attention of a decision maker, the amount of information that can be processed by them increases. This increase may lead to more sufficient decision results as more information can be considered (Clor-Proell et al., 2014).

Since the attention of individuals is limited and information is vast, individuals use heuristics and, thus, only process a subset of information. Especially in a financial reporting context, researchers find that investors concentrate on few salient stimuli instead of trying to process several provided information (Fiske & Taylor, 1991; Libby et al., 2002). In a financial statement context, this means that an investor will not review all information that a financial statement contains but rather make an investment decision based on the firm's earnings performance. Investors consequently focus on accounting profitability represented by cash profitability first and net assets second. They further consider the cumulative difference between free cash flow and operating income, which measures the extent by which over-optimism occurs. In this context, net operating assets scaled by total assets can be seen as a negative predictor of stock returns in the long run (Hirshleifer et al., 2004).[20] Hirshleifer and Teoh (2003) are the first to examine reporting choices and accounting disclosures specifically in this context. They argue that information aggregation can be helpful for investors as they may face trouble in processing disaggregated information. A different presentation of information eases the processing redundancy, which can also be helpful to make the information more accessible for different users. They state that the specific structure of financial reporting and regulation could be driven by the limited attention of investors (Hirshleifer & Teoh, 2003).

NPIs are more likely to rely on heuristics when they make an investment decision compared to professional investors. Thus, NPIs are especially likely to miss the deeper understanding of accounting information but save cognitive effort by easing the stream of attention and memory on the other hand. Consequently, NPIs are likely to focus on the bottom line earnings that are displayed more saliently than other (disclosed) accounting figures (Clor-Proell et al., 2014; Hirst & Hopkins, 1998). This research translates the long-established psychological findings described in the previous chapters (chapters 3.6.1 to 3.6.4) into a financial reporting context. While research in the field of psychology focuses on the decision of an individual without a specific context (Payne et al., 1993; Simon, 1955), financial statement users and decision makers in a financial reporting context have specific information needs and background knowledge (Hirst & Hopkins, 1998).

3.6.5 Actors on the capital market and information behavior

According to the Conceptual Framework, the IFRS are designated for a variety of user groups. Potential users and their information needs are displayed in the following table.

[20] Hirshleifer et al. (2004) chose firms listed at the New York Stock Exchange (NYSE)/American Stock Exchange (AMEX) and National Association of Security Automated Quotations Dealers (NASDAQ) for their sample selection, which covers a broad range of different industries.

User group	Main information needs
Investors	Need detailed information on the future development of the company regarding the height and timely manner of future cash-flows. This is relevant to assess the risk-return-structure of their investment. They are further interested in periodical information that show how the management of the company is dealing with the supplied resources.
Creditors	Since they bear the default risk, they are mainly interested in information about the possibility of current and future liquidity problems of the company.
Employees	They are primarily interested in the company's stability and profitability as they potentially conclude in job security. They might further see stability and profitability as an indicator for possible wage and salary demands.
Suppliers and other Creditors	Due to the receivables they are interested in the economic situation of the company.
Clients	The economic dependence of clients, especially with regard to long-term business relations between suppliers and clients, leads to an enhanced interest in the economic situation as well as going concern for the company.
Government and other institutions	Companies operate in public. Thus, public institutions are interested in information about the economic situation of companies to regulate the activities of a firm or to determine the tax policy.
Public	Further, user groups that don't have a direct contractual relationship with the company could be interested in the economic situation of a company as they can be taken into account as a (future) potential part of the user group.

Table 3: Main information needs of financial reporting user groups[21]

The ED /2015/4 defines the primary users of financial reports as potential and existing investors, creditors, and other lenders who are not in the position to require information to be provided directly to them (IASB, 2015, BC1.11). This definition is picked up by several discussants arguing that this primary user group is too narrow. They propose a wider definition including employees, customers, suppliers, regulators, and others (IASB, 2015, BC1.12). On the other side, discussants claimed that the definition was too broad and that the primary user group should be defined as the holders of equity claims against the entity (IASB, 2015, BC1.13). The Board of the IASB states in their Basis for Conclusion on Conceptual Framework for Financial Reporting (BCIN) that renunciation on a primary user group can lead to the risk of the conceptual framework becoming vague or unduly abstract (IASB, 2015). The usage of decision heuristics distinguishes between professional and NPIs in most research contributions (Clor-Proell et al., 2014; Cohen et al., 2015; Hirst & Hopkins, 1998; Maines & McDaniel, 2000) which is why their approach is being followed.

[21] Author's own illustration based on Pellens et al. (2014) and IASB (2015).

3.6.5.1 Nonprofessional investors

How individuals process information when it comes to making judgements and decisions is a major topic in research in the field of psychology (Payne et al., 1993). When viewed from an economical perspective, individuals seem to maximize their subjective utility in this process. Yet, viewing from a psychological perspective, individuals suffer from limited cognitive capacity, and thus, have to make trade-offs when it comes to information processing (Clor-Proell et al., 2014; Simon, 1978). For example, if individuals would indeed maximize their subjective utility, they would convert information into a (more) useful form more often. Hence, individuals often process information in the form in which it is displayed to them. The existing literature on this subject matter presumes that this is caused by the thought process of individuals that suggest to them that altering the information in its original form may lead to more costs than benefits for them (Clor-Proell et al., 2014; Payne, 1982). The use of this heuristic may save individuals' cognitive effort, but it may also lead to a suboptimal decision caused, inter alia, by the presentation of information (Payne et al., 1993).

The use of heuristics to save cognitive effort is also relevant against the background of disclosure overload. The term refers to information overload that is strongly linked to the publication of financial statements. Generally, the individual decision performance (i.e., the quality of decisions) is positively correlated with the amount of provided information (Beerbaum, 2016). Yet, this only holds to a certain point from when on the usefulness of additional information becomes negative. Consequently, information that is provided to investors beyond this point will not be integrated into their decision-making process (Schick & Gordon, 1999). Guay et al. (2016) discover a significant positive correlation between financial statement complexity and voluntary disclosure. They also point out that during the past 20 years (1995-2015), the amount of voluntary disclosures steadily increased. Taking these findings, together with the fact that individuals only have a limited amount of cognitive capacity, constitutes a problem.

Changes to the presentation format can enhance attention and can, ultimately, lead to an increase in the amount of information being processed (Maines & McDaniel, 2000). This behavior is especially relevant to NPIs because they tend to use simplified decision heuristics, however, it also keeps them from gaining a deeper understanding of the information presented (Clor-Proell et al., 2014). Consistent with this line of argument, Maines and McDaniel (2000) develope a psychology-based framework around the specific ways to display accounting information to ease information processing. The main components of the framework include NPIs' information acquisition, information evaluation, and the information weighting process as depicted below.

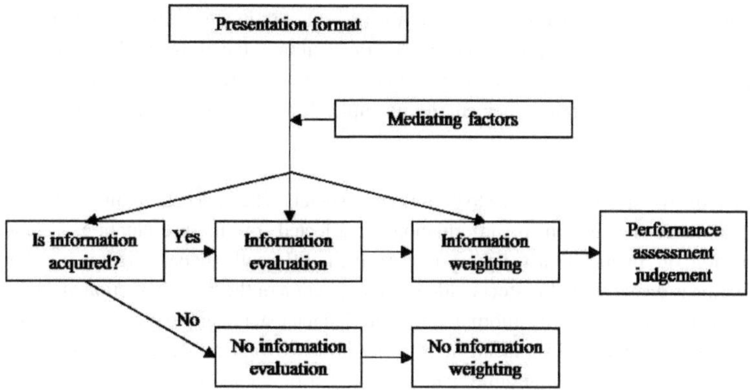

Figure 4: Effect of presentation format on investors' performance assessment judgements[22]

The framework by Maines and McDaniel (2000) proposes that the presentation format of information affects the performance assessment judgement of investors. The performance assessment judgement is particularly affected by the acquisition, evaluation and/or weighting of information. The framework was originally proposed for the information processing of comprehensive-income information. Information acquisition refers to an investor reading a specific item of financial statement information, e.g., unrealized gains and losses, and storing this item of information in its memory. The term further implies that the investor can recall the information by memory and consequently can state where the information appeared in the financial statement. Information evaluation requires an investor to assess the characteristics of the acquired financial statement information. Hence, unrealized gains and losses would be evaluated in terms of volatility in this step of information processing. The last step of information processing is the weighting of information. In this step, an investor places a certain weight on the evaluated information characteristics. This placed weight partly represents the importance of this information characteristic for the judgement of the management performance as well as the corporate performance (performance assessment). As mentioned earlier, if information is not acquired, evaluation and weighting of the information is not possible.

Besides the three steps of information processing, the authors further identify five differences between the format dimensions of financial statement information. These differences in dimensions help identify the format that will produce the greatest level of information weighting. Each dimension can affect the NPIs' judgement because it either affects the cognitive costs evoked by processing information or signals the importance of the information. Two out of five dimensions affect the cognitive costs evoked by processing the information. Information *isolation* facilitates the process of information processing by separating the different information types. It is, for example, easier for investors to process the information

[22] Author's own illustration based on Hogarth (1989), Dawes & Corrigan (1974) and Maines & McDaniel (2000).

pertaining to comprehensive income when it is presented in its own separate statement (Clor-Proell & Warfield, 2009). Information *aggregation* facilitates the disassembling of information and marks the second cognitive cost dimension of the model. Presenting gross changes instead of net changes in the income statement, for example, disassembles information (Clor-Proell & Warfield, 2009).

Three out of five dimensions relate to performance signals. The idea behind this category is that the importance perception of information is affected by its presentation. Accounting information on financial instruments is perceived differently depending on whether this information is displayed in the stockholders' equity section or the liability section of the balance sheet. A certain *placement* of information in the financial statement expresses the importance of information, for e.g., by placing it in a performance rather than in a non-performance statement. Therefore, important information can rather be found in the income statement than in the statement of the stockholder's equity (Clor-Proell & Warfield, 2009). By *labelling* the information, e.g., with the term income, its importance is affected. The last signaling dimension is *linkage*. It expresses that the importance of the information is affected by a direct association between the different information items, for e.g., placing two items of the same category on the financial statement, like the fixed assets accounts bank and cash.

The changes proposed in this experiment relate to three of the above described five dimensions. I create an extra column in the balance sheet to present the fair value hierarchy, sensitivity analysis, or the reconciliation between the carrying amounts between prior year and current year. By presenting this information, I am signaling the importance of this information to the NPIs. Thus, the cognitive costs of the users spent on processing the information decreases by explicitly *labelling* them. Furthermore, by presenting the information in a separate column, I am *isolating* it for the user. Additionally, the fair value of an investment property is *linked* to the profit and loss statement since the change in the fair value compared to the prior year is realized through profit and loss. Consequently, all dimensions that relate to performance signals are covered by my experimental design. I take the other category of dimension related to cognitive costs into account with this experimental design, since I make the information more salient for the user. This suggested salient presentation reduces the cognitive costs expended in processing the information and signals its importance to the financial statement users (Clor-Proell et al., 2014).

I take prior accounting research into account to evaluate how a change in the financial statement format will affect the judgement of NPIs (Clor-Proell & Warfield, 2009). Numerous reporting contexts have been investigated by the existing research and it has found that, generally, both professional and nonprofessional financial statement users are affected by the changes relating to the format of the financial statements (Clor-Proell & Warfield; Hirst & Hopkins, 1998; Maines & McDaniel, 2000). Specifically, research in this field examines the effect of format changes on information evaluation and weighting, finding that a specific format can affect both nonprofessional (Clor-Proell et al., 2014; Clor-Proell & Warfield, 2009; Hodge et al., 2004) and professional (Hirst & Hopkins, 1998) financial statement users. I follow the research by Clor-Proell et al. (2014), who examine how changes in presentation affect the use of disclosures and not the number itself, e.g., the subjectivity (fair value-hierarchy) with which the number is measured. My hypotheses in line with the framework of Maines and McDaniel (2000) are presented in chapter 4.1.

3.6.5.2 Professional investors

Institutional investors provide the most financial capital (Ferreira & Matos, 2008) and are, thus, one of the main user groups of financial reporting. Institutional investors are professional analysts and fund managers and proxy in the literature for professional investors (Hirst & Hopkins, 1998; Reimsbach et al., 2017). While I use the framework provided by Maines and McDaniel (2000) for the information processing for NPIs, Hirst and Hopkins (1998) provide the results for professional investors. Maines and McDaniel (2000) use their results to build the framework. Hirst and Hopkins (1998) choose to observe the detection of earnings management of investments of firms in the electronic manufacturing sector. They find that earnings management is only detected when the information on unrealized gains and losses is presented in a statement of comprehensive income.

While half of the participants in the study of Hirst and Hopkins (1998) received information on unrealized gains and losses in the statement of comprehensive income, the other half received a statement of stockholders' equity where the information on unrealized gains and losses is present. The authors find that, of the participants who received the statement of stockholders' equity, 50% could not indicate that the term comprehensive income was presented. Still, it would be possible for professional investors to see the term comprehensive income but not capture several components of it, such as information on unrealized gains and losses. Based on this result, the authors argue that the professional investors did not acquire the information on unrealized gains and losses. Maines and McDaniel (2000) remark that a manipulation test on the acquisition of information on unrealized gains and losses was absent in the experiment by Hirst and Hopkins (1998). Thus, it is not clear if analysts who state that they saw the term comprehensive income did read the information on unrealized gains and losses included in the comprehensive income (Maines & McDaniel, 2000). Keeping this in mind, professional investors' information acquisition is affected by the format of presentation. Professional investors will use valuation models and, thus, will directly search for the information they need to fill these models. Consequently, they will not read the presentation fully in the order of the presentation (like NPIs) but rather skip back and forth between the financial statement information until they have the information they need for their valuation models (McEwen & Hunton, 1999). Finally, professional investors are unlikely to read financial statement information that is not relevant to their valuation model (Maines & McDaniel, 2000).

Because the information needs of NPIs and professional investors differ as well as their information processing, most research contributions focus on one type of investor. In my research context, I focus on NPIs as earlier research finds that NPIs, especially, face difficulties in incorporating disclosures on fair value measurements while professional investors do not seem to have these problems. Particularly, Kolev (2009) and Song et al. (2010) find that professional investors can incorporate fair value disclosures into their decision-making process. NPIs, on the other hand, face difficulties when trying to enclose fair value disclosures into their decision-making process (Clor-Proell et al., 2014; Dietrich et al., 2001; Harper et al., 1987; Hodge et al., 2004). Thus, this research focuses on NPIs as prior research shows that they currently seem unable to incorporate the disclosures into their decision-making process and calls for future research to find ways to compensate this detriment.

4 Theoretical background and predictions on facilitating the usage of disclosures for investors

There are different types of disclosures mandated for the financial reporting of assets according to the IFRS. In the following chapter, I will introduce a classification system for the different types of disclosures by taking into account the existing literature on this topic. Also, I will point out different ways that information facilitation can be increased for financial statement users and which way seems most effective and reasonable especially for NPIs. I will then deduce my research questions and hypotheses for the conducted experiment.

4.1 Investors' information processing of fair value disclosures for investment decisions

To provide more understandable and relevant information for financial statement users, the FASB was the first to introduce fair value information for several components of the balance sheet (FASB, 2010; IASB, 2010). Thus, the FASB places information for assets and liabilities measured at fair value above information measured at the cost-model (Barth, 2006; Clor-Proell & Warfield, 2009; FASB, 2007). Still, there were inconsistencies regarding fair value definition, measurement, and reporting. These inconsistencies were addressed by the Statement of Financial Accounting Standards (SFAS) No. 157 Fair Value Measurements in September 2006. Since then, a common definition of fair value exists; defining fair value as "the price that would be received to sell an asset or paid to transfer a liability in an orderly transaction between market participants at the measurement date" (SFAS 157-8). The mentioned price provides investors with information that increases their decision usefulness in comparison to historical costs (Botosan & Huffman, 2015). This conclusion even holds true when the fair value is imperfectly determined. Besides the definition of the fair value itself, a framework for fair value measurement was established. In May 2011, the IASB and the FASB issued new guidance on fair value measurement and disclosure requirements for the IFRS. For the FASB and IASB, the issuance of a new standard was seen as the conclusion to a major convergence project as well as an element of response to the financial crisis. The guidance set out in the IFRS 13 Fair Value Measurement as well as the update to Topic 820 in the FASB's Accounting Standard Codification (formerly referred to as SFAS 157) intended to improve the IFRS' fair value accounting (FASB, 2011).

4.1.1 Types of fair value disclosures

The initial application of the IFRS 13 referred to annual periods beginning after 1 January 2013. The definition of fair value in the framework of the IFRS 13 remained the same as stated in the SFAS 157. The main goals of the IFRS 13 are to increase comparability and consistency of fair value measurements and disclosures through the implementation of the fair value hierarchy. Within the frame of this hierarchy, input parameters used in valuation techniques are categorized into three levels. The highest priority is given to (unadjusted) quoted prices in an active market, where assets or liabilities are identical. The lowest priority in this hierarchy is given to unobservable inputs (IFRS 13.72). Following this principle, quoted prices in an active market for identical assets or liabilities are classified as level 1 inputs. Level 2 inputs include

T. Herrmann, *The Decision Usefulness of Additional Fair Value Disclosures*, Controlling und Rechnungslegung – Managerial and Financial Accounting, https://doi.org/10.1007/978-3-658-24832-1_4

quoted prices for similar assets or liabilities in active markets or quoted prices for identical or similar assets or liabilities in markets that are not active. In addition, inputs other than quoted prices that are observable can be classified as level 2 inputs. When inputs are unobservable for the valuation of assets or liabilities, the inputs are classified as level 3. These level 3 inputs occur when the target market of the asset or liability has little, if any, activity at the measurement date. Level 3 inputs are the best available information under these circumstances and can even involve the entity's own data. To meet the requirements of the standard setter, the input level itself needs to be disclosed, but the disclosure requirements for the respective input level also needs to be considered. Clearly, inputs classified as level 3 contain the highest information risk for financial statement users, leading to the highest requirements in terms of disclosures. Future development of level 3 inputs is difficult to predict, especially compared to level 1. To address this, the SEC encourages voluntary disclosures for fair value estimates (SEC, 2008).

The main goal of disclosing input parameters and other supporting information for fair value is to make information more understandable and reliable for financial statement users. To be (decision-) useful, information must be both relevant and reliable (FASB, 1980a). Ceteris paribus, financial statement users would rather use reliable information than non-reliable information when making an investment decision (Clor-Proell et al., 2014). Yet, reliability remains an elusive and a complex construct (Gassen & Schwedler, 2010; Maines & Wahlen, 2006). Thus, it may be difficult for financial statement users to differentiate between highly reliable, e.g., inputs classified at level 1, and non-reliable information, e.g., inputs classified at level 3.

Compared to the historical cost accounting of recognized assets, which often contains hidden management reserves, assets measured at fair value narrow this gap between the market value and the book value (Hitz, 2007). Hence, fair values classified at level 2 and 3 often use model-based estimates that rely heavily on projections and expectations of the management. These projections and expectations can be subject to earnings management. Mazza et al. (2011) argue that, for level 3 input parameters, the measurement guidance in accordance with the SFAS No. 157 (FASB, 2010) falls into the "unstructured and imprecise category of standards" introduced by Nelson et al. (2002). The authors find that managers are more likely to attempt earnings management when assets are accounted for according to imprecise standards compared to more precise standards (Nelson et al., 2002). Thus, performance-based incentives could motivate managers to exploit the flexibility of level 3 fair value estimates to produce unreliable and biased accounting figures (Mazza et al., 2011). These findings are in line with McEwen et al. (2008), who study management biases related to level 3 fair value estimates in the context of impairment losses and find that managers take advantage of the leeway in terms of discretionary valuation. Moreover, analysts ignore these biases caused by earnings management, even though they know that the management exploits their flexibility with level 3 estimates. Besides the fair value itself, voluntary disclosures can also be used opportunistically by managers (Blacconiere et al., 2011).

Hence, the decision to incorporate such non-reliable (disclosure) information in an individual's investment decision may, as a result, suffer from the difficulty involved in determining the reliability level of the information. Given the fact that many financial statement users are unable to differentiate between highly reliable and non-reliable information, they tend to rely on contextual factors to ascertain the reliability of the financial statement information (Hirst et al., 1995; Maines & McDaniel, 2000). By initiating the fair value hierarchy, the FASB not only makes it simpler for investors to detect highly uncertain information using the level-label for the input parameters of the fair value but also works toward making highly uncertain information more decision-useful by mandating additional disclosures. Latest research finds that level 3 fair values are as value-relevant for an investment decision as level 1 and level 2 fair values (Lawrence et al., 2016) while earlier research finds that level 3 fair value measurements are significantly less value-relevant than level 1 and level 2 measurements (Kolev, 2009; Song et al., 2010). Level 3 and level 2 fair values are especially relevant for real estate firms. These firms are economically significant and have highly relevant assets measured at fair value. Investment properties are an important example in this context. Investment properties represent over 75% of the average total assets of real estate firms in the EU member states (Müller et al., 2015). Thus, looking at the disclosures for these firms, it can be concluded that measuring fair value with level 3 inputs has a high impact and practical relevance in the EU.

Apart from the disclosures that must be part of a financial statement according to the IAS 17 when the investment property is a leased asset (operating lease), there are additional disclosures for investment properties re-measured at fair value. Among the criteria used to distinguish investment property from owner-occupied property as well as from property held for sale, the disclosure of methods and assumptions used to determine the fair value of an investment are mandatory. Rental incomes, direct operating expenses arising from the investment properties that generated rental income during the period, as well as expenses arising from an investment property that did not generate rental income during the period have to be recognized in profit and loss. The changes in fair value recognized when an investment property is sold also have to be recognized through profit and loss followed by disclosed information on the sale of the investment properties (IAS 40.75). Additionally, a reconciliation between the carrying amounts of an investment property at the beginning and at the end of the period, showing any additions or disposals as well as adjustments made in fair values and transfers from owner-occupied property to inventories or back must be disclosed (IAS 40.76). If there was an outside valuation that required significant adjustments made to the fair value, it would also need to be recognized (IAS 40.77).

In the occasion that the investment property is measured at fair value on a recurring basis after its initial recognition, the methods applied, the assumptions made to determine the fair value, and its impact on profit and loss as well as on other comprehensive income (OCI), especially for investment properties categorized within the level 3 hierarchy, are to be disclosed according to the IFRS 13. This ensures that the financial statement users may assess the provided information more efficiently. Thus, the IFRS 13 provides guidance on disclosures concerning investment properties categorized within the level 3 hierarchy. These mentioned disclosures required by the IFRS 13 and IAS 40, which are the relevant standards for investment properties, can be categorized into the following different types of information: qualitative information, range values, and change values. The fair value of the investment properties can be classified as a point value. Thus, the point value is the fair value measurement of an investment property at the end of the reporting period (IFRS 13.93).[23] Fair values and, thus, the fair value point information are value-relevant and, thus, play an important role for investors' decision-making (IASB, 2010; Lawrence et al., 2016). Qualitative information, in terms of investment properties, is represented by the fair value hierarchy and the resulting fair value level. The description of the sensitivity of the fair value on potential effects to changes in the key input parameters of the fair value determination can be summarized as a range value (IFRS 13.93). The standard setter requires a narrative description of the sensitivity of the fair value to changes in unobservable inputs (IFRS 13.93). When looking at disclosures of European real estate firms (e.g., the financial statement of LEG Immobilien AG), the sensitivity is often displayed as a numerical range (Kile et al., 1998). The reconciliation between the carrying amounts of investment properties at the beginning and the end of the period, according to IAS 40.75, can be classified as a change value. Following this classification of fair value disclosures, the subsequent category tree evokes the following figure:

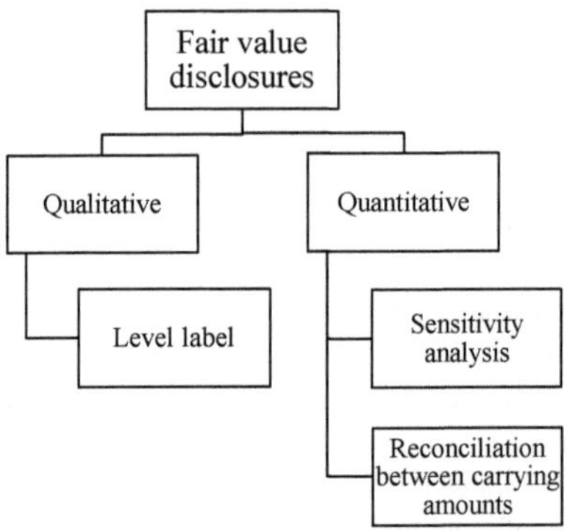

Figure 5: Types of fair value disclosures[24]

I am the first to introduce this type of disclosure categorization within an accounting context. Still, there are other literature streams (e.g., forecasting literature) that have introduced classifications of information. In terms of disclosure overload, it is often criticized that too many disclosures are provided, and investors are unable to incorporate all of them into their investment decision (Beerbaum, 2016). I intend to address this problem with my research and find out what type of disclosure brings along the greatest benefits in term of decision usefulness for its users. Especially NPIs face difficulties in incorporating disclosure information on fair values into their decision-making process, even though research finds that these information are value-relevant for investors (Lawrence et al., 2016). In line with the IASB (2010), decision-useful fair value financial statement information can be defined as value-relevant and, thus,

[23] For a detailed classification of disclosure information, see Appendix S1.
[24] Author's own illustration.

being useful to existing and potential investors. Besides, these disclosures have the greatest proportion for assets where the input parameters are classified at level 3 of the fair value hierarchy. Consequently, my first research question (RQ) reads as follows:

RQ1: *What type of fair value disclosure information leads to the highest perceived reliability and decision usefulness for NPIs?*

My first research question addresses the reliability and decision usefulness of different types of disclosures. Nevertheless, other impacts can affect the reliability and decision usefulness and, consequently, the incorporation of disclosure information on fair value estimates into the decision-making process of the NPIs as well. How the reliability and, thus, decision usefulness of financial statement information can be improved is widely discussed in the literature over a period of several years (Clor-Proell et al., 2014; Hodge et al., 2004; Maines & McDaniel, 2000; Pitt, 2001) and will be examined in the following.

4.1.2 Incorporating fair value disclosures into the decision-making process

In the prior literature, two main approaches can be identified when it comes to increasing the reliability and, consequently, decision usefulness for investors. One approach discussed by Pitt (2001) and Hodge et al. (2004) is to enclose additional information to the financial statement into the notes and, thus, try to increase the reliability for financial statement users. This earlier approach, however, concludes that enclosing additional information does not (always) lead to a higher perceived reliability of the accounting data and that it might result in disclosure overload (Beerbaum, 2016). The other and more recent approach tries to increase the reliability for financial statement users by proposing format changes of the enclosed information (Clor-Proell & Warfield, 2009; Maines & McDaniel, 2000). These changes can be of different nature and affect the interpretation of the provided information. Different ways that can facilitate the information usage of investors and, thus, increase decision usefulness are presented in the figure below:

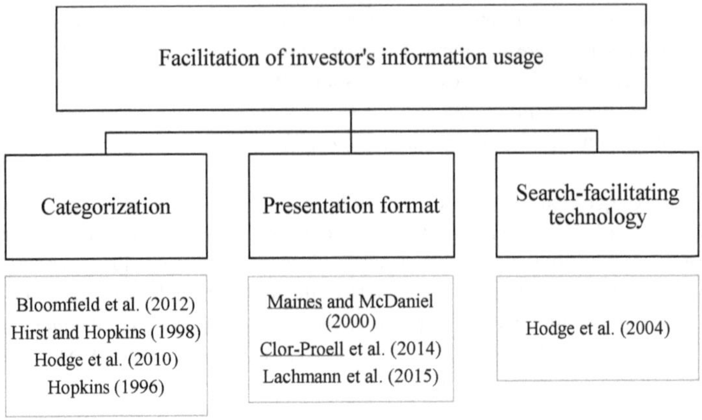

Figure 6: Approaches to facilitate information usage of NPIs[25]

Hopkins (1996) investigates the classification of financial instruments in the balance sheet in his paper. These instruments can be attributed to both equity and debt and, thus, might affect the judgement of stock prices by buy-side analysts. The author takes earlier psychology research (Chi et al., 1981; Spivey, 1989) into account, which suggests that individuals mentally try to access knowledge on related or similar situations when making judgements. Thus, if decision-relevant information is classified as related or similar, this classification can influence the knowledge of new information and its assessment and usage by investors. The author tests this hypothesis for financial analysts, who proxy for professional investors in the context of classifying balance sheet information. The paper finds, when manipulating the balance sheet classification in a laboratory experiment, that the manipulation of accounting classification affects the stock price judgements of financial analysts. Thus, changes in the classification, which can be summarized under the term of categorization, facilitate the information usage of professional investors.

Bloomfield et al. (2012) also test categorization as a way to facilitate information usage for investors. They use an experiment to examine if professional-credit analysts are better able to evaluate information when the information is disaggregated and classified. They find that if the information is classified, the analysts are better able to identify the operating structures of a firm. Consequently, they add up to earlier research (Hirst & Hopkins, 1998; Hodge et al., 2010) that related information should be presented in close proximity within the financial statement. Bringing their results to a more common level, the authors state that financial statement users respond more when information is presented in the face of the financial statement compared to when the information is provided in the footnotes (Bloomfield et al., 2012).

[25] Author's own illustration.

Maines and McDaniel (2000) also use an experiment to test if alternative *presentation formats* could affect the information processing of NPIs. The authors chose the context of the SFAS No. 130 for their experiment, which not only requires comprehensive income in a primary financial statement but also allows the firm to present the accounting information on unrealized gains and losses in either a statement of stockholders' equity or statement of comprehensive income (FASB, 1997). They find that the judgement on the corporate and management performance of NPIs only reflect the volatility if the statement of comprehensive income presents the comprehensive income of the firm. Consequently, the authors provide evidence that the presentation format of information affects the information weighting of NPIs. The different options of the presentation format that are tested in the experiment are optional in accordance with the applicable accounting framework at that time. Thus, the authors tested differences in the presentation format in accordance with the legitimate presentation formats of comprehensive income.

Clor-Proell et al. (2014) draw onto the information processing research (e.g., Maines & McDaniel, 2000) and evaluate how the change in presentation with regard to the income statement can affect the reliability of the mandated supplemental disclosures. The authors take prior research into account, which finds that some investors (namely NPIs) have difficulties in assessing the nature of the inputs of fair value accounting figures (Dietrich et al., 2001; Harper et al., 1987). To manipulate the presentation format, the authors add an additional column to the income statement and call the presentation of accounting information in this additional column "salient." They find that the reliance of nonprofessional financial statement users on mandated supplemental disclosures can be improved by making a change to the presentation format of the information and presenting it in an additional column in the income statement. These findings, thus, extend earlier findings in this stream of literature by Maines and McDaniel (2000). Compared to the earlier research contributions in this literature stream, the authors are the first to introduce a new presentation format that is not yet applicable according to the IFRS. The authors aim to point out new ways on how the reliability of income statements can be increased.

Hodge et al. (2004) introduce another approach to facilitate the information usage of investors. They examine if a search engine that facilitates direct searches and allows the simultaneous presentation of related footnote and financial statement presentation helps users acquire financial statement information and integrate them into their investment decision process. As a context, the authors choose the recognition vs. disclosure of stock option compensation. They find that several users do not use the technology but that those who do, are more likely to acquire the information and integrate it into their investment decision. This results in different investment decisions of individuals depending on whether or not they have made use of the search engine. The research results implicate that the usage of a search facilitating technology can increase the transparency of financial statement for potential investors as well as managements' choices to report that information. Still, a lot of people do not seem to know about either the existence of such technologies or how to assess them.

The facilitation of information usage for investors can not only be distinguished between different ways such as categorization, presentation format, and search-facilitating technologies but also in terms of different types of investors. Though the FASB and IASB mandated fair value disclosures to make fair value estimates with high uncertainty levels more reliable and consequently more decision-useful, various literature shows that especially NPIs have difficulties in using the disclosed information (Harper et al., 1987; Hodge et al., 2004). Professional investors, on the other hand, are more likely to incorporate value-relevant fair value disclosures into their decision-making process, since the value-relevant disclosures are reflected in stock prices (Kolev, 2009; Song et al., 2010). By extension, recent research suggests that the NPIs are at a disadvantage compared to professional investors when it comes to the processing of fair value disclosures (Clor-Proell et al., 2014). Relevant research on improving the reliability of accounting figures by categorizing them focuses on professional investors (Bloomfield et al., 2012; Hopkins, 1996).

The change in the presentation format is applied in a research context with NPIs (Clor-Proell et al., 2014; Lachmann et al., 2015; Maines & McDaniel, 2000). The research by Hodge et al. (2004) focuses on the benefits and usage of search engines among NPIs. Even though I choose NPIs as research subject, I decide not to use a search engine as a way to possibly increase information usage and reliability due to two reasons: first, Hodge et al. (2004) find that half of their NPIs in the experiment did not use the search engine at all as they possibly felt that they were not familiar with this type of technology. Second, for my research, I could not have used this approach because I conducted a paper-based experiment. Consequently, I followed the research approach by Clor-Proell et al. (2014), who make changes to the salience of the information. The authors take prior research, especially the one by Maines and McDaniel (2000) into account, when they display income statement information in an additional column in the income statement, thus, making it salient to financial statement users. I also consider the research of Lachmann et al. (2015) who evaluate if the presentation of changes in firms' credit risk presented in net income vs. OCI affects information processing of knowledgeable NPIs. When the content of information is constant, they find that information processing only slightly differs between different presentation formats while the risk of misinterpreting the credit risk is not affected by the presentation format. The evaluation of the overall firm performance is affected by the presentation format though. Further, the authors identify that information processing is affected by the profitability of the firm. Thus, they determined that the content of information (e.g., the profitability of the firm) can affect the information processing of NPIs, while the format can affect the performance evaluation, which is mediated by information processing steps according to Maines and McDaniel (2000).

Summarizing these earlier research contributions, format effects were researched in the context of (voluntary) disclosures, profit and loss statement, as well as comprehensive income (Clor-Proell et al., 2014; Lachmann et al., 2015; Maines & McDaniel, 2000). So far, none of the research contributions in this field evaluated format and content effects by presenting information in an additional column in the balance sheet. By displaying the information in the balance sheet in an additional column, I attempt to make disclosure information on the fair value salient, and thus, aim to research if the presentation format facilitates users' abilities to process the disclosed information. This is in line with the finding that NPIs are better able to understand management subjectivity that is part of uncertain fair value estimates, in higher salience condition (Pitt, 2011).

Besides the variation of the format of information, several research contributions also evaluate the effect of a variation of the *content of information* (Clor-Proell et al., 2014; Lachmann et al., 2015; Maines & McDaniel, 2000). Maines and McDaniel (2000) manipulate the volatility of unrealized gains and losses in their primary experiment. Specifically, they use a mixed pattern where they manipulate a high, low, and medium level of unrealized gains and losses' volatility in a three-year time series. By doing so, they manipulate the content of the information. They find that investors correctly evaluate information on unrealized gains and losses' volatility in all presentation formats. Thus, the authors argue that besides the format, the content of information does affect the information evaluation. The unrealized gain and loss of stocks, however, is unrealized and, thus, not directly comparable to a realized gain or loss. Clor-Proell et al. (2014) manipulate the measurement subjectivity of fair values (level 1 vs. level 3 inputs) and, thus, also the content of information besides the format (more salient vs. less salient). Though, the authors focus on fair value gains only, the results indicate that the content can affect information processing even though this effect is only significant when the format is more salient. Lachmann et al. (2015) manipulate the content of the information by using the firm's profitability (profit vs. loss). They find that the correct evaluation of credit risk is affected by the content of information when the change in credit risk is presented in net income. Moreover, the weights placed on credit risk information differ when the change in credit risk is presented in net income. The results indicate, that content affects the information processing of NPIs.

To sum up, the results of prior research show that the information processing of NPIs is affected by both the format and the content of the information presented. As mentioned above, research has not yet examined if these results hold for fair value balance sheet items. Pertinent research points out ways for NPIs to increase information usage and help them to incorporate the information into their decision-making process. What remains unclear is what causes the difficulties for NPIs to take decision-useful financial statement information into account, which forms my second research question:

RQ2: *Why do NPIs have difficulty including fair value disclosures in their decision-making process? Is it due to the format or the content of the information?*

Information that is incorporated into the decision-making process and, thus, the investment process of NPIs is supposed to be decision-useful. Both practical and theoretical literature on this topic find and argue that higher reliability of accounting information would lead to higher decision usefulness (Clor-Proell et al., 2014; IASB, 2015, 2010). The following chapter will take a closer look at the relationship between reliability and decision usefulness and how manipulations to the format and changes in the fair value of material accounting figures may influence these two considering the theoretical framework on information processing by Maines and McDaniel (2000).

4.2 Decision usefulness of fair value disclosures

In the following chapter, I will deduce the hypotheses of my research. My hypotheses can be split into four different subtopics dealing with improving the decision usefulness of disclosure information of fair value estimates. I start with hypotheses block one, which focuses on the connection of reliability and decision usefulness of accounting data on the fair value and financial statement level, and continue to my hypotheses block two with differences in information acquisition, evaluation, and weighting among treatments and relationships between the different stages of information processing. In my third hypotheses block, I will cover the different types of disclosures that can be classified and look at moderating effects of the change in fair value (gain vs. loss). The last hypotheses block focuses on the resulting investment decision of NPIs, taking the theoretical framework and differences between treatments into account.

4.2.1 Relation between reliability and decision usefulness

To provide financial reporting information of high quality is the primary objective of financial reporting (Gagnon, 2010). Information is high in quality when it is useful to economic decision makers. Thus, providing financial reporting of high quality may influence potential investors in a positive manner, which means that it will be easier for investors to make an investment decision, if decision-useful financial accounting information is provided to them (IASB, 2008a). Qualitative characteristics contribute to the usefulness of financial statements. These characteristics are the faithful representation of accounting figures and the relevance of these (IASB, 2015, 2008b, 2008c). Faithful representation was formerly known as reliability and a qualitative characteristic of useful financial information (IASB, 2015). The term was introduced by the conceptual framework 2010 due to a lack of common understanding about the term reliability. Many respondents commented on this proposed change by the IASB and would favor the standard setter to keep the original term of reliability. They argue that the original term (reliability) is better understood than the new term. Furthermore, if disclosures are provided in a sufficient manner, any information can be presented faithfully. Consequently, faithfulness does not fulfill its role as an effective filter to distinguish between information that should be presented in the financial statement or not. In addition, faithful representation and reliability can be subject to earnings management (van Tendeloo & Vanstraelen, 2005). Taking this into account, the recognition of financial statement items that lack reliability would be possible. They further argue that the term reliability indicated a trade-off between reliability and relevance. The original term, therefore, considered that relevant information might be less reliable and reliable information might me be less relevant. Many respondents felt that this trade-off was not represented with the introduction of the new term of faithful representation (IASB, 2015).

Following the new conceptual framework, researchers in the international financial reporting context used the new term of faithful representation in their research (Clor-Proell et al., 2014). Still, later contributions continue to use the term reliability in their research (Müller et al., 2015). Following the approach of European research contribution in this area of study by Müller et al. (2015), I use the term reliability in this experiment and, consequently, throughout my research for the following reason: I follow the argumentation of several respondents in terms of the introduction of the new term, who argue that the trade-off between reliability and relevance is of high importance. This trade-off is important for my research topic as the asset which the participants in this experiment assess in terms of reliability is relevant due to materiality. Specifically, I choose the setting of a real estate firm where the financial properties represent 90% of the average total assets in both years. Thus, I have a relevant asset value in terms of materiality that is, however, potentially less reliable than other accounting figures in my balance sheet as the investment properties measured at fair value are classified as level 3 input parameters.

Recent research in this area of study argues that faithfulness (earlier: reliability) is one of the main characteristics of decision-useful information. Still, hypotheses often fail to look at the correlation between faithfulness and decision usefulness in a financial accounting context. Clor-Proell et al. (2014) even argue that decision usefulness should be higher for specific income statement information that is measured more reliable but only include reliability and not decision usefulness into their hypotheses. This approach of considering only one of the qualitative characteristics of decision-useful information by looking at the reliability of a certain financial statement item or a certain income statement item is used by several authors (e.g. Bhat & Ryan, 2015; McDonough & Shakespeare, 2015; Müller et al., 2015). By doing so, only one of the qualitative characteristics of decision usefulness is considered in recent research even though both qualities coexist (FASB, 1980b).

Though both the FASB and IASB emphasize the importance of high quality financial reporting information and, thus, high decision usefulness, one of the key problems is that measuring this quality is challenging. Since different financial statement user groups (professional investors vs. NPIs) have dissimilar preferences, usefulness may vary among them (Braam et al., 2009). This variation makes measuring quality directly in this context problematic (Botosan, 2004). Thus, many researchers measure financial reporting quality by focusing on its attributes, such as timeliness, financial restatements, or earnings quality (Barth et al., 2008; Cohen et al., 2004; Schipper & Vincent, 2003). Using indirect measures, however, often leads to puzzling results on the decision usefulness of accounting data and standard setting (Barth et al., 2008; Barth, 2006; van der Meulen et al., 2007). These results strengthen my approach to measure quality directly to avoid puzzling results. Since even individuals among the same financial statement user group may have a differing perception of decision usefulness, it is a subjective but direct measure (Clor-Proell et al., 2014). Thus, decision-useful financial information should be perceived to be more reliable. All else equal, NPIs should consider information that is measured reliable to be more decision-useful. I take the two primary qualitative characteristics of accounting information into account and hold relevance constant. Based on this reasoning I make the following prediction for a financial statement asset measured at fair value[26]:

H1a: *At the <u>fair value level</u>, higher reliability leads to higher decision usefulness for NPIs.*

Financial statement information (e.g. the balance sheet item of investment properties measured

[26] Fair values that are recognized in the financial statement will be entitled with "fair value level" for simplification reasons hereafter.

at fair value) and the corresponding accounting rules and regulations affect investors' valuation of a firm (Lee, 1999). Specifically, the decision-useful measurement information on assets plays an important role in an investor's firm valuation (Barth, 2014; Nissim & Penman, 2008). Also, asset measurement information is important for investor's to estimate firm value (Botosan & Huffman, 2015). In more detail, Botosan and Huffman (2015) argue that assets create value for a firm in two ways: either in use or in exchange. The value of the assets varies along with the way the assets are expected to realize value for the firm. For in-use assets (e.g., investment properties measured at fair value as part of the financial statement of a real estate firm), investors need to determine the value expected to be realized in the use of the asset by letting it out to others. Thus, the future cash flow that is expected to be generated by the asset needs to be forecasted by investors. The asset valuation is the measurement basis for a business valuation. For the business valuation of real estate firms, Müller et al. (2015) state that these kinds of firms usually have an economically significant primary operating asset (e.g., investment properties measured at fair value). This asset strongly influences the structure of the balance sheet of real estate firms in Europe. Consequently, research indicates that the assessment of a firms' performance at the financial statement level is strongly influenced by the assessment of the key asset of a firm measured at the fair value level. Thus, if higher reliability leads to higher decision usefulness for the key asset of a firm measured at fair value, I predict that this effect will also hold for the financial statement level.

***H1b**: At the financial statement level, higher reliability leads to higher decision usefulness for NPIs.*

For the valuation of a business that considers the financial statement of a firm, the measurement of a key asset plays an important role (Botosan & Huffman, 2015; Müller et al., 2015). If an asset is perceived to be reliable at the fair value level, it is likely to be perceived reliable at the financial statement level as well. Keeping in mind that higher reliability leads to higher decision usefulness, I predict the following:

***H1c**: Higher reliability at the fair value level leads to higher reliability at the financial statement level.*

While the first hypotheses block focused on the correlation between reliability and decision usefulness at both fair value-level and the financial statement level, the second hypotheses block will focus on information processing that ultimately plays a role when individuals make an investment decision.

4.2.2 Differences in information processing

Generally, investment decisions require cognitive capacity and thus can be seen as a cognitive task (Hirshleifer & Teoh, 2003). This cognitive task is highly complex as the process of information processing of investors is hardly observable. To shed light into this area of research, Maines and McDaniel (2000) introduce a framework that breaks down the decision-making process into three stages: information acquisition, information evaluation, and information weighting. In the first stage, the investors need to store and recall specific information. The second stage of the model requires the investor to assess characteristics and, thus, evaluate the provided information (Maines & McDaniel, 2000). By evaluating the information, the investor will be able to use it (Hirshleifer & Teoh, 2003). The third stage requires the investor to judge a particular piece of information that is related to its investment decision. The framework is based on earlier findings of psychological research (Simon, 1955), widely used in recent accounting literature (Clor-Proell et al., 2014; Lachmann et al., 2015; Müller et al., 2015; Reimsbach et al., 2017) and seen as influential in contemporary research (Dunbar & Weber, 2014; Reimsbach et al., 2017).

Maines and McDaniel (2000) propose in line with Hogarth (1989), that the presentation format affects the judgements of investors on corporate performance. Specifically, a change in the presentation format influences the information processing of investors and, thus, might lead to different investment decision results. By doing so, the information acquisition, evaluation, and weighting of NPIs is affected. In addition, information weighting depends on information acquisition and evaluation. Compared to professional investors, NPIs have difficulties in identifying specific data needed for financial analysis. This is caused by the fact that they assimilate information in a relatively unstructured manner. The result is that NPIs and less-experienced investors will read the financial statements in the order of appearance (Maines & McDaniel, 2000). This indicates that they lack preconceived ideas about financial statement items as well as on the relationship between these items (McEwen & Hunton, 1999; Ungson & Braunstein, 1982). Maines and McDaniel (2000) claim to find that NPIs will acquire and evaluate information correctly regardless of the presentation format being used.

Hence, they state in a footnote of their research that 22% of the NPIs in one of the three tested formats[27] failed to acquire the information of unrealized gains and losses. They even suggest that these results indicate that format changes may have an effect on information acquisition for NPIs. Specifically, the different formats they use for their research are different types of comprehensive income statements: statement of comprehensive income in its original form, statement of stockholders' equity, or statement of comprehensive income according to the SFAS No. 130. The prediction that NPIs acquire information regardless of the presentation format is in line with the argumentation that NPIs read through all information and would thus process all types of income statements.

The change of format I test in this experiment differs from the one proposed by Maines and McDaniel (2000) in two ways: first, I make a format change to the balance sheet and not the income statement and, second, I do not change the format by providing a completely different statement in addition but rather add an additional column to the balance sheet and thus highlight information that is presented in the disclosures in all formats. Moreover, my research context is different. While Maines and McDaniel (2000) evaluate the role of the financial statement presentation format for NPIs, I research on how to improve the decision usefulness of disclosures for NPIs. I make the format changes primarily to increase the probability of

[27] Maines and McDaniel (2000) tested three different formats for the presentation of unrealized gains and losses: 115EQ (presentation requirements according to the SFAS No. 115), 130EQ (presentation format requirements according to the SFAS No. 130 - with gross changes of unrealized gains and losses in a statement of changes in stockholders' equity), and 130IS (presentation format requirements also according to the SFAS No. 130 - with gross changes of unrealized gains and losses in a statement of comprehensive income). In the format 130EQ, 22% of the NPIs failed to acquire information.

information acquisition. This is in line with the reasoning of Clor-Proell et al. (2014) who argue that even a small format change can ease information processing and thus the acquisition, evaluation, and weighting of information. This is because the salient presentation of a financial statement item can provide a signal of attention for the user and, thus, ease the cognitive strain. This can ultimately increase the financial statement users' ability to incorporate the underlying measurement information of balance sheet items into their judgements.

While Maines and McDaniel (2000) propose the two dimensions "isolation" and "aggregation" of information related to the cost of information processing, Hodge et al. (2010) introduce the third dimension of proximity. The proximity compatibility principle is first introduced by Wickens and Carswell (1995) and explains the relationship between visual presentation and cognitive processing during the decision-making process. The authors further distinguish between task and display proximity. When multiple sources of information are required for a specific judgement or task, task proximity is high. On the other hand, a great distance between different display features describes display proximity. It further describes whether different objects can be perceived (e.g., read or used) by the information user in a similar manner (Hodge et al., 2010; Reimsbach et al., 2017). In this context, Hodge et al. (2010) find that it is difficult for individuals to acquire multiple pieces of information concurrently. Besides, they find that cognitive costs are lower for individuals when display proximity is high. Lachmann et al. (2015) also use the dimension of isolation (degree of isolation) as originally proposed by Maines and McDaniel (2000). While isolation originally referred to whether comprehensive income was the sole type of information that was presented in the financial statement (Maines & McDaniel, 2000), Lachmann et al. (2015) distinguish between a lower and higher degree of isolation. They distinguish between the presentation of credit risk in net income and other comprehensive income and argue that the net income has more items than the statement of other comprehensive income.

Reimsbach et al. (2017) take this prior research into account and predict that the cognitive costs for information acquisition will be lower for integrated reports compared to a spate reporting format. By presenting my additional disclosure information on fair values in an additional column in the balance sheet, I ensure a high display proximity. Consequently, the information I present to the NPIs is isolated in the spate column, aggregated compared to the original disclosure in the current format mandated under the IFRS and still high in proximity. Specifically, the proximity is high because the additional disclosure on the fair value of the investment property is presented in the balance sheet. I thus fulfill all requirements that have been tested by earlier research contributions up to this date to maximize information acquisition of the additional disclosure information. Based on this reasoning, I make the following prediction:

H2a: *<u>Acquisition</u> of fair value information is more likely if the related information is presented salient (i.e., in the balance sheet) compared to when it is not presented salient.*

The probability for a fair value to vary is high (Barth et al., 1995; Song, 2015). Compared to the prior year, a fair value can vary in three possible ways: the fair value can increase (gain), decrease (loss), or stay the same. The third option, however, is unlikely to happen in this research context as I choose investment properties as key operating assets. These assets are usually classified with level 3 input parameters to their valuation models. Thus, it is unlikely that there will be no change at all in any input parameters into the valuation model compared to the prior period (Barth et al., 1995; Song, 2015). Prior research on investors' fair value judgements focuses on fair value gains compared to the prior year. In the context of the income statement, fair value gains are examined because they are more prevalent than fair value losses after the issuance of the FASB 157 (Clor-Proell et al., 2014). Still, the issuance of losses is shared by almost all firms (Hayn, 1995; Manchiraju et al., 2015). Prior research indicates that investors examine these positive and negative changes of fair values differently (Shefrin & Statman, 1985).

Investors generally notice fair value gains more than fair value losses and react differently to a favorable or positive revision (gain) and unfavorable or negative revision (loss) of stocks (Hou et al., 2014). Maines and McDaniel (2000) introduce the isolation of information as a dimension related to cognitive costs. Specifically, they argue that cognitive costs for processing information will be less if the information is presented rather isolated. The processing of information required the information to be acquired first. By presenting information rather isolated, the authors present the information in a salient manner. This approach is also used by Clor-Proell et al. (2014) who isolate fair value gains and present them in an additional column to make them salient for investors. Lachmann et al. (2015) find that that a change in credit risk was more likely to be acquired when the change was presented in the other comprehensive income rather than net income. They also find that information acquisition varies if a profitability development arose concurrently with a downgrade (loss) or not (profit). In the other comprehensive income presentation format (more isolated and thus more salient presentation), the change in credit risk was more likely to be acquired with a loss compared to a profit even though this finding is not significant. According to Hodder et al. (2001), financial statement users interpret losses as negative signals and gains as positive signals. Hou et al. (2014) find investors generally notice fair value gains more than fair value losses and react differently to them. Thus, in line with the findings of Hodder et al. (2001) and Hou et al. (2014), I predict the following:

H2b: *<u>Acquisition</u> of fair value information is more likely if the related information is presented salient (i.e., in the balance sheet) with a fair value <u>gain</u> compared to a fair value <u>loss</u>.*

After having acquired the fair value information, investors will evaluate and weight the information next. Lachmann et al. (2015) argue that they do not predict changes in information evaluation between their different presentation formats (other comprehensive income (more isolated) and net income (less isolated)). They justify their prediction by arguing that an increase in the firm's credit risk would lead to a gain independent of the presentation format used. Hence, they also argue that the typical interpretation of losses as negative signals and gains as positive signals does not hold for changes in credit risks. In terms of investment properties, a negative development of the fair value, however, is a negative sign for investors as it implies that the value of the asset has decreased compared to the prior period. Due to this,

I argue that if information acquisition is more likely when the fair value information is presented salient, information evaluation is also more likely to be correct, when the fair value information is presented salient.

H2c: *NPIs are more likely to evaluate fair value information correctly if related information is presented salient (i.e., in the balance sheet) compared to when it is not presented salient.*

Maines and McDaniel (2000) do not predict different results for format effects for information acquisition and evaluation. They argue that information that is acquired will also be evaluated correctly. In line with the reasoning for H2b that information acquisition is more likely when the related information is presented salient with a fair value gain compared to a fair value loss, I predict the same perception for the second step in the information processing process:

H2d: *NPIs are more likely to evaluate fair value information correctly if related information is presented salient (i.e., in the balance sheet) with a fair value gain compared to a fair value loss.*

The weight investors place on information can be affected in two ways: In line with the argumentation for H2a and H2b that refer to the acquisition of information, H2a states that the presentation format (salient vs. non-salient) of information affects acquisition, while H2b predicts that information acquisition is also affected by the development of the fair value estimate (gain vs. loss). Specifically, I argue that the acquisition of fair value information is more likely if the related information is presented salient (i.e., in the balance sheet) with a fair value gain compared to a fair value loss.

In the context of my research, the proposed change in the presentation format exhibits similarities with the format change between recognition versus disclosure. Most studies find that investors weigh recognized amounts more heavy than disclosed amounts when determining a firm value (e.g., Davis-Friday et al., 1999; Gopalakrishnan, 1994). This is in line with the findings that investors will place greater weight on information that is displayed in a more salient manner (Maines & McDaniel, 2000). Specifically, the disclosed estimate of the anticipated liability for retiree benefits other than pensions is valued differently by firms than the subsequent value of the same reliability. Thus, recognized retiree benefits other than pensions receive more weight than disclosed liabilities of the same type (Davis-Friday et al., 1999). Further, research indicates that investors consider information on pensions that is disclosed in the footnotes as value-relevant, when the prepaid pension liability is also recognized in the balance sheet (Gopalakrishnan, 1994). To sum up, investors find recognized values more relevant than disclosed values for decision-making even though recognized values are not more reliable than disclosed values (Michels, 2017). In the context of investment properties measured at fair value, the recognized and, thus, salient, investors will place more weight on fair values in determining the firm value (Israeli, 2015). Also, information weighting is affected by the presentation format (Lachmann et al., 2015). Specifically, information that is presented salient (e.g., with a higher degree of isolation) will be weighted more by investors compared to formats with lower salience (Nisbett et al., 1981). Thus, I predict the following:

H2e: *Weighting of fair value information is higher if related information is presented salient (i.e., in the balance sheet) compared to when it is not presented salient.*

The development of the fair value is predicted to influence information acquisition. Prior research finds that investors generally notice fair value gains more than fair value losses (Hou et al., 2014). When combining this with the findings on information weighting, in terms of the presentation format, the results would indicate that investors would place more weight on fair value gains that are presented salient. In line with this reasoning, I make the following prediction:

H2f: *Weighting of fair value information is higher if related information is presented salient (i.e., in the balance sheet) with a fair value gain compared to a fair value loss.*

After shedding light on the literature stream of information processing of NPIs and predicting results of format change effects for the components of the information processing approach by Maines and McDaniel (2000) and Hodge et al. (2010), the following chapter will evaluate the effects of format changes on the perceived reliability and decision usefulness. Thus, the reasoning on the correlation between perceived reliability and decision usefulness for my hypotheses 1a-1c is taken into account. The next chapter will provide further detail on the different types of disclosures I have tested in this experiment.

4.2.3 How changes in fair value affect different types of disclosures

Earnings forecasts occur in the two following forms: qualitative and quantitative. Qualitative forecasts are nonnumeric, while quantitative forecasts are numeric, and thus, can occur as numerical point, range, minimum, or maximum estimates (Hirst et al., 2008). When the quoted prices in an active market are not available, an entity may rely on valuation techniques. These valuation techniques often include the prediction of future cash flows, for e.g., by using the DCF method. By applying this method, the value of an asset or liability as the present value is calculated using the expected future cash flows that are discounted with a risk adjusted discount rate (see chapter 2.4.1). In this context, risk refers to the volatility of the expected future cash flows. If input parameters of investment properties measured at fair value are classified at level 3 (income approach), the future cash flows of the property, usually the rental income, are discounted. This shows that measuring the investment properties estimated at fair value with level 3 is mainly driven by earnings forecasts.

Management earnings forecasting literature divides information into two broad categories: hard and soft information. While hard information is quantitative, soft information is of a qualitative nature. The literature stream highlights the importance of qualitative information as most corporate announcements contain a higher amount of soft than hard information. Further, both soft and hard information are value-relevant for investors (Brockman & Cicon, 2013). Specifically, the literature of several management earnings studies finds that stock prices are significantly affected by soft information during earnings announcements. This effect of soft information affecting stock prices can even be greater than the effect of the announcement of hard information during earnings announcements (Tetlock, 2007). The literature also finds that it takes investors less time to interpret hard information compared to soft information. This is because it is harder for investors to interpret soft information compared to hard information (Brockman & Cicon, 2013). In the context of investment properties measured at fair value, I classify the disclosed fair value hierarchy as qualitative information. In line with the framework of Maines and McDaniel (2000) and the literature on management earnings, I conclude that it is necessary to highlight the disclosed information for NPIs because they only have limited cognitive capacity and rely heavily on decision heuristics (Clor-Proell et al., 2014). Thus, I assume that if I present qualitative, value-relevant disclosure information in the form of additional fair value information saliently in the balance sheet, the perceived reliability and decision usefulness will increase for both the fair value of investment properties as well as the financial statement as a whole. The manipulation to the presentation format when presenting an additional qualitative fair value disclosure information in the balance sheet is shown in the figure below.

Assets

	t=1	t=0		Fair Value Hierarchy
	kEUR	kEUR	Discolsure	
Non-current Assets				
Investment Properties	33.169	31.312	D1	**Level 3**
PP&E	1.351	1.382	D2	
	34.520	32.694		
[...]				
Total Assets	36.248	34.624		

Figure 7: Excerpt from the balance sheet of XY Corp., when presenting additional qualitative disclosure information salient[28]

Apart from qualitative value-relevant forecasting information, I also test quantitative information since many disclosures are classified as this type of information. Management earnings forecasting literature divides forecasts into point and range forecasts (Rapaport et al., 1990). Range forecasts are seen to be less precise than point forecasts because ranges are generally seen as an expression of uncertainty by investors (Rapaport et al., 1990; Wallsten et al., 1986). A point value in the context of investment properties is the fair value displayed in the balance sheet. While such a point estimate only provides one anchor value, range estimates provide additional information for both better and worse possible values (Highhouse, 1994). Accounting research suggests that the uncertainty perception of range forecasts is driven by the assumptions of investors that these kinds of forecasts are issued if the business environment is uncertain and if the earnings are not predictable. A range (e.g., earnings will be $1.50-$2.00 per share) has a maximum (e.g., $2.00 per share) and a minimum (e.g., $1.50 per share) in a numeric form and will, therefore, be seen as an adequate variation to the point forecast (Kile et al., 1998). In the existing literature on the subject matter, there are different opinions about whether

[28] Author's own illustration. For the entire financial statement, see Appendix S3.

investors will distinguish between range and point forecasts, which may be driven by different samples, design, and dependent variables used throughout the research (Hirst et al., 1999). Confidence was earlier identified as a key input parameter for an investment decision (Bloomfield et al., 1996), and it is influenced by the form of the management earnings forecast. This influence is particularly present when the accuracy level of the prior forecasts is high. Confidence in this research context is interpreted as the confidence of investors in their own earnings forecasts. If investors feel they can trust their own earnings forecasts, they feel that they can rely on the underlying information for the prediction. Thus, it can be concluded that if a firm's management uses range instead of point estimates, this potentially signals high uncertainty to investors (Hirst et al., 1999). In the field of accounting, firms do not have the choice of reporting range values as they are mandatory disclosures, e.g., the description of the sensitivity analysis of a fair value caused by changes in unobservable (key) inputs for the valuation of the investment properties. Following the forecasting literature stream, the reliability and decision usefulness would be lower when presenting the sensitivity analysis saliently in addition to presenting the fair value point value as currently mandated under the IFRS only. Still, I argue that the additional information makes the financial statement more reliable, as indicated by the standard setter and, thus, I predict that the reliability and decision usefulness will increase. The manipulation to the presentation format when presenting an additional range fair value disclosure information in the balance sheet is shown in the figure below.

Assets

	t=1	**t=0**		**Sensitivity analysis (t=1)**
	kEUR	kEUR	Discolsure	
Non-current Assets				
Investment Properties	33.169	31.312	D1	**31.676-34.662**
PP&E	1.351	1.382	D2	
	34.520	32.694		
[...]				
Total Assets	36.248	34.624		

Figure 8: Excerpt from the balance sheet of XY Corp., when presenting additional range value disclosure information salient[29]

Besides management earnings forecasting literature, there is also a large literature stream focusing on analysts' forecasts. Analysts are told to have the ability to provide high-quality information to investors as they are sophisticated users of financial information (Chava et al., 2010). Market participants use these forecasts because they transform the financial statement information along with additional information about the economy, future earnings predictions, as well as information about the industry and firm strategy (Wieland, 2011). In the case of

[29] Author's own illustration. For the entire financial statement, see Appendix S3.

investment properties, the fair value of an investment property contains this information. The investment properties reflect the predictions pertaining to future earnings, particularly the rent generated with the investment properties, along with the predicted economic development (e.g., the development of the household income and the ability to pay the rent in the case of a residential investment property). Information about the industry, such as the predicted housing market development and the firm strategy (e.g., maximized returns of the investment properties by increasing rents) are considered. The fair values of investment properties often vary over time, which is why a revision to the fair value becomes necessary. The equivalent of the same revision on the fair value of an investment property in the forecasting literature is an analysts' earnings forecast revisions.

While the literature streams agree on the finding that there is a stock price reaction to a revision of an analysts' forecast, Hou et al. (2014) are the first to address whether the stock price reaction is different for positive and negative forecast revisions. They find that the difference between unfavorable and favorable revision is greater for stocks with higher uncertainty and that the upwards-revised forecasts receive higher positive returns. Following Hou et al. (2014), I predict that there will be a reaction by NPIs to a revision in the fair value of investment properties with regard to reliability and decision usefulness. The revision of the fair value is the disclosed reconciliation between the carrying amounts of investment properties at the beginning and the end of the period according to the IAS 40.75, which I classify as a change value. I, thus assume, based on the findings by Hou et al. (2014) that if the change value is presented prominently in the balance sheet and closely linked to the point value, the perceived reliability and decision usefulness will increase. The manipulation to the presentation format when presenting an additional change fair value disclosure information in the balance sheet is shown in the figure below.

Assets

	t=1	t=0		**Reconciliation between carrying amounts from**
	kEUR	kEUR	Discolsure	**t=0 to t=1**
Non-current Assets				
Investment Properties	33.169	31.312	D1	**1.857**
PP&E	1.351	1.382	D2	
	34.520	32.694		
[...]				
Total Assets	36.248	34.624		

Figure 9: Excerpt from the balance sheet of XY Corp., when presenting additional change value disclosure information salient[30]

[30] Author's own illustration. For the entire financial statement, see Appendix S3.

Bringing together the literature streams for qualitative disclosure information, range value, and change value, I argue that presenting information in a higher salience condition, which means presenting the disclosure information in an additional column in the balance sheet,[31] increases the perceived reliability and decision usefulness. This builds up on my reasoning for the predication of hypothesis H1a-H1c. Also, I take into account the research by Clor-Proell et al. (2014), who find that measurement subjectivity is more likely to be deciphered by NPIs in higher salience conditions. Thus, perceived reliability judgements are significantly different in higher salience conditions but not in lower salience conditions. This indicates that NPIs are better aware of the drivers of perceived reliability in higher salience conditions. To ensure a higher salience condition, the authors added an additional line to the income statement. Based on this approach and the theoretical framework of Maines and McDaniel (2000) on information processing, I make the following prediction:

H3a: *Presenting fair value information salient (i.e., in the balance sheet) leads to an increase in the perceived reliability and decision usefulness for NPIs.*

While hypotheses 3a is a general prediction for the increase in perceived reliability and decision usefulness, the following hypotheses will provide a more detailed view on additional salient disclosure information and different ways of the corresponding fair value development. As shown in Figure 5, mediating variables may affect the decision processing on investors. Maines and McDaniel (2000) test if different types of investors (professional vs. NPI) mediate the information processing. In addition, they also test if the type of business activity (core vs. noncore) has a mediating effect. The authors argue that NPIs' decision-making will differ only in term of information weighting but not in terms of information acquisition and evaluation. They argue this is because NPIs are not able to distinguish between core and noncore activities of the firm. They find that NPIs tend to rely on the financial statement to evaluate the core activities because the statement signals the importance of information for them. Hodge et al. (2010) mediate the extensiveness of feedback on forecast accuracy (limited feedback vs. extensive feedback) for low and high proximity. Again, proximity is high when the information is presented closely (e.g., on the same page). Since I do not plan to incorporate any type of feedback into my research, this research approach and findings is of subordinate importance for my experiment, however, I ensure that proximity is high.

Clor-Proell et al. (2014) mediate information salience (lower vs. higher) for less and more subjectivity of inputs to measure gains. The fair value of a firm's trading securities is associated with the gain in their experiment. They find that participants are more likely to decipher the degree of input-subjectivity to measure gains in higher salience conditions. I take these findings on mediating effects in a financial accounting experiment research context into account and introduce a mediating effect that is not yet subject to this stream of literature: the development (gain vs. loss) of the core asset compared to the prior period measured at a fair value. There is an extensive stream of experimental research on fair value gains (Clor-Proell et al., 2014; Hodge et al., 2010; Maines & McDaniel, 2000), while fair value losses so far have been largely

[31] For reason of presentation, I introduce the term additional disclosure for disclosure information that is presented salient in the balance sheet. I use both terms "salient disclosure information" and "additional disclosure information" as synonyms in this thesis.

ignored. The latest experimental research finds that NPIs become more aware of the measurement subjectivity of fair value gains in higher salience conditions (Clor-Proell et al., 2014). Taking into account these findings, I predict the following for a fair value gain:

***H3b**: Presenting fair value information salient (i.e., in the balance sheet) with a fair value gain leads to an increase in the perceived reliability and decision usefulness for NPIs.*

Mediating variables like extensiveness of feedback, proximity, and salience affect the information processing of NPIs (Clor-Proell et al., 2014; Hodge et al., 2010; Maines & McDaniel, 2000). So far, these mediating variables have only been used in the context of a fair value gain. I extend this literature and introduce the variable of fair value development. A fair value can develop in two ways: gain and loss. The probability for a fair value to vary over time is likely, as fair values are regularly subject to high volatility (Barth et al., 1995; Song, 2015). This change in fair value can also be negative, as almost all firms face losses over time (Hayn, 1995; Manchiraju et al., 2015). Investors examine these positive and negative changes of fair values differently (Shefrin & Statman, 1985).

Investors generally notice fair value gains more than fair value losses and react differently to a favorable or positive revision (gain) and unfavorable or negative revision (loss) of stocks (Hou et al., 2014). This is driven by the fact that losses are less informative for investors as they perceive them as extreme level of earnings (Hayn, 1995; Kahneman & Tversky, 1979). Besides, shareholders hold a liquidation option, which limits the informativeness of losses with regard to future cash flows (Hayn, 1995). Nevertheless, future cash flows are an important aspect of investors' investment decisions even though the cause of the relation and its strength are subject to debate (Kaplan & Zingales, 1997; Lewellen & Lewellen, 2016). An investor's perception of risk is low when earnings are smooth relative to the extreme levels of earnings (e.g., losses). Consequently, investors will evaluate company risk to be higher when the volatility of earnings is high (Erickson et al., 2017). I argue that this high perception of risk of extreme levels of earnings, namely fair value losses, is emphasized by the presentation of additional disclosures. Therefore, the presentation of the additional disclosure of the sensitivity analysis would highlight the low reliability compared to the current format with a fair value loss. Hence, I predict the following:

***H3c**: Presenting fair value information salient with a fair value loss leads to a decrease in the perceived reliability and decision usefulness for NPIs.*

In line with my reasoning for hypothesis 3b and hypothesis 3c, I argue that if the fair value information is presented salient in the balance sheet with a fair value gain, perceived reliability and decision usefulness will increase. Since investors are averse to loss, with a loss and a gain of the same amount, investors will weigh the loss heavier than the gain. This phenomenon describes the loss aversion of investors (Kahneman & Tversky, 1979; Liu et al., 2017). Thus, with a fair value loss, I predict that the perceived reliability and decision usefulness will decrease as losses have a lower level of informativeness than gains. Since NPIs will spend more cognitive effort on the additional information presented with a fair value loss, the uncertainty of the fair value will be highlighted. Based on this reasoning, I predict the following:

H3d: *Perceived reliability and decision usefulness for NPIs is higher when fair value information is presented salient with a fair value gain than with a fair value loss.*

After bringing together the theoretical framework of Maines and McDaniel (2000) and Hodge et al. (2010) on information processing and information salience together with the findings of Clor-Proell et al. (2014) and my newly introduced mediating variable "fair value development" (gain vs. loss), my fourth hypothesis block deals with the last component of the information processing model (cf. Figure 5): performance assessment judgement, resulting in an investment decision.

4.2.4 Investment decisions of NPIs

Compared to the information processing model, which was introduced in the first place for an income statement information processing approach (Maines & McDaniel, 2000), this experiment focuses on the balance sheet. Thus, the performance of the firm in terms of income statement evaluation is a part of this experiment, but the presentation of additional information is linked primarily to the balance sheet, even though gains and losses due to valuation differences of the investment properties will be realized in the income statement. Hence, the participants in this experiment were asked to evaluate the performance of the firm.

Maines and McDaniel (2000) predict for their research context that the weighting of the different formats will have similar results (as in similar differences between the different formats) in investors' performance judgements. In this context, I argue that NPIs are more likely to weight the information higher if additional fair value information is presented salient in the balance sheet. Thus, with a fair value gain, I expect NPIs to evaluate the performance more positive when fair value disclosure information is presented salient in the balance sheet. In line with the reasoning of Maines and McDaniel (2000) that the weighting differences due to format changes will come along with similar differences in investors' performance judgements, NPIs will be more likely to purchase shares of a firm if they evaluate the performance of the firm in a positive way. Clor-Proell et al. (2014) predict that the perceived reliability judgements of NPIs mediate their Price/Earnings (P/E) judgements. Thus, the degree of reliability an investor awards to the accounting figures drives the P/E multiples, a ratio to value a firm, measuring the current share price relative to the per-share earnings. Higher P/E ratios may indicate higher firm growth in the future. This behaviour is driven by the fact that changes in judgements affect share prices (Kolev, 2009; Song et al., 2010). Because I reason that additional information presented in the balance sheet will lead to higher perceived reliability and decision usefulness for NPIs with a fair value gain, I predict the following:

H4a: *If the decision usefulness of fair value information is high, NPIs will feel more able to make an investment decision compared to when decision usefulness is low.*

The objective and general purpose of financial reporting is to provide decision-useful financial information to existing and potential investors to make investment decisions. These decisions include the buying and selling of equity and instruments (IASB, 2010). Socea (2012) argues that financial accounting information needs to be decision-useful to be suitable for decision-making (e.g., the purchase of shares). Thus, providing high-quality financial reporting information is important because it will positively influence capital providers (IASB, 2008a). Consequently, no or less decision-useful financial accounting information would not be as relevant for decision-making as highly decision-useful financial information. Taking this into account, I predict the following:

***H4b**: If the decision usefulness of fair value information is high, NPIs will rather buy shares of a firm compared to when decision usefulness is low.*

After the derivation of two research questions and 15 hypotheses, the following chapter will sum up the hypotheses and point out interfaces between them.

4.2.5 Summary of predicitions

Bringing the previous chapters together, the first hypotheses block deals with the relationship of financial statement positions and the financial statement as a whole and perceived reliability of these. The second hypotheses block focuses on the information processing and potential impacts on this process for NPIs like the display of salient fair value disclosures as well as different developments of the fair value (gain vs. loss). The third hypotheses block marks the relation between the first and the second hypotheses block. It deals with the impact of salient disclosures on the perceived decision usefulness of NPIs and takes into account the relationship between reliability and decision usefulness predicted in the first hypotheses block. Moreover, the third hypotheses block uses the mediating variables introduced in the second hypotheses block: the positive and negative development of the fair value (gain vs. loss). The fourth hypotheses block builds onto the predictions of the hypotheses block two on information processing of NPIs. It takes a look at the relationship between the perceived decision usefulness of investors and the investment decision. This decision is split into two parts: first, the judgement of the firm's performance by the investor and second, the ultimate decision to buy shares. All hypotheses as well as their relationship are depicted in Figure 10 on the following page.

The next chapter will describe the method I used to test the hypotheses above by providing information on the experimental setting, the participants, my research design, as well as materials and procedures.

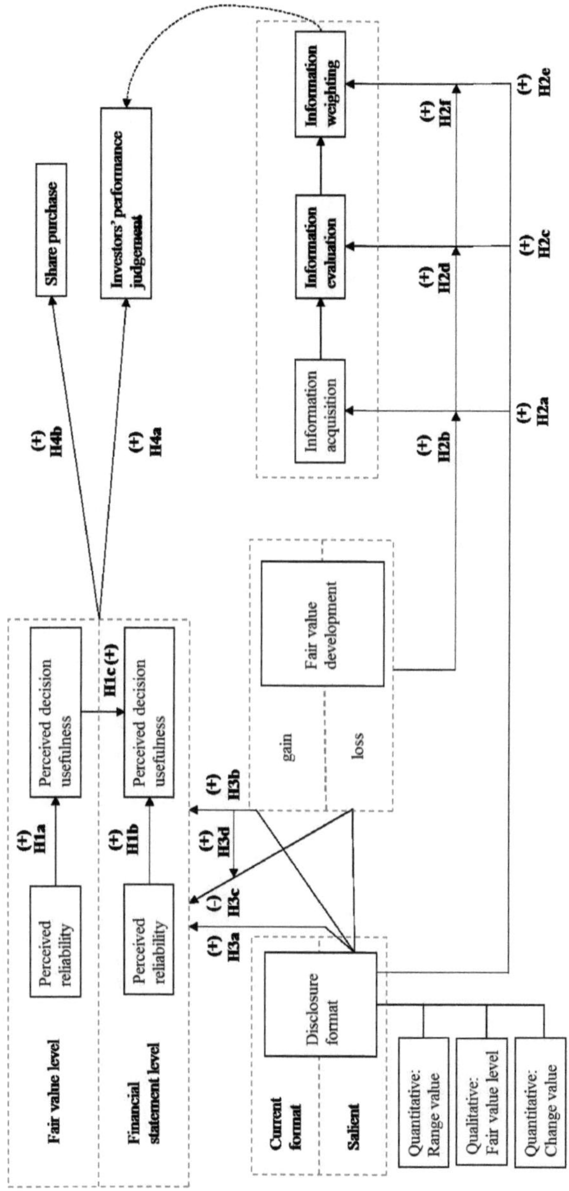

Figure 10: Hypotheses summary[32]

[32] Author's own illustration.

5 Method

This chapter will describe the method used for my research in this thesis. First, different experimental approaches in the accounting literature will be explained and then information about statistical tests used to analyze the data obtained from this experiment will be provided. Additionally, the choice to conduct an experiment in my research setting will be reasoned. This chapter will also describe the participants in this experiment and argue why they are a suitable proxy for NPIs. This chapter will be closed with further information on the design chose for this experiment.

5.1 Research design

The research design reveals the general plan behind the aim of answering my research questions and address my hypotheses. Further, the section will contain information on my objectives that derive from my research questions and specify the source from which the data is intended to be collected. Moreover, the plan will be proposed to analyze the data - once collected - and discuss it in line with this research design. The first necessary choice is of methodological nature as the research design can follow quantitative, qualitative, or a mixed method research design. Moreover, the nature of the research projects needs to be determined, differentiating between exploratory, descriptive, explanatory, evaluative, and a combination of these. These choices also affect the time horizon of the research. In addition, the research design may be subject to ethical concerns (Saunders et al., 2016).

5.1.1 Experimental research strategies

Experiments have got their roots in natural science and are forms of research that, even though often feature psychological and social science, owe much to natural sciences (Saunders et al., 2016). Generally, experiments are studies that involve the intervention by researchers beyond of what is necessary for measurement. An intervention in this context is to manipulate a variable in a certain setting and observe the effects of the manipulation in people or physical entities (Blumberg et al., 2014). The independent or explanatory variable is manipulated, and the researcher then observes if or how the manipulation affects the hypothesized dependent variable. In a causal relationship, there is at least one independent and one dependent variable (Blumberg et al., 2014).

The goal of many research approaches is to uncover casual relationships, which is why experiments are recently used in the literature to establish such causality between variables (Floyd & List, 2016). When researchers try to establish this causality in a real world-setting, the may face the problem - independent of the fact if the treatment is given or not - that they can never directly observe what would happen in the alternative state. Thus, generating an appropriate counterfactual is a problem that arises when using empirical archival studies. Further, this problem should be seen in the context that researchers often distinguish between either given or not given treatments even though the real world is much more complex. The markets have a high complexity and several parts of a market are moving simultaneously. Building onto existing literature on related works of Fréchette and Schotter (2015) and List

T. Herrmann, *The Decision Usefulness of Additional Fair Value Disclosures*, Controlling und Rechnungslegung – Managerial and Financial Accounting, https://doi.org/10.1007/978-3-658-24832-1_5

(2004), Floyd and List (2016) introduce the following measure of a treatment effect for an individual:

$$\tau_i = y_{i1} - y_{i0}$$

Equation 2: Treatment effect for person $\boldsymbol{i}$[33]

The key behind this equation is to construct the proper counterfactual. In the equation, y_0 is generally defined as the outcome without treatment, whereas y_1 is defined as the outcome with treatment. Thus, $T = 0$ when not treated and $T = 1$ when treated. The treatment effect for one person is thus the outcome with treatment minus the outcome without treatment. The challenge that arises from this equation by Floyd and List (2016) is that person i cannot be observed in with and without treatment but only in one of the two states. To still be able to estimate counterfactual, social scientists developed deductive models that assume rationality. These models offer grounds for criticism as a large range of assumptions is necessary for the models to establish causality. Floyd and List (2016) argue that this leads in many cases to the question of what assumptions need to be made in order to assume that the naturally occurring data results from a valid experiment. Thus, it can be hard to prove causality with certainty. Still, an experiment comes closer than any other method in terms of accomplishing this goal (Blumberg et al., 2014).

Libby et al. (2002) argue that experiments have the comparative advantage to untangle variables that are jumbled in natural settings. In line with this reasoning, conducting an experiment has at least three main general advantages as proposed by Blumberg et al. (2014): First, an experiment comes closer than any other research method to achieve the goal of evaluating the probability of one variable being linked to another (causality). This is because a researcher can manipulate the independent variable in an experiment. Thus, changes in the dependent variable are driven by the manipulation of the independent variable. Second, the contamination from extraneous variables can be controlled in an experiment very effectively. Consequently, the impact of the variables over time can be evaluated more precisely. Third, the costs and convenience of conducting an experiment is often superior to other research methods. Still, an experiment can also be subject to disadvantages such as limited generalization in terms of proxies. Moreover, experiments are most effective to target problems in the present or the near future. Last, there are ethical issues that can arise when studying people in an experiment (Blumberg et al., 2014).

To exploit the advantages of an experiment, a number of activities are necessary to ensure a successful experiment: selecting relevant variables, specifying the level(s) of treatment, controlling the experimental environment, choosing the experimental design, selecting and assigning subjects and performing some pilot tests, revising, and testing. Relevant variables are the variables that are the best to operational representations of the original concepts. These need to be determined before a design is chosen to appropriately measure the selected variables. The

---

[33] Cf. Floyd & List (2016), p. 440.

number of variables is determined by several reasons such as the budget, time, availability, and number of subjects (Blumberg et al., 2014). For statistical reasons, the latter should include between 10 to 30 subjects for each treatment level (Campbell & Stanley, 1966). In this experiment, the number of subjects varies between 23 to 24 per treatment group without the application of manipulation checks.

To specify the level(s) of treatments of the independent variable, distinctions need to be made by the researcher between the different conditions. The assigned levels should be simple and common sense. For researchers to obtain strong evidence on the casual relation, the subjects should be assigned randomly (Cook & Campbell, 1979; Libby et al., 2002). A control group can provide a basis level for comparison. The subjects of this control group are not exposed to the independent variables compared to those participants who receive experimental treatments (Blumberg et al., 2014). This experiment consists of six experimental and two control group treatments. Thus, a level for comparison is ensured.

To control the experimental environment, the physical environment in which the experiment is conducted should be held constant (Blumberg et al., 2014; Floyd & List, 2016). I ensure that all experimental groups receive the same written and verbal instructions. In addition, environmental control is ensured by the same arrangement of the room, the same amount of time where the experimental subjects receive their instructions as well as the interaction with them. Another form of controlling the experimental environment involves both subjects and experimenters. Subjects are labeled as "blind" if they do not know whether they receive the experimental treatment or not. If even experimenters do not know if they are giving a treatment to certain participants, the experiment is said to be "double blind." Both the approaches ensure that unwanted reactions such as subjects' reaction to expected condition or the influence of the experimenter occur (Blumberg et al., 2014). The experiment conducted for this thesis is of double bind nature.

The choice of the experimental design is strongly related to positional and statistical plans to designate the relationships that wish to be observed. In general terms, an experiment should be designed efficiently and effectively (Libby et al., 2002). Still, experimental designs vary widely in terms of their power to ensure that the relationship between the independent and dependent variable is not contaminated (Bloomfield et al., 2016; Blumberg et al., 2014). True experimental designs can be described with two cornerstones. First, they consist of a control group and an experimental group, the so-called treatment group, and second, it needs to be assured that the two groups are equal in terms of relevant characteristics of the participants. Specifically, this equality can be achieved by randomly assigning subjects to one of the two groups or through matching. The random assignment of subjects is the basic form of a true experiment and can be described as completely randomized design, whereas the matching which is especially relevant for small samples of less than 18 individuals per treatment is called randomized block design (Blumberg et al., 2014). In this experiment, the participants are randomly assigned to one of the eight treatments, which represents a completely randomized experimental design.
This true experimental design has nowadays two basic designs that are based on early experimental education: the pretest-posttest control group design and the posttest-only control

group design (Campbell & Stanley, 1966; Saunders et al., 2016). The pretest-posttest control group design indicates that a measure is made before and after the treatment effect (Blumberg et al., 2014). This design is subject to several internal and external validity problems (Blumberg et al., 2014; Campbell & Stanley, 1966). The post-test-only control group design is also known as between subject design. In this design the pre-test measure is omitted. Thus, the measurement is only made after the treatment. With this research design, pre-test is not really necessary as it is possible to randomize (Blumberg et al., 2014; Saunders et al., 2016). In this experiment, I use a post-test-only control group design (between subject design). More specifically, a factorial design is used to manipulate more than one independent variable at a time. Consequently, this research design is a 4 x 2 between subject factorial design. Two independent variables are manipulated: one with four levels and the other with two levels of intensity, resulting in eight randomized treatments. The treatments are presented in more detail in section 5.4. With an experimental design like this, it is possible to estimate the main effects deriving from each of the two independent variables as well as the interactions between them (Blumberg et al., 2014).

5.1.2 Internal and external validity of experiments

Even with an ideal research design, an experiment cannot be conducted without problems. The question if the results are true, will always remain and thus validity issues will comprise. While internal validity raises the question if the conclusion that is drawn about the demonstrated experimental relationship truly implies the cause, external validity raises the question if the observed causal relationship is generalizable across time, people, and settings (Blumberg et al., 2014; Chan et al., 2011). Moreover, external validity is established by extending research in terms of environmental contingencies that limit the generalizability of the initial hypotheses (Libby et al., 2002). Consequently, each type of validity has several threats that need to be avoided. An overview of threats to internal and external validity for experimental research is listed below.

Threats to internal validity	Threats to external validity
• History • Maturation • Testing • Instrumentation • Selection • Statistical regression • Experiment mortality	• Reactivity of testing on X • Interaction of selection and X • Other reactive factors

Table 4: Threats to internal and external validity for experimental research[34]

The threats of internal validity which are most present in the literature on experimental research are as follows: history, maturation, testing, instrumentation, selection, statistical regression, and experimental mortality (Blumberg et al., 2014; Campbell & Stanley, 1966; Saunders et al., 2016). *History* describes that events may occur during the experiment that can confuse the relationship that is studied in the experiment. This is especially relevant for a pretest-posttest experimental design as the difference between the two measures is attributed to be caused by the manipulation (Blumberg et al., 2014). *Maturation* describes the possibility that changes can also occur within the subject. These changes are likely to occur in long-time periods but can also be factors that should be considered for shorter-time periods, like an hour. If a test subject, e.g., becomes hungry, bored, or tired during the experiment, this condition can affect the subjects' response. *Testing* refers to the threat that taking one test may affect the score of a participant in a second test. The background of this threat is that the experience of taking one test may lead to a learning effect that can influence the second test. Thus, when performing a pre-test and post-test, it is difficult to ensure that the measured affect arises from the manipulation of the variable only. *Instrumentation* describes the threat that changes in the instrumentation used in the experiment may cause problems for the internal validity, such as a change of the observer or the use of different questions throughout the experiment. The *selection* of test subjects for experimental research can be a threat to internal validity. For validity reasons, the experimental groups (treatment and control groups) should be equivalent. Yet, when experimental subjects are randomly assigned to either a treatment or a control group, this aspect can be overcome (Blumberg et al., 2014). *Statistical regression* as a threat to internal validity is controlled for when mean differences are concerned and the treatment groups and the control group are randomly assigned from the same pool. By doing so, the control group regresses as much as the treatment group. *Mortality* describes the phenomenon of incomplete data due to lost cases or cases where only parts of the data are available (Campbell & Stanley, 1966). Mortality is less likely to happen in the control group as the subjects do not face the

[34] Author's own illustration based on Blumberg et al. (2014), p. 326-328.

testing situation. This could ultimately distort the comparison between the treatment groups and the control group. Besides the already mentioned main threats to internal validity in experimental research, there are additional threats, such as imitation (people from one treatment group talking to people from another treatment group) (Blumberg et al., 2014).

While internal validity observes if the source of observation differences is caused by the experimental treatment (*X*) or other extraneous factors (Cook & Campbell, 1979), external validity observes the interaction of experimental treatments with other factors (Calder et al., 1981). This is done with the aim of generalizing the observations across persons, settings, and time. The reactivity of testing *X* refers to the performance of a pre-test to ensure that the test subject reacts to the experimental stimulus of *X* and evaluate the way in which they react to it. If this pre-test is conducted before the measurement of a test subject's knowledge on specific information, it may lead to the situation that the test subject becomes more aware of a certain aspect later tested in the experiment. This before-measurement (e.g., the measurement is conducted in a pre-test and post-test design) can be a threat to external validity, especially for experiments where a change in the attitude of the test subjects is the change in the independent variable that is measured. The interaction of selection and *X* describes the threat to external validity that test subjects might be selected in a way that brings strong limitations to the generalization of results. Thus, the population group which is used as test subjects may not be the same type of population group that the researcher wished to generalize. Besides, if a researcher, e.g., only conducts an experiment with people who agree to participate, a self-selection bias may arise. Thus, the selection of subjects for an experiment can raise external validity concerns (Chan et al., 2011). Other reactive factors summarize biases that the experimental setting itself may cause. For instance, if participants know that they are taking part in an experiment, they may have the tendency to play a role and thus act differently which ultimately distorts the effects on *X* (Blumberg et al., 2014).

In this experiment, the threats to internal and external validity were addressed as follows: since a post-test-only control group design (between subject design) was chosen, a pre-test with the same individuals was not conducted, thus addressing the issues of history and testing. Maturation was addressed because this experiment did not exceed a time frame of 30 minutes. Furthermore, no changes were made in observations or measuring to address the threat of instrumentation. When analyzing the results, it was ensured that the mortality in the control group was not higher compared to the treatment groups. In terms of external validity, again a pre-test was not performed to avoid a bias in the reactivity of testing *X*. With regard to selection issues, career starters were used with some investment experience as proxies for NPI with a sound knowledge in accounting. Lachmann et al. (2015) argue that auditors are a suitable proxy for knowledgeable NPIs as they have reasonable knowledge to understand financial statement information as requested by the IASB (IASB, 2010). Also, career starters are suitable proxies for NPIs because they have the requisite academic degrees and professional experience to qualify for tasks with high integrative complexity (Elliott et al., 2007). Even though all of the participants worked at the same firm when the experiment was conducted, they all have a different background and no common investments.

In the context of business and management, and thus accounting, most experiments are conducted in a laboratory environment rather than in the field. Conducting a laboratory experiment has the general advantage of greater control over aspects of the sample selection. However, while conducting a laboratory experiment improves internal validity, external validity is more difficult to establish. Still, the feasibility of using a certain experimental strategy (such as laboratory vs. field) depends on the nature of research questions and hypothesis (Saunders et al., 2016). The experimental strategy of this research will be described in the next chapter.

5.1.3 Laboratory vs. field experiment

At the different ends of the empirical spectrum, the literature differentiates between the following forms of experimentation: laboratory experiment, artefactual field experiment, framed field experiment, and natural field experiment. The goal of laboratory experiments is to create a small-scale environment in a laboratory to ensure adequate control. This current practice relies on the economic experiments of Kmenta and Ramsey (1980). Floyd and List (2016) state that laboratory experimentation in some sense is the most convincing method as researchers can record and structure data provoked from participants as a response to their manipulation of an independent variable in a controlled setting (Bloomfield et al., 2016). Further, Bloomfield et al. (2016) state that one of the main advantages to exploit from laboratory experiments is that the control setting allows researchers to capture specific constructs.

Field experiments generate data outside of a laboratory environment. While earlier experimental research rather used laboratory experiments, in the last two decades many creative ways were introduced for researchers to generate economic data outside the laboratory environment (Floyd & List, 2016). Smith (1982), for example, proposes percepts for laboratory experiments. Building onto that research, Harrison and List (2004) propose six factors that determine field experiments: the subject pool, the type of information the participants in the experiment bring to the task, commodity, the task itself, the stakes, and the environment in which the participants of the experiment operate. Within the field experiments, the artefactual field experiment is closest to a laboratory experiment. The difference lies in the participants. While laboratory experiments use standard subjects, artefactual field experiment uses nonstandard subjects, e.g., participants drawn from the market of interest rather than college students. An example of artefactual field experiments in accounting literature is the work of Libby and Brown (2013). The authors use professional auditors as their research questions addresses the behavior of auditors directly.[35]

Data is originated more naturally in a framed field experiment (Harrison & List, 2004). Framed field experiment thus builds up on artefactual field experiment but is set within a field context. Consequently, this type of experiment tries to progress toward the natural environment of the participants, which is regularly the environment of ultimate interest. Alvey et al. (2007) use a

[35] Floyd & List (2016) argue that the research by Libby & Brown (2013) could also be classified as an FFE with the argumentation that the auditors perform tasks that are close to the type of tasks they typically perform.

framed field experiment in a financial market context and show that students and financial market professionals behave differently. Libby et al. (2002) argue that professional settings and subjects should only be used in experiments when this is necessary to address the research question. Furthermore, the use of professional participants is costlier (Floyd & List, 2016). Finally, a natural field experiment is a framed field experiment undertaken in the natural environment in which the participant usually performs the task.

An artefactual field experiment best describes the type of experiment used for this research. The participants in this experiment are employees at an accounting firm. I needed to ensure that the participants in this experiment have a deeper understanding of fair value accounting and knowledge about investment properties. As the materials which the participants received throughout the experiment are financial statements according to IFRS and as I wanted the participants to proxy for knowledgeable NPIs, I needed to ensure that they are used to working with financial statements. Moreover, they had to exhibit some investment experience, even though not to the extent of professional investors. Still, this experiment was not set into a field context as the participants did not act in their natural environment which would have been an audit of a financial statement. Instead, I attended an introductory training for career starters at this audit firm.

5.2 Setting

Conducting an experiment in this setting has numerous advantages. Since perceived reliability and decision usefulness are indirect measures, till date no archival dataset exists that could have been used for the purpose of this study. In addition, accounting research has not yet come up with an undisputed measure of decision usefulness (Gassen & Schwedler, 2010). This encouraged the employment of an experiment because with this research method, there was the opportunity to measure the decision usefulness and the relation to reliability of fair value estimates directly. To test my predictions, I chose to examine a setting where the investment property represents more than 90% of the average total assets of a firm. Using this approach, I not only followed Müller et al. (2015) but also take into account the practical structure of real estate investment company's balance sheets' reporting according to the IFRS. The investment properties of the real estate investment company are measured at fair value with input parameters classified at level 3. These input parameters are considered to be the most subjective within the fair value hierarchy. For these, fair value disclosures are especially relevant to make the value presented in the balance sheet more reliable for NPIs. Moreover, investment properties are relatively easy to understand for NPIs compared to, for example, a given firms' trading securities (Clor-Proell et al., 2014). The financial statement of the real estate investment firm is simplified, following experimental research works that have already been conducted, which utilize simplified decision contexts for the acquired test subject and examine that even after the information acquisition has occurred, differences in the personal judgement of information can persist (Clor-Proell & Warfield; Hirst & Hopkins, 1998; Hodge et al., 2004; Maines & McDaniel, 2000). It is subsequently examined whether differences in the presentation format of fair value estimates with high uncertainty levels affect NPIs' personal information evaluation and weighting by following earlier contributions to this research field (Clor-Proell et al., 2014; Clor-Proell & Warfield).[36] I chose investment properties because they can be associated with fair values with high uncertainty levels. Disclosures mandated for investment properties measured at fair value with recurring level 3 input parameters are, among others, the fair value hierarchy of the input parameter, the sensitivity analysis (IFRS 13.93), and the reconciliation between the carrying amounts between the prior and the current year (IAS 40.75).

Prior to the final experiment, a pre-test was conducted with 84 participants who had the same background as the final participants. The same setting and surroundings like those in the final experiment was ensured. The assessment of the data showed mixed results for reliability and decision usefulness of the financial statement. I argue that this was due to the two following main reasons: First, a definition of perceived reliability and decision usefulness was not provided to the participants, and second, the reliability was not distinguished from the decision usefulness for the fair value of the investment properties and the reliability and the decision usefulness for the financial statement as a whole. This issue is also a limitation of the research conducted by Clor-Proell et al. (2014) and Clor-Proell and Warfield (2009) as they did not differentiate between decision usefulness of the financial statement position and the financial statement as a whole. Thus, these issues were considered in the final experiment. I further examine a setting in which the fair value both increased (fair value gain) as well as decreased (fair value loss) compared to the prior year. By doing so, I can measure if there are different effects on reliability and decision usefulness that depend on the fair value development.

5.3 Participants

Participants for this experiment were recruited through a Big Four accounting firm. I attended an introductory training for career starters at this audit firm. As a part of this training, the participants took part in this paper-based experiment that lasted 30 minutes. The training management staff did not participate in the experiment, and the experiment was conducted completely anonymously so the participants would not feel performance pressure from their employer. I ruled out potential environmental biases by conducting all experimental treatments in the same facilities, at the same time of the day and during the same phase of the training. The participants received writing materials and a calculator. Career starters are suitable proxies for NPIs because they have the requisite academic degrees and professional experience to qualify for tasks with high integrative complexity (Elliott et al., 2007).[37] For this experimental setting, I ensured that the proxies had sufficient knowledge of accounting, according to the IFRS.

In total, 190 participants took part in this experiment. The participants were on average 25.8 years old and had an average of 10.5 month of business experience. They were predominantly

---

[36] With this line of argument, I follow Clor-Proell and Warfield, who acknowledge that disclosures will be a greater concern in more (complex) experimental settings. They argue that it is not necessary to provide an empirical test to confirm this assertion.

[37] US-based experiments often use MBA students as proxies for NPIs (e.g., Clor-Proell; Proell, and Warfield (2014)). The prerequisites to take part in an MBA programme in the US are different from Germany. While most US programmes require a minimum of five-year work experience, several MBA-programmes in Germany require a minimum of two-year work experience. I ensure that the participants in this experiment do not have work experience exceeding five years.

women (68.9%), and 96.8% of all participants work in the field of auditing, while the rest work in other service lines at the same company. The participants had private investment experience with an average of 5.33 years and therefore represented an adequate proxy of knowledgeable NPI. The academic degrees of the participants are distributed as follows: 58.7% of the participants had a bachelor's degree, 39.2% had a master's degree, and 2.1% have a diploma degree (former German master's degree). The subjects in which the participants graduated were mostly from the field of business (90.1%), followed by law (9.4%) and other fields (0.6%).

5.4 Design

To test my hypotheses, I use a 4 x 2 between-subjects mixed design. The first independent variable is the format of the disclosure information, which I manipulated at four levels: (1) the format currently mandated under IFRS (control group), or a salient presentation of (2) the fair value hierarchy, (3) the sensitivity analysis or (4) the reconciliation between the carrying amounts. The format currently mandated under the IFRS contains the fair value of the investment property in the balance sheet and the additional information appears only in the disclosures, as mandated by the standard setter. This format is also my control group. For making information salient in this experiment, an additional column in the balance sheet is used to highlight the disclosed information for NPIs (Clor-Proell et al., 2014)[38]. The second independent variable is the development of the fair value compared to the prior period, namely the gain or loss of the fair value. Thus, my experimental design results in eight treatments as displayed in Table 5 below.[39]

	Disclosure format			
	Non-salient	Salient		
	Current format (IFRS) *(point value)*	Fair value hierarchy *(qualitative)*	Sensitivity analysis *(range value)*	Reconciliation between carrying amounts *(change value)*
Gain	Treatment one	Treatment two	Treatment three	Treatment four
Loss	Treatment five	Treatment six	Treatment seven	Treatment eight

Table 5 Treatment overview[40]

The participants were randomly assigned to one of the eight treatments. They received a financial statement according to the treatment, with all other information equal among the

[38] Clor-Proell et al. (2014) had added an additional column to the income statement. In this experiment, I add a column to the balance sheet.

[39] For an overview of all treatments see Table 1.

[40] Author's own illustration.

treatments. Questions to measure information acquisition, weighting, and evaluation did not vary across treatments, following Maines and McDaniel (2000), Lachmann et al. (2015), and Clor-Proell et al. (2014). The participants further answered questions about perceived reliability and decision usefulness of both the fair value of investment properties and the financial statement overall, as well as questions about a potential investment. The experiment concluded with manipulation checks and questions regarding the demographic data.

5.5 Materials and procedure

The experiment was conducted paper-based. The task of this experiment required participants to evaluate financial statement information about XY Corporation (Crop.), a fictional public company in the real estate industry, wherein 90% of the company's assets in t=0 were investment properties. Managing the investment properties was the purpose of the real estate investment firm, which did not employ its own personnel. The XY Corp. reported according to the IFRS. The participants were asked to look at the company's financial statements from an investment perspective. The duration of the experiment was approximately 30 minutes, and the participants were kept anonymous. Thus, all participants were assigned a unique participation number. The following figure gives an overview on the procedure of the experiment:

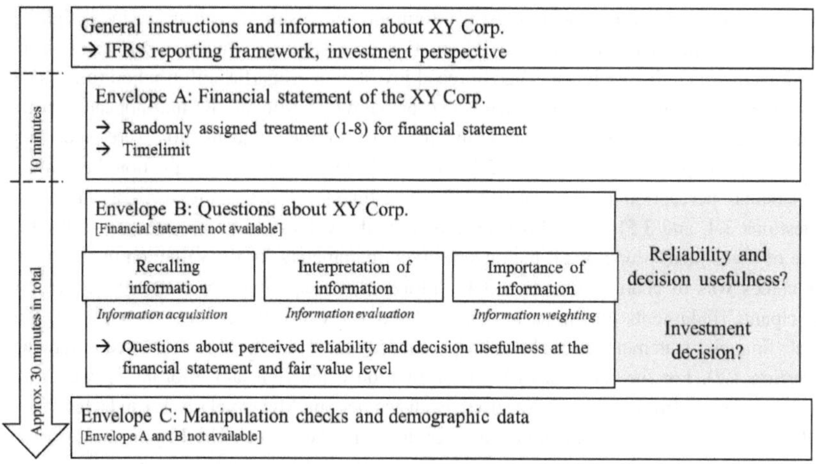

Figure 11: Procedure of the conducted experiment[41]

First, the participants received general instructions and information about the further approach of the experiment and the XY Corp., which included the IFRS reporting framework and the investment perspective. In the second part of the experiment, the participants were provided with the financial statement of the XY Corp. according to the assigned treatment (envelope A).

[41] Authors' own illustration.

Along with the statement, the participants received general information on how long they can assess the statement and that the statement would not be available for answering the questions afterward. A time limit for the evaluation of the financial statement of the XY Corp. was necessary to carry out this experiment in the context of disclosure overload. Since there are hardly enough topics in international accounting that lead to a higher level of unity amongst its originators than the level of detail and the high complexity of the disclosures of consolidated financial statements according to IFRS, this issue was addressed in this experiment. Even though the IASB addresses this issue with its disclosure initiative, which now comprises first results and clears the way for a focused disclosure reporting, it is a recurrent issue that companies face when reporting according to the IFRS. The financial statement of the XY Corp. starts with accounting principles, e.g., regarding investment properties and the fair value hierarchy, followed by a balance sheet and income statement. The financial statement is complimented by disclosures according to the IFRS. By providing the time limit of 10 minutes, I ensured that participants did not have enough time to look at every item of the financial statement and disclosures in detail. The length of a meaningful time limit was evaluated prior to the experiment when conducting pre-tests. When the time was up, the participants were asked to put the financial statement back into the envelope A and seal it.

In the next step, the participants received the envelope B. This envelope contained questions about the XY Corp.[42] formulated to test if information acquisition, evaluation, and weighting varied among the treatments. To test information acquisition, I examined responses to the questions in which the participants had to recall investment properties information (e.g., is the fair value of the investment properties above or below 25 Mio. EUR) that appeared in the balance sheet (Question 3.1). The questions that test information acquisition were given only two answering options (Questions 3.1, 3.2 and 3.3). To test information evaluation, I examined participants' perception of the volatility for investment properties measured at fair value (Questions 3.4, and 3.5). I asked participants, e.g., if there would be a correction to the fair value of investment properties if the material input parameters for the valuation model of the fair values was to change (Question 3.4). Information weighting was tested by asking for participants' judgments on the performance of the XY Corp. (Question 1.1) and analyzing which financial statement information they primarily used for their performance judgments (Question 1.2). For the retrieval of both information evaluation and information weighting questions, a scale from zero to 11 was used. Both Maines and McDaniel (2000) and Clor-Proell et al. (2014) use a 14-point scale for the answers in their experiments. The 14-point scale ranges from one to 14, where one, e.g., indicates "low risk", while 14 indicates "high risk" (Maines & McDaniel, 2000). In this experiment, I follow the approach of Lachmann et al. (2015) and use a 12-point scale ranging from zero to 11. Like Maines and McDaniel (2000) and Clor-Proell et al. (2014), Lachmann et al. (2015) use a scale with even numbers. In the 11-point scale, zero indicates, e.g., "not at all important", and 11 indicates "extremely important". Addressing experimental questions to measure acquisition, evaluation, and weighting, I followed the experiment by Maines and McDaniel (2000). The scale from zero to 11 was also used to measure the perceived reliability and the decision usefulness of both the fair value of investment

[42] For a detailed overview of all experimental questions please see Appendix S6.

properties as well as the financial statement as a whole, where zero signified "not reliable/decision-useful" and 11 signified "very reliable/decision-useful". I provided definitions on reliability and decision usefulness to the participants to ensure that they all understood the terms in the same way. For the definitions, I used the conceptual framework for financial reporting ED/2015/3 (IASB, 2015). Reliability was defined as having a high degree of objectivity and thus, a low level of subjective inputs. Light was also shed on how decision-useful information enables existing and potential investors to evaluate the amount, timing, and uncertainty of future net cash inflows to the entity. The participants were further asked if they felt that they could make an investment decision with regard to purchasing shares of the XY Corp., and if yes, which information in the financial statement they especially used in their decision-making process. If the answer to the question was negative, I asked the participants to list the additional information they would have needed to revise their investment decision. Participants were then asked to put the questions back into the envelope B and seal it. By doing so, I ensured that the participants cannot subsequently alter their answers to these questions once they saw the manipulation check questions in the envelope C.

In the last step of the experiment, the participants were asked to open envelope C, which contained manipulation check questions as well as questions pertaining to demographic data. At the end of the experiment, the participants were asked to put all envelopes (A, B, and C), as well as the instructions, writing material, and calculator back into one big envelope with their participation number on it, and were asked to seal it. With their participation number, the participants could participate in a lottery for winning Amazon vouchers. Since the experiment was paper-based, I used a four-eye-principle when digitalizing the data to control for transmission errors. Libby et al. (2002) state that the decision if monetary incentives should be paid in financial accounting experiments primarily depends on the goal of the experiment. Thus, e.g., if experiments focus on incentives, they will rely on the participation of professionals. These professionals are supposed to bring their knowledge into the experimental context. Yet, in the real world, they would receive incentives for this knowledge. The tasks the subjects dealt with in this experiment are not linked to the task audit professionals perform in the real world (e.g., auditing financial statements). Besides, many questions in this experiment did not have "one" correct answer to which I could have linked performance incentives. Due to the fact that the experiment was conducted as part of an introductory training of a Big Four accounting firm, the participants did not have any opportunity costs. This was also the reason why the participants did not receive a show-up fee.

6 Results

In the following chapter, the results of this research will be described. I will first describe and present the results of my manipulation checks followed by the results of my first hypotheses block on the perceived reliability and decision usefulness on both the fair value and the financial statement level. The second hypotheses block will then focus on the framework by Maines and McDaniel (2000) and present results on information acquisition, evaluation, and weighting among treatment groups' gain vs. loss and salient vs. non-salient information. In the third hypotheses group, the effect of the different treatment formats as well as the development of gain and loss on perceived reliability and decision usefulness will be examined. Along with this hypotheses block, the content-related research questions will be answered. In the last hypotheses block, I will focus on the weighting of information and the investment decisions of NPIs. I will further present some additional analysis on information that NPIs would value in financial statements besides the already presented information. Last, a depicted and written summary of the results on all hypotheses will be presented.

6.1 Manipulation checks

In total, 190 subjects took part in the experiment. I follow the approach by Gaynor et al. (2011) also used by Lachmann et al. (2015) and use manipulation check questions to ensure that the participants understood the corresponding manipulation of their treatment. I first asked them to recall, if the fair value of investment properties that was presented in the financial statement did increase or decrease compared to the prior year. For participants that were assigned to treatments one to four, the correct answer was a positive development of the fair value (gain), while for participants assigned to treatments five to eight, the correct answer was a negative development of the fair value (loss). Four people that participated in this experiment did not complete the manipulation check questions. Of the remaining 186 participants, 168 answered this nominal scaled (positive vs. negative) manipulation check question correctly. Thus, 9.68% failed the manipulation check. Treatment four (gain: reconciliation between carrying amounts) was the only treatment where all participants assigned to this treatment answered the first manipulation check question correctly, followed by treatment three (gain: sensitivity analysis) where one participant failed the manipulation check question. For treatments one (gain: current format), five (loss: current format), seven (loss: sensitivity analysis), and eight (loss: reconciliation between carrying amounts), three participants in each treatment failed the manipulation check. For treatments two (gain: sensitivity analysis) and six (loss: fair value hierarchy), four participants answered incorrectly. Consequently, eight participants answered the question incorrect with a fair value gain, while 13 people answered incorrect with a fair value loss.

As a supplemental test, the participants were asked which information was displayed salient in the balance sheet. The participants were asked to select one of the four presented answers: no additional information, the level label according to the fair value hierarchy, the sensitivity analysis data, or the reconciliation between carrying amounts. Depending on the treatment assignment, only one answer was correct. By applying this filter to the data, I discover that only

T. Herrmann, *The Decision Usefulness of Additional Fair Value Disclosures*, Controlling und Rechnungslegung – Managerial and Financial Accounting, https://doi.org/10.1007/978-3-658-24832-1_6

87 participants passed this supplemental test, which marks 53.22% of the participants. In my opinion, this result was caused by the two following main reasons: first, to ensure that the participants had cognitively noticed the manipulations, the manipulation checks were performed when the financial statement of the XY Corp. was not available to participants any more. Second, the manipulation checks were conducted at the end of the experiment so that the participants could answer the questions concerning reliability, decision usefulness, acquisition, evaluation, and weighting from an investor's perspective without actively knowing which manipulation they are dealing with. As the concentration levels of the participants decrease as the time progresses, this might have caused some participants to answer the manipulation checks incorrectly. Further, descriptive statistics show that most supplemental check questions were answered incorrectly when there was a fair value gain compared to the prior year. This could indicate that the participants were more aware of manipulations to the financial statement in the case of a fair value loss compared to the prior year. I state that using the full sample would have added statistical noise to my analysis. In line with this argument, I chose to evaluate the results for the sample including only those participants independent of their supplemental test results. This approach is in line with several research contributions in this field (Asay et al., 2017; Clor-Proell et al., 2014).

6.2 Hypotheses test

For reasons of clarity, I group my hypotheses into four blocks. Block one deals with the perceived reliability and decision usefulness of accounting information as proposed by the IASB. The second block deals with the theoretical framework introduced by Maines and McDaniel (2000) on information processing, and the third block with the impact of the fair value development on the salient and non-salient presentation of disclosures. The fourth block addresses the performance assessment judgements of NPIs and their final investment decision on buying shares. An overview of the results of all hypotheses will be provided at the end of this chapter.

For all my results, I ensure that only data of participants who passed the manipulation check are taken into account when testing for correlations. Hence, I ensure that the results remain significant when I consider all participants. Following this approach, all results for all the hypotheses remain significant for the sample with all participants unless indicated otherwise. When the data is not normally distributed, non-parametric tests were performed but ensure the robustness of the results by performing parametric tests as well. To analyse differences in means between groups, I perform non-parametric one-way ANOVAs on ranks (referred to hereafter as one-way ANOVA). I use a parametric one-way ANOVA (referred to hereafter as ANOVA) when data is distributed normally. ANOVAs are relatively robust to infringements of the normality distribution, which is why I use them as robustness test when the data is not distributed normally (Kirk, 2013). All reported *p*-values are two-tailed unless indicated otherwise.

6.2.1 Hypotheses on perceived reliability and decision usefulness

I take prior literature and information provided by the standard setter into account and argue that higher reliability will lead to higher decision usefulness. While most researchers so far look at reliability and decision usefulness at a more aggregated level (e.g., the financial statement level), I am the first to test the perceived reliability and decision usefulness at the fair value level. For this context, I predict in my hypothesis **H1a** that higher reliability leads to higher decision usefulness for NPIs at the fair value level. Before testing this hypothesis, the collected data is explored to see if a normal distribution of data presence. The data is not distributed normally, but has a slight tendency toward a normal distribution. Due to that, I will present the results for both parametric and nonparametric test in the following.

First, I use a nonparametric test to check for the predicted correlation. Spearman's rank correlation coefficient measures the rank correlations, and in turn, the statistical dependence between two variables. The test examines how well a monotonic function can be described using the relationship between two variables. Using this test to evaluate the correlation between the perceived reliability and the decision usefulness at the fair value level, I determine a strong significant positive correlation between both variables with a correlation coefficient of 0.451 (p=0.000, see Panel B of Table 6). The result is statistically significant at the two-tailed 1%-level. Thus, a significant positive correlation between the two variables with a weighted statistical connection is found. This positive tendency is moderately pronounced and implies that there are cases that show opposing results as well. To ensure the robustness of the results, I also test the correlation using a parametric test. Since my data shows a tendency for a normal distribution, I use a Pearson correlation. Again, the results of Panel B of Table 6 indicate a significant positive correlation between perceived reliability and perceived decision usefulness at the fair value level with a value of 0.452 (p=0.000) for the Spearman's rho. Likewise, the result is significant at the two-tailed 1%-level. Overall, I ascertain a robust significant positive correlation between the perceived reliability and perceived decision usefulness of NPIs at the fair value level. On this account, I can support my hypothesis H1a.

Hypothesis **H1b** predicts that higher reliability leads to higher decision usefulness at the financial statement level. Again, I first explore if the data is normally distributed. In line with my findings for H1a, the data is not distributed normally but a tendency toward normally distributed data existed. Consequently, and according to the approach for H1a, I first conduct a nonparametric correlation and yet again find a strong significant positive correlation between the two variables at the financial statement level. The Spearman's rho correlation coefficient is 0.521 (p=0.000) as presented in Panel B of Table 6 and significant at the two-tailed 1%-level. Again, I use a parametric correlation to ensure that the significance of the result remains robust even when I assume the normal distribution of the data. The correlation coefficient remains highly significant with a value of 0.526 (p=0.000) as indicated in Panel B of Table 6. Following my approach for H1a, I further ensure that the results remain significant after considering all participants and not only the ones that pass the manipulation check. Again, I find a significant positive correlation between the perceived reliability and decision usefulness of NPIs at the financial statement that is robust when I use both parametrical and non-parametrical tests.

Consequently, I can support my hypothesis H1b, which is in line with findings of previous literature (Clor-Proell et al., 2014).

Finally, for my hypotheses **H1c,** I bring the reasoning for the predicted correlations for hypotheses 1a and 1b together and argue that a higher perceived reliability at the fair value level will lead to higher perceived decision usefulness at the financial statement level. I discover a significant positive correlation between the perceived reliability of the fair value and the perceived reliability of the financial statement with a correlation coefficient of 0.406 (p=0.000) and decision usefulness with a correlation coefficient of 0.361 (p=0.000) as indicated in Panel C of Table 6, which is significant at the 1%- level. According to prior procedure in this hypotheses block, I again first perform a non-parametric correlation. The results for the parametric correlation that are presented in Panel C of Table 6 with a correlation coefficient of 0.397 (p=0.000) for reliability and 0.355 (p=0.000) for decision usefulness, which are significant at the 1%-level. The results of both tests indicate that higher levels of perceived reliability for the fair value lead to higher levels of perceived reliability of the financial statement. Thus, I can support my hypothesis H1c because I determine a robust and highly significant positive correlation between the perceived reliability at the fair value level and the perceived reliability at the financial statement level.

Panel A: Descriptive statistics for reliability and decision usefulness measures-mean [standard error]			
		n	Mean
Reliability	Fair value	168	4.79 [0.20]
	Financial statement	168	5.81 [0.16]
Decision usefulness	Fair value	168	5.61 [0.21]
	Financial statement	168	6.22 [0.17]

Panel B: Correlation between reliability and decision usefulness				
	Spearman's rho		Pearson	
	ρ	*p*	r	*p*
Fair value	0.451	0.000	0.452	0.000
Financial statement	0.521	0.000	0.526	0.000

Panel C: Correlation between reliability at fair value and financial statement level				
	Spearman's rho		Pearson	
	ρ	*p*	r	*p*
Reliability	0.406	0.000	0.397	0.000
Decision usefulness	0.361	0.000	0.355	0.000

Table 6, Panel A presents participants' mean ratings of reliability and decision usefulness at fair value and financial statement level. Participants rated reliability and decision usefulness on a 12-point scale (0= not at all reliable/decision-useful; 11= highly reliable/decision-useful). Panel B presents the parametric and non-parametric correlation between NPIs perceived reliability and decision usefulness at the fair value and financial statement level. Panel C presents the correlation between reliability at the fair value level and financial statement level.

Table 6: Relation between reliability and decision usefulness[43]

To sum up, all hypotheses on the relationship between perceived reliability and decision usefulness can be confirmed. Furthermore, all of them show a highly statistically positive correlation. The results remain robust when I use parametric test, even though my underlying data only shows a slight tendency toward a normal distribution. Also, all test show a significant positive correlation with and without the application of my manipulation check. Generally, the results correspond to my argumentation and findings from my pre-test, suggesting that the perceived reliability of a financial statement summarizes the perceived reliability of several financial statement positions. For my fair value level, I use the investment property of a real estate firm as they have a prominent height among the assets in the balance sheet for those firms. I take practical implications into account and ensured that the average total assets in both years marked at least 90%[44] of the average total assets of the firm. This further implicates that the level of perceived reliability of a firm's key operating asset is positively correlated with

[43] Author's own calculation.

[44] When looking at the composition of assets in the balance sheets of European real estate firms (e.g., financial statement of LEG Immobilien Aktiengesellschaft (AG)), I ascertain that average total assets will usually exceed 85%.

both the overall reliability of the financial statement and the perceived decision usefulness at financial statement level.

6.2.2 Hypotheses on information processing

For my second hypothesis block, I focus on the framework of information processing of NPIs introduced by Maines and McDaniel (2000). The model divides information processing into three steps: information acquisition, evaluation, and weighting. The authors propose in line with Hogarth (1989), that the presentation format affect the judgements of NPIs. Thus, I argue in my first hypothesis of this block, **H2a,** that the acquisition of information of fair value information is more likely if information on fair value estimates is presented salient in the balance sheet compared to when it is not presented salient. In the experiment, the participants were asked three different types of questions on information acquisition (cf. Appendix S6 question 3.1, 3.2 and 3.3). All three questions had two answering options ("yes" and "no"). Information acquisition is defined as the ability of individuals to store and recall information (Maines & McDaniel, 2000). Therefore, individuals can either store and recall information or not. In order to display this background, all three (sub-) variables were transferred into the new variable information acquisition. The participants acquired the information when the variable information acquisition was greater than or equal to two. Reimsbach et al. (2017) use information acquisition questions as their manipulation checks. Thus, in the context of this experiment, two of the three information acquisition questions need to be answered correctly for information acquisition to occur as the participants considered in my calculations already passed a manipulation check. Since in my hypotheses, I want to test differences between two groups of fair value information presentation in the financial statement (salient vs. non-salient), I also have to group my variables. I group treatments one (gain: current format) and five (loss: current format) as in both treatments no salient information is presented. In addition, I group treatments two (gain: fair value hierarchy), three (gain: sensitivity analysis), four (gain: reconciliation between carrying amounts), six (loss: fair value hierarchy), seven (loss: sensitivity analysis), and eight (loss: reconciliation between carrying amounts) and refer to them as the salient treatment group.

Of the 168 participants that passed the manipulation check, 152 answered at least two of the information acquisition questions correct which is why information acquisition is greater than or equal to two for the participants. Like prior hypotheses, I test my results concerning robustness with and without manipulation checks. The data is not normally distributed, which is why my primary test for this hypothesis is the non-parametric Mann-Whitney-U test. This test can be used to test the null hypothesis for non-parametric data as the assumption of normal distribution is not required. Still, as I see a slight tendency toward a normal distribution of the data as well as to ensure the robustness of the results, I also use the t-test as the parametric version of the Mann-Whitney-U test. When using a non-parametric test, I find a difference between information acquisitions of salient vs. non-salient presentation of information. Even though the p-value of 0.186 is not significant, it indicates that a subgroup analysis on this could be interesting as indicated in Panel B of Table 7. The result remaines insignificant when using a parametric test. This adds robustness to my results as I also consider the Levene's test for homogeneity of variances. I conjecture that due to the high aggregation level of my hypothesis

I do not find significant results at this point, which is why a subgroup analysis is conducted. According to my treatments overview in Table 5, I group treatments. This grouping results in treatment "non-salient" with treatments one (gain: current format, n=20) and five (loss: current format, n=19), as these treatments do not contain additional disclosures and treatment "salient" with all remaining treatments. Panel A of Table 7 presents descriptive statistics on information acquisition for participants that answered at least two information acquisition questions correct. To gain deeper insights into participants' information acquisition, I perform additional subgroup analyses among treatments. As a post-hoc test for the subgroup-analysis, the Mann-Whitney-U test is used. The test indicates that significant differences at the lay between groups one (gain: current format) and three (gain: sensitivity analysis) significant at the 5%-level, one (gain: current format) and four (significant at the 1%-level), and one (gain: current format) and seven (loss: sensitivity analysis) significant at the 10%-level, as well as four (gain: reconciliation between carrying amounts) and five (loss: current format) significant at the 10%-level. This indicates, further, that there are significant differences in information acquisition depending on the presentation of fair value information.

When comparing the mean ranks of the treatments, I ascertain that the presentation of fair value information as an additional disclosure in the balance sheet receives higher mean ranks for information acquisition than the presentation in the current format mandated under IFRS. Therefore, even though I do not find support for my hypothesis H2a when using a high-level statistical test (Kruskal-Wallis test) at first, the results of the test gives an indication to perform a subgroup analysis. This analysis shows a significant positive difference in information acquisition between treatments without additional disclosure presentation (treatments one and five) and treatments with additional disclosure presentation (treatments two, three, four, six, seven and eight). Consequently, I find evidence, as indicated in Panel C of Table 7, that participants who receive certain disclosures in a more salient manner are more likely to acquire this information. Especially, the presentation of the sensitivity analysis or the reconciliation between carrying amounts in an additional column in the balance sheet facilitates information acquisition. These results ultimately provide some weak support for H2a.

Panel A: Descriptive statistics for information acquisition with salient and non-salient presentation format

		n	Mean
Information acquisition >=2	Non-salient	39	2.53 [0.08]
	Salient	113	2.65 [0.04]
	Σ	152	2.74 [0.48]

Panel B: Information acquisition between salient and non-salient information

	SS	df	MS	F	*p*
ANOVA	0.399	1	0.399	1.75	0.187
Levene's test		150		4.26	0.041
Welch test		62.279			0.206
One-way ANOVA		1			0.186

Panel C: Information acquisition of salient and non-salient information (subgroup analysis)

Treatments	n	*p*	Mean rank	Mean
one/two	20/17	0.582		
one/three	20/21	0.050	19.59/26.35	2.40/2.76
one/four	20/20	0.001	16.55/27.71	2.40/2.95
one/six	20/17	0.259		
one/seven	20/17	0.073		
one/eight	20/21	0.307		
five/two	19/17	0.275		
five/three	19/21	0.841		
five/four	19/20	0.073	19.07/23.93	2.74/2.95
five/six	19/17	0.602		
five/seven	19/17	0.932		
five/eight	19/21	0.371		

Table 7, Panel A presents participants' information acquisition depending on the presentation format. Participants answered three questions on information acquisition. Participants acquired the information correctly when they answered at least two of the questions correctly. Panel B presents the parametric and non-parametric tests on differences of participants' information acquisition between salient and non-salient conditions. Panel C presents non-parametric analyses on differences between subgroups.

Table 7: Information acquisition between treatments[45]

When it comes to the development of a fair value compared to the prior year, researchers agree that differences in investment decision depend on whether the firm has a profit or loss (Kahneman & Tversky, 1979; Shefrin & Statman, 1985) and thus on the fair value development. The favourable and thus positive revision of a value requires less of the limited cognitive capacity of individuals. This is why I predict in my hypothesis **H2b** that information acquisition of fair value information is more likely if relevant balance sheet information is presented salient with a fair value gain compared to a fair value loss. To address this hypothesis, my treatments are now grouped differently. While treatments two (gain: fair value hierarchy), three (gain: sensitivity analysis), and four (gain: reconciliation between carrying amounts) contain a fair

[45] Author's own illustration.

value gain with salient fair value related information in the balance sheet, treatments six (loss: fair value hierarchy), seven (loss: sensitivity analysis), and eight (loss: reconciliation between carrying amounts) contain the same salient information with a fair value loss.

The descriptive statistic for this hypothesis is presented in Table 8, Panel A. Again, my data is not distributed normally; to ensure the robustness of results, I use both parametric and non-parametric tests. It is discovered that p=0.000 when I use both Kolmogorov-Smirnov and Sharpio-Wilk test, which indicate that the null-hypotheses on normal distribution assumption needs to be rejected (see Table 8, Panel B). I find a significant difference at the 10%-level (p=0.072) with the non-parametric test as well as when testing the hypothesis with a parametric test (p=0.072) between the salient presentation of disclosure information with a fair value gain and a fair value loss as presented in Table 8, Panel B. Again, I use a subgroup analysis as I have to group treatments together to test this hypothesis at an aggregated level. The subtest in Table 8, Panel C shows that with a fair value gain, information acquisition of additional disclosure information on the reconciliation between carrying amounts is significantly more likely than with a fair value loss (p=0.001). Even though I do not find statistically significant results between the remaining treatments, the results for the treatment comparison between two (gain: fair value hierarchy) and six (loss: fair value hierarchy) as well as four (gain: reconciliation between carrying amounts) and eight (loss: reconciliation between carrying amounts) indicate the direction of my prediction that information acquisition is more likely with a fair value gain and less likely with a fair value loss.

Panel A: Descriptive statistics for information acquisition of salient information measures-mean [standard error]

		n	Mean
Information acquisition	Gain	58	2.76 [0.06]
	Loss	55	2.60 [0.07]
	Σ	113	2.68 [0.04]

Panel B: Information acquisition of salient information between gain and loss

	SS	df	MS	*F*	*p*
ANOVA	0.710	1	0.710	3.310	0.072
Levene's test		111		12.037	0.072
Kolmogorov-Smirnov test		113		0.433	0.000
One-way ANOVA		1			0.072

Panel C: Information acquisition of salient information between corresponding treatments gain vs. loss (subgroup analysis)

Treatments tested	n	*p*	Mean rank	Mean
two/six	17/17	0.492	16.50/18.50	2.53/2.65
three/seven	21/17	0.700	19.98/18.91	2.76/2.71
four/eight	20/21	0.001	25.98/26.26	2.95/2.48

Table 8, Panel A presents participants' information acquisition of salient information presented either with a fair value gain or loss. Thus, n=113 because only treatments two, three and four as well as six, seven and eight are considered. Treatments one (n=20) and five (n=19) of the sample n=152 for information acquisition are not considered. Participants answered three questions on information acquisition. Participants acquired the information correctly when they answered at least two of the questions correctly. Panel B presents the parametric and non-parametric tests on differences of participants' information acquisition between gain and loss conditions. Panel C presents analyses on differences between subgroups.

Table 8: Information acquisition of salient disclosures gain vs. loss[46]

While the first two hypotheses of the second hypotheses block deal with the information acquisition during the information processing process of NPIs and thus the first step in the process, hypotheses **H2c** and **H2d** addresses the second step of information processing: information evaluation. The originally introduced framework by Maines and McDaniel (2000) does not make different predictions for information acquisition and information evaluation. Still, they state in their model that only information that has been acquired previously can be evaluated by investors. I test the information evaluation by asking the participants whether there is a change to the fair value of the investment properties when the input parameters of the valuation of the investment properties change. Key input parameters in the DCF calculation is discount rate (cost of equity, cost of capital), cash flows (in the case of investment properties the market rent), as well as the future growth (growth in firm's earnings). By making changes to these main input parameters of the valuation method, the value of the investment properties measured at fair value using DCF valuation will change. This information was given to the participants along with the information that all current rents of the XY Corp. were equal to market rents. Another information evaluation question used in the experiment was to rate the rental price development in context of the market development. The participants obtained the

[46] Author's own illustration.

information that the rental prices, the XY Corp. receives from their investment properties, were equal to the market rents. This assumption is necessary in order to test information evaluation with regard to the rental market development. To answer this question, the participants had the choice to select a number for the rental market development ranging from minus eleven "strong decrease of rental prices" to plus 11 "very strong increase of rental prices". For treatments groups that received a financial statement with a negative development of the investment properties measured at fair value (treatments: five, six, seven, and eight), the rental prices would have consequently decreased, while for treatments groups with positive developments of assets (treatments: one, two, three, and four), the rental prices would have increased.

I use a cross tabulation to analyse the distribution of market development predictions across all treatments. To determine whether the participants in this experiment evaluated the provided information correctly, I asked them to answer two questions (cf. Appendix 6, questions 3.4 and 3.5). The answer to the first question is scaled nominal. For all treatments, "yes" (coded with the value of one) would be the correct answer. In the second question, the participants were asked to rate the development of the rental prices in the seven biggest cities in Germany on a scale from minus 11 to plus 11 from t=0 to t=1. To transform both variables on information evaluation into one, the second question was recoded. Information evaluation can be considered correctly for the second question, where participants rated the rental price development with a value of one or more (one to 11) when they were in one of the gain treatments which were one to four. For treatments with a fair value loss, which were five to eight, values between one and minus 11 showed that participants evaluated the information presented to them correctly. The value of zero would indicate that no change in the rental prices had occurred. This answer would not be correct for the treatments with either a fair value gain or a fair value loss, which is why the information was not evaluated correctly for both gain and loss when the participants rated the rental price development at zero. Following the approach for the tests on information acquisition, I argue that information evaluation was performed correctly when the participants answered both information evaluation questions correctly.

Panel A of Table 9 presents the descriptive statistics for information evaluation that addresses **H2c**. Of the 168 participants that passed the manipulation check, 152 acquired the information in their treatments successfully. Of these 152 participants, 104 evaluated the information in their treatments correctly. Information is presented salient in treatments two and six (fair value hierarchy), three and seven (sensitivity analysis), as well as four and eight (reconciliation between carrying amounts) independent of the fair value development. The analysis of the descriptive statistics in Panel A of Table 9 indicates that on a higher level, the correct evaluation of information does not depend on the presentation format with a fair value gain as 85.0% of the participants evaluated the information in the current format correctly (treatment one) while 89.5% of the participants evaluated the information correctly when the related fair value information was presented salient in the balance sheet (treatment two, three, and four). Thus, with a fair value gain, information evaluation seems rather independent of the presentation format. With a fair value loss, 36.8% of the participants evaluated the information correctly in the current format (treatment five), while a higher proportion of the participants (52.8%) evaluated the information correctly in presentation formats with salient presentation of related fair value information (treatments six, seven and eight). Consequently, with a fair value loss, salient presentation formats seem to facilitate the correct evaluation of information as more people evaluate the information correctly in formats six, seven, and eight.

Panel B of Table 9 presents, in line with the results of the descriptive statistics, the results of the cross tabulation between information evaluation and the presentation format. With a salient presentation format, more participants evaluate the presented fair value information correct (n=76) than incorrect (n=37). The results of the statistical test in Panel C and D of Table 9 show that there is no significant correlation between the correct evaluation of information and the presentation format independent of the fair value development (p=0.133 and p=0.135). In line with these results, I could not find sufficient support for H2c that NPIs are generally more likely to evaluate fair value information correctly (and independent of the development of the fair value) if related information is presented salient.

Panel A: Descriptive statistics for information evaluation and acquisition measures-mean [standard error]

		Acquisition		Evaluation			Difference
		n	Mean (n)	n	Mean (n)	%	n
Gain	one	20		17		85.0	3
	two	17		14		82.4	3
	three	21	19.33	21	17.00	100	0
	four	20		16		80.0	4
	Σ	78		68		87.2	10
Loss	five	19		7		36.8	12
	six	17		10		58.8	7
	seven	17	18.33	9	9.67	52.9	8
	eight	21		10		47.6	11
	Σ	74		36		48.6	38
Σ Gain and loss		152		104		68.4	48

Panel B: Cross tabulation for information evaluation and presentation format (non-salient vs. salient)

	Information evaluation (n)		
Presentation format (n)	Incorrect	Correct	Σ
Non-salient	18	21	39
Salient	37	76	113
Σ	55	97	152

Panel C: Chi-squared test results on information evaluation and presentation format (non-salient vs. salient)

	Value	df	*p*
Pearson χ 2	2.258	1	0.133

Panel D: Logistic regression results on information evaluation and presentation format (non-salient vs. salient)

	Regression coefficient	Standard error	Wald	df	*p*	Exp (B)
Presentation format	-0.566	0.379	2.232	1	0.135	0.568

Table 9, Panel A presents descriptive statistics on participants' evaluation of information. Participants answered two questions: one nominally scaled questions and one metrically scaled question. Participants evaluated the information when they answered both of the questions correct. Evaluation % indicates the proportion of participants that evaluated the information correctly after acquiring them. Panel B presents the results of the cross tabulation between information evaluation and presentation format. Panel C presents the statistic results of the Chi-squared test. Panel D presents the results of the logistic regression.

Table 9: Descriptive statistics on information evaluation and relationship between information evaluation and presentation format[47]

For **H2d**, it is further predicted that NPIs are more likely to evaluate fair value information correctly if the related fair value information is presented with a fair value gain compared to a

[47] Author's own illustration.

fair value loss. Fair value information is presented salient with a fair value gain in treatments two (fair value hierarchy), three (sensitivity analysis), and four (reconciliation between carrying amounts) and with a fair value loss, in treatments six (fair value hierarchy), seven (sensitivity analysis), and eight (reconciliation between carrying amounts).

The results of the descriptive statistic in Panel A of Table 9 indicate that with a fair value gain 89.5% of the participants evaluate the information correctly when it was displayed salient, while 52.8% of the participants evaluate the information correctly with a fair value loss when it was displayed salient. Specifically, with a fair value gain, all participants in treatment three (sensitivity analysis) who acquired the information also evaluate them correctly. Moreover, with a fair value gain, treatment four (reconciliation between carrying amounts) seems to contribute least to a correct evaluation of information (Information acquisition n=20; Information evaluation n=16). With a fair value loss, the salient presentation of the reconciliation between carrying amounts (treatment eight) seems to narrow the correct evaluation of information as well. In this treatment, 21 participants acquire the information but only 10 (47.6%) of them evaluate the information correctly. Besides, treatments six (fair value hierarchy) contributes the most to a correct evaluation of information (Information acquisition n=17; Information evaluation n=10 (58.8%)). With a fair value loss, the current format contributes least to a correct evaluation of information (Difference n=12 (36.8%)).

These results are in line with the results of the cross tabulation between information evaluation and the salient presentation of gain vs. loss presented in Panel A of Table 10. The Chi-squared test results presented in Panel B of Table 10 point out that a logistic regression between the two variables can be performed (p=0.000). Finally, Panel C of Table 10 shows that the fair value development (gain vs. loss) has a significant effect on the correct evaluation of information. Thus, the correct evaluation of information strongly depends on the development of the fair value. To sum up, I ascertain support for H2d that the evaluation of information is more likely to be correct when the related fair value information is displayed salient with a fair value gain compared to a fair value loss.

Panel A: Cross tabulation for information evaluation and salient presentation with a fair value gain vs. loss

Presentation format (n)	Information evaluation (n)		
	Incorrect	Correct	Σ
Gain	9	49	58
Loss	28	27	55
Σ	37	76	113

Panel B: Chi-squared test results on information evaluation and salient presentation with a fair value gain vs. loss

	Value	df	*p*
Pearson χ 2	16.619	1	0.000

Panel C: Logistic regression results on information evaluation and salient presentation with a fair value gain vs. loss

	Regression coefficient	Standard error	Wald	df	*p*	Exp (B)
Presentation format	1.731	0.452	14.668	1	0.000	5.646

Table 10, Panel A presents the results of the cross tabulation between information evaluation and the salient presentation of gain vs. loss. Panel B presents the statistic results of the Chi-squared test. Panel C presents the results of the logistic regression.

Table 10: Relationship between information evaluation and salient presentation of fair value gain vs. loss[48]

The hypothesis **H2e** addresses the third part of the framework on information processing by (Maines & McDaniel, 2000): the weighting of information. Participants were asked to weight information they considered for their assessment of firm performance. They were asked to place weighs on the balance sheet items of “Property, Plant and Equipment (PP&E),” “Investment Properties,” “Equity,” “Other Accruals,” and “Liabilities due to Banks.” First, I expect that the participants place greater weights on investment properties compared to other balance sheet items. Second, and for H2e, I make the prediction that participants would place higher weights on investment properties, when the related fair value information would be presented salient in the balance sheet compared to the current format (non-salient). In line with the framework by Maines and McDaniel (2000), participants need to acquire information and evaluate them correctly before they weigh them.

Panel A of Table 11 presents the descriptive statistics for mean measures of the weights the participants placed on the different balance sheet items. The mean measures indicate that participants place the highest weight (ranging from zero to 11) on the balance sheet item of investment properties, followed by equity, liabilities due to banks, PP&E, and accruals. Therefore, my first prediction that participants place higher weights on investment properties in this experiment compared to other balance sheet items is confirmed. For H2e, I predict that

[48] Author’s own illustration.

the presentation format would affect the participants' weighting of information. Panel B of Table 11 presents the descriptive statistics on the mean weights. The results show that, consistent with the prediction of hypothesis H2e, participants place higher weight on investment properties when related fair value information was presented saliently (mean=8.46) than when it was not presented saliently (mean=8.17). However, the difference in the weighting of information between the salient and non-salient presentation format for both gain and loss is not significant (p=0.652). This result is verified by post-hoc tests between treatment groups according to H2a (cf. Table 7) that also indicates no significant differences between any of the treatment groups. Thus, the results do not support H2e.

Panel A: Descriptive statistics for information weighting measures-mean

		n	Mean				
			PP&E	IP	Equity	Accruals	Liabilities
Gain	one	17	4.35	8.35	6.53	4.20	6.00
	two	14	6.00	8.00	5.57	4.56	7.07
	three	21	5.62	8.24	7.57	4.71	7.14
	four	16	3.94	8.00	7.76	5.75	7.06
Loss	five	7	4.71	8.71	6.86	4.57	6.29
	six	10	6.30	8.40	5.40	2.90	6.00
	seven	9	2.66	6.78	5.33	4.11	4.67
	eight	10	5.60	9.60	7.70	3.80	5.60
	Σ	104					

Panel B: Descriptive statistics for information weighting of salient vs. non-salient information measures-mean [standard error]

		n	Mean
Information weighting	Salient	24	8.46 [0.47]
	Non-salient	80	8.17 [0.31]
	Σ	104	8.24 [0.26]

Panel C: Information weighting between salient vs. non-salient information

	SS	df	MS	*F*	*p*
ANOVA	1.482	1	1.482	0.205	0.652
Levene's Test		102		0.378	0.540

Panel A of Table 11 presents the descriptive statistics of the weights the participants placed on different items of the balance sheet. PP&E represents property, plant and equipment, IP stands for investment properties, Accrual refers to other accruals and liabilities are due to banks. Panel B presents the descriptive statistics for the weights participants placed on investment properties differentiating between the salient vs. non-salient presentation of related fair value information. Panel C presents the variance analysis on differences in weights between salient and non-salient treatment groups. When performing a subgroup analysis on the results of Panel C all differences between salient and non-salient treatment groups remain insignificant.

Table 11: Information weighting of salient vs. non-salient information[49]

For the last hypothesis (**H2f**) of my second hypotheses block, I predict that the weighting of information will be higher if the related information on the financial statement is presented salient with a fair value gain compared to a fair value loss. Panel A of Table 12 shows the descriptive statistics of salient information with a fair value gain and loss. Since now only the participants that acquired and evaluated the information correctly are taken into account that were in the treatment groups with salient presentation of related information, the number of participants reduces from 104 to 80. With a fair value gain, 51 participants were in a treatment group with salient presentation (cf. n of treatment groups two (n=14), three (n=21), and four (n=16) as of Panel A, Table 11) while 29 participants were in a treatment group with salient information with a fair value loss (cf. n of treatment groups six (n=10), seven (n=9), and eight (n=10) as of Panel A, Table 11).

[49] Author's own illustration.

Panel B of Table 12 presents the parametric analysis of differences between the salient presentations of related information with a gain compared to a loss. The data is normally distributed and indicates no significant differences between gain and loss (p=0.853). The subgroup analysis in Panel C of Table 12 shows that only the difference between treatment four (gain: reconciliation between carrying amounts) and eight (loss: reconciliation between carrying amounts), where the reconciliation between carrying amounts is presented salient, is significant at the 10%-level (p=0.099). The differences between the treatments groups two and six (gain vs. loss: fair value hierarchy) and three and seven (gain vs. loss: sensitivity analysis) are not significant. Taken together, the results do not provide sufficient support for H2f.

Panel A: Descriptive statistics for information weighting of salient information measures-mean gain vs. loss [standard error]

		n	Mean
Information weighting	Gain	51	8.10 [0.36]
	Loss	29	8.31 [0.59]
	Σ	80	8.19 [0.34]

Panel B: Information weighting of salient information between corresponding treatments gain vs. loss

	SS	df	MS	*F*	*p*
ANOVA	2.315	2	1.158	0.159	0.853
Levene's Test		78		1.396	0.241

Panel C: Information weighting of salient information between corresponding treatments gain vs. loss (subgroup analysis)

Treatments tested	n	*p*	Mean
two/six	14/10	0.681	8.00/8.40
three/seven	21/9	0.381	8.23/6.78
four/eight	16/10	0.099	8.00/9.60

Panel A of Table 12 presents the descriptive statistics on information weighting of salient information for a fair value gain and loss. Panel B presents the variance analysis on differences of participants' weighing of salient information between gain and loss treatment groups. Panel C presents the results of the subgroup analysis.

Table 12: Information weighting of salient information with a fair value gain vs. fair value loss[50]

While the second hypotheses block presented the results on predicted relationships on the information processing model by Maines and McDaniel (2000), the following hypotheses block will present the results on the predicted relationships between format changes on perceived reliability and decision usefulness.

[50] Author's own illustration.

6.2.3 Hypotheses on correlation between additional disclosures and reliability

In my third hypotheses block, I combine the topic of my hypotheses block on reliability and decision usefulness at the fair value and financial statement level with the different types of disclosure information and different fair value developments (gain vs. loss). My first hypothesis of this block, **H3a,** predicts in line with the findings of Clor-Proell et al. (2014) that the salient presentation of fair value information (i.e. as an additional disclosure in the balance sheet) will lead to an increase in perceived reliability and decision usefulness for NPIs. Because the results of H1c indicate that higher levels of perceived decision usefulness at the fair value level lead to higher decision usefulness at the financial statement level, I concentrate on the fair value level for hypothesis H3a. Moreover, H1a and H1b indicated that higher perceived reliability leads to higher decision usefulness both at the fair value and financial statement level. The treatments that present salient disclosures in the balance sheet are two and six (fair value hierarchy), three and seven (sensitivity analysis), as well as four and eight (reconciliation between carrying amounts). Thus, they are grouped and recoded into one variable. The treatments without salient presentation of fair value information are one and five (both current format), which are also grouped together into a new variable. This procedure achieves that the two groups of information (salient vs. non-salient disclosure information) can be compared in terms of perceived reliability and decision usefulness on both fair value and financial statement level.

The descriptive statistics on the reliability and decision usefulness for salient and non-salient disclosures is presented in Table 13, Panel A. Of the 186 participants, 168 answered the manipulation check correct and thus remain in the sample. The experiment consists of two treatments where no information is displayed salient independent of the fair value development (treatment one and five). Therefore, 43 participants in the experiment received a financial statement without salient information (gain: treatment one, n=22; loss: treatment five, n=21). Besides the two treatments with no salient information, the experiment contained six treatments where salient information was displayed. Consequently, 125 participants received salient information in their financial statement (gain: treatment two, n=20; treatment three, n=23 and treatment four, n=23. loss: treatment six, n=19; treatment seven, n=19 and treatment, n=21). Before addressing my hypotheses, I test the normal distribution of my data as presented in Table 13, Panel B. I discover that neither reliability nor decision usefulness are normally distributed, which is why I use primarily one-way ANOVA on ranks (non-parametric) to address my hypotheses. Hence, in line with my other hypotheses blocks, I also perform parametric tests (ANOVA) to ensure the robustness of my results. The results in Table 13, Panel B indicate a significant difference at the 10%-level in the perceived decision usefulness between non-salient presentation and salient presentation of fair value information (p=0.080) using a one-way ANOVA (Kruskal-Wallis test). Due to the grouping necessary to test this hypothesis and the resulting subordinate level of data, a subtest between groups in necessary. The results of the subgroup test are presented in Table 13, Panel C. For reasons of clarity, Table 13, Panel C only presents the significant results between treatments. For the perceived reliability at the financial statement level, I determine significant differences between treatments one (gain: current format) and seven (loss: sensitivity analysis) as well as five (loss: current format) and seven (loss: sensitivity analysis). When comparing the mean ranks of the treatments, I ascertain that the mean rank of treatment seven is significantly lower than the mean rank of treatments one and five, which are both treatments without the presentation of salient information. In terms of decision usefulness, I find in line with my results on H1b, that higher reliability leads to higher decision usefulness. Consequently, Table 13, Panel C presents significant differences between treatments one (gain: current format) and seven (loss: sensitivity analysis) as well as five (loss: current format) and seven (loss: sensitivity analysis) for decision usefulness. Additionally, for decision usefulness, I determine significant differences between treatments five (loss: current format) and eight (loss: reconciliation between carrying amounts). When comparing mean ranks, I discover that the mean rank is lower for treatments with the salient presentation of disclosure information like treatment seven (loss: sensitivity analysis) and eight (loss: reconciliation between carrying amounts) compared to treatments without salient presentation of disclosure information like treatment one (gain: current format) and five (loss: current format).

The results indicate that the salient presentation of disclosure information does play an important role in terms of reliability and decision usefulness, even though this role is not independent of the development of the fair value as predicted for hypothesis H3a. This is because the results show that the change in reliability and decision usefulness is driven not only by the presentation format of disclosures (salient vs. non-salient) but also by the development of the firms' key asset (gain vs. loss). Consequently, I test gain and loss separately in hypothesis H3b and H3c before testing differences between them with H3d. I find significant differences between treatments with salient presentation of disclosure information and treatments without salient presentation. Yet, the results do not indicate that the salient presentation of related information leads to an increase in perceived reliability and decision usefulness independent of the fair value development. Specifically, the results of the subgroup analysis in Panel C of Table 13 indicate that the salient presentation of related fair value information decreases the reliability and decision usefulness compared to the current non-salient format. These results are significant when presenting the sensitivity analysis salient (treatment seven) and the reconciliation between carrying amounts (treatment eight). Consequently, the data does not support H3a and the hypothesis has to be rejected. Nevertheless, the data indicates that these results could be driven by the differences in information processing of individuals depending on gain and loss environments which I will analyse next.

Panel A: Descriptive statistics for reliability and decision usefulness measures-mean [standard error]			
	Presentation format	n	Mean
Reliability	Non-salient	43	6.07 [0.33]
	Salient	125	5.72 [0.18]
	Σ	168	5.81 [0.16]
Decision usefulness	Non-salient	43	6.70 [0.35]
	Salient	125	6.06 [0.20]
	Σ	168	6.22 [0.17]

Panel B: Variance analysis for reliability and decision usefulness						
		SS	df	MS	F	*p*
Reliability	ANOVA	3.914	1	3.914	0.942	0.333
	Levene's test		166		1.252	0.353
	Kolmogorov-Smirnov test		168		0.167	0.000
	One-way ANOVA					0.212
Decision usefulness	ANOVA	13.173	1	13.173	2.674	0.104
	Levene's test		166		0.648	0.144
	Kolmogorov-Smirnov test		168		0.119	0.000
	One-way ANOVA					0.080

Panel C: Salient vs. non-salient disclosure (non-parametric subgroup analysis)					
	Treatments tested	n	*p*	Mean rank	Mean
Reliability	one/seven	21/19	0.019	24.99/16.39	6.27/4.53
	five/seven	21/19	0.047	23.93/16.71	5.86/4.53
Decision usefulness	one/seven	22/19	0.023	24.91/16.47	6.36/5.00
	five/seven	21/19	0.008	25.10/15.42	7.05/5.00
	five/eight	21/21	0.006	24.95/18.05	7.05/5.76

Panel A of Table 13 presents participants' mean ratings of reliability and decision usefulness at the financial statement level with a fair value loss. Participants rated reliability and decision usefulness on a 12-point scale (0= not at all reliable/decision-useful; 11= highly reliable/decision-useful). Panel B presents the variance analysis of reliability and decision usefulness with and without additional disclosures independent of the development of the firms' key asset (gain and loss). Panel C presents the non-parametric subgroup analysis between treatments without or with additional disclosures. For reasons of clarity the subgroup analysis only presents differences between treatment groups with significant p-values at the 5%-level.

Table 13: Impact of presentation salience on reliability and decision usefulness[51]

Hypothesis **H3b** predicts that the salient presentation of fair value disclosure information with a fair value gain compared to the prior year in the balance sheet leads to an increase in the perceived reliability and the decision usefulness. Panel A of Table 14 presents the descriptive statistics on reliability and decision usefulness for financial statements with and without salient fair value disclosures for a fair value gain. Of the 168 participants that completed the manipulation check correctly, 88 participants received a financial statement with a fair value gain of investment properties and 80 received a financial statement with a fair value loss. Of the 88 participants with a fair value gain, 22 received a non-salient presentation format (gain:

[51] Author's own illustration.

treatment one) and 66 received a presentation format with salient disclosures (gain: treatment two (n=20), treatment three (n=23), and four (n=23)).

Table 14, Panel B indicates that the data is not distributed normally for either reliability or decision usefulness. Thus, the null hypotheses on variance homogeneity for reliability (p=0.000) and decision usefulness (p=0.000) is rejected. Consequently, I use a one-way ANOVA on ranks to determine differences between my four treatment groups. Hence, in line with my other hypotheses blocks, I also perform parametric tests (ANOVA) to ensure the robustness of my results. Both procedures show that there is no significant change in reliability or decision usefulness when additional fair value disclosures are presented in the balance sheet. Specifically, the results of my analysis of variance (one-way ANOVA), presented in Panel B, indicate that participants who receive an additional disclosure do not rate reliability (p=0.656) and decision usefulness (p=0.880) of accounting data significantly higher than in the current format.

Still, to address this hypothesis, I again had to group my treatments. Treatment one is the treatment that presents the balance sheet and corresponding disclosures in the format currently mandated under IFRS (non-salient). Treatments two, three, and four present salient disclosures in the balance sheet, which is why they are grouped together to test salient vs. non-salient disclosure effects on reliability and decision usefulness. All treatments (one to four) show a fair value gain for the company's key assets compared to the prior year. The analysis in Panel C of Table 14 analysis detects no significant differences between any of the treatments. When comparing the mean ranks, I discover that the means of reliability are higher when disclosures on the fair value are presented salient in the balance sheet compared to when they are not. Yet, this weak evidence could not support H3b.

Panel A: Descriptive statistics for reliability and decision usefulness measures-mean [standard error]					
	Presentation format	n	Mean		
Reliability	Non-salient	22	6.27 [0.46]		
	Salient	66	6.24 [0.24]		
	Σ	88	6.25 [0.21]		
Decision usefulness	Non-salient	22	6.36 [0.40]		
	Salient	66	6.42 [0.27]		
	Σ	88	6.41 [0.22]		
Panel B: Variance analysis for reliability and decision usefulness					
		SS	df	MS	F	*p*
Reliability	ANOVA	0.015	1	0.013	0.004	0.951
	Levene's test		86		0.430	0.954
	Kolmogorov-Smirnov test		88		0.169	0.000
	One-way ANOVA					0.656
Decision usefulness	ANOVA	0.061	1	0.061	0.013	0.908
	Levene's test		86		0.257	0.908
	Kolmogorov-Smirnov test		88		0.156	0.000
	One-way ANOVA					0.880
Panel C: Salient vs. non-salient disclosure (non-parametric subgroup analysis)						
	Treatments tested	n	*p*	Mean rank	Mean	
Reliability	one/two	42	0.389	23.02/19.83	6.27/6.05	
	one/three	45	0.755	22.39/23.59	6.27/6.52	
	one/four	45	0.556	24.16/21.89	6.27/6.13	
Decision usefulness	one/two	42	0.444	20.14/23.00	6.36/6.75	
	one/three	45	0.917	22.80/23.20	6.36/6.48	
	one/four	45	0.663	23.86/22.17	6.36/6.09	

Table 14, Panel A presents participants' mean ratings of reliability and decision usefulness at the financial statement level with a fair value gain. Participants rated reliability and decision usefulness on a 12-point scale (0= not at all reliable/decision-useful; 11= highly reliable/decision-useful). Panel B presents the variance analysis of reliability and decision usefulness with and without additional disclosures with a fair value gain. Panel C presents the non-parametric subgroup analysis between treatments without and with additional disclosures and a fair value gain compared to the prior period.

Table 14: Effects of additional disclosures on reliability and decision usefulness with a fair value gain[52]

My first research question (**RQ1**) aims to find out what type of disclosure information leads to the highest perceived reliability and decision usefulness for NPIs. As the results of H1a, H1b and H1c (cf. Table 6) indicate that higher reliability leads to higher decision usefulness at both the fair value and financial statement level. Therefore, to evaluate the results for RQ1, I will focus on the most aggregated level, the decision usefulness of the financial statement. Panel A of Table 15 presents the mean values for decision usefulness at the financial statement level for all treatments. The values are ranked according to their height. Treatment five (loss: current

[52] Author's own illustration.

format) receives the highest mean values by participants in terms of decision usefulness followed by the salient presentation of the fair value hierarchy with a fair value gain (treatment two). The third highest mean values occur with treatment three, the presentation of the sensitivity analysis with a fair value gain. Except for treatment five (loss: current format), the mean values for decision usefulness are higher with a fair value gain compared to a fair value loss. The differences between all treatment combinations are displayed in Panel B of Table 15. The greatest difference in mean values lies between treatment five (loss: current format) and seven (loss: sensitivity analysis). To sum up, I answer my first research question on what type of fair value disclosure information leads to the highest perceived reliability and decision usefulness as follows: The current disclosure format mandated under IFRS overall leads to the highest perceived reliability and decision usefulness (mean=7.05). Yet again, the results also indicate that the development of the fair value plays an important role for the perceived decision usefulness of different disclosure formats. Thus, I further analyse the answer to my RQ1 separately for a fair value gain and loss.

Panel A of Table 14 indicates that with a fair value **gain,** decision usefulness is highest when the quantitative disclosure on the sensitivity analysis is presented salient. The decision usefulness is lowest when the reconciliation between carrying amounts is presented salient. The results indicate that range value disclosures (gain: sensitivity analysis, treatment three) and qualitative disclosures (gain: fair value hierarchy, treatment two) analysis can improve decision usefulness the most. The loss component of RQ1 will be evaluated in line with hypothesis H3c.

Panel A: Descriptive statistics of decision usefulness at the financial statement level for all treatments

Treatment	n	Mean	Rank	Rank gain vs. loss
one	22	6.36 [0.40]	4	3
two	20	6.75 [0.48]	2	1
three	23	6.48 [0.30]	3	2
four	23	6.08 [0.59]	6	4
five	21	7.04 [0.58]	1	1
six	19	6.16 [0.51]	5	2
seven	19	5.00 [0.42]	8	4
eight	21	5.76 [0.49]	7	3

Panel B: Differences between treatments in decision usefulness

Treatments	n	Mean	Treatments	n	Mean
one/two	22/20	6.36/6.75	three/five	23/21	6.48/7.04
one/three	22/23	6.36/6.48	three/six	23/19	6.48/6.16
one/four	22/23	6.36/6.08	three/seven	23/19	6.48/5.00
one/five	22/21	6.36/7.04	three/eight	23/21	6.48/5.76
one/six	22/19	6.36/6.16	four/five	23/21	6.08/7.04
one/seven	22/19	6.36/5.00	four/six	23/19	6.08/6.16
one/eight	22/21	6.36/5.76	four/seven	23/19	6.08/5.00
two/three	20/23	6.75/6.48	four/eight	23/21	6.08/5.76
two/four	20/23	6.75/6.08	five/six	21/19	7.04/6.16
two/five	20/21	6.75/7.04	five/seven	21/19	7.04/5.00
two/six	20/19	6.75/6.16	five/eight	21/21	7.04/5.76
two/seven	20/19	6.75/5.00	six/seven	19/19	6.16/5.00
two/eight	20/21	6.75/5.76	six/eight	19/21	6.16/5.76
three/four	23/23	6.48/6.08	seven/eight	19/21	5.00/5.76

Panel A of Table 15 presents the descriptive statistics on decision usefulness at the financial statement level. Panel B presents the differences in means of all treatment combinations. The parametric subgroup analysis is presented in Table 14 for a fair value gain and in Table 16 for a fair value loss.

Table 15: Descriptive statistics on decision usefulness at the financial statement level for all treatments[53]

I argue that the decrease of an asset accounted for at fair value is comparable to an unfavourable revision of other financial statement items (e.g., stocks) measured at fair value. I predict that with an unfavourable revaluation of company assets, NPIs will become more aware of the underlying measurement subjectivity of assets measured at fair value when the corresponding disclosure information is presented salient. Therefore, I predict for my hypothesis **H3c** that if salient disclosures are presented with a fair value loss, the perceived reliability and decision

[53] Author's own illustration.

usefulness will decrease. Panel A of Table 16 presents descriptive statistics on reliability and decision usefulness with and without additional disclosures when a fair value loss occurs. 80 participants of the experiment received a financial statement with a fair value loss of the investment properties. Of these 80 participants, 21 received a financial statement in the current format mandated under IFRS and thus without salient disclosure information. The remaining 59 participants received financial statement with different salient disclosure information (loss: treatment six (n=20), treatment seven (n=23) and treatment eight (n=23)).

Table 16, Panel B indicates that the data is not distributed normally for either reliability or decision usefulness. As a result, the null hypotheses on variance homogeneity for reliability (p=0.000) and decision usefulness (p=0.002) is rejected. Consequently, I use a one-way ANOVA on ranks to determine differences between my four treatment groups. Hence, in line with my other hypotheses blocks, I also perform parametric tests (ANOVA) to ensure the robustness of my results. As predicted, the results of the analysis of variance (one-way ANOVA) in Panel B show that the differences between some of the medians of reliability (p=0.091) and decision usefulness (p=0.039) are statistically significant. The subgroup-analysis in Panel C shows significant differences between the means of reliability for treatment five and seven (p=0.047). In line with the findings on reliability, there are significant differences for the means of decision usefulness between treatments five (current format) and seven (sensitivity analysis) (p=0.008). Further, the difference between the means of treatments five (current format) and eight (reconciliation between carrying amounts) (p=0.066) is statistically significant. The results indicate that reliability and decision usefulness decrease when financial statements contain additional disclosures along with a fair value loss. NPIs become aware of the low reliability the most with quantitative disclosures, like the disclosure on the sensitivity analysis, signal high uncertainty. Since the current format is most decision-useful for NPIs with a fair value loss, it seems that the participants become aware of the low reliability and consequently the decision usefulness of the fair value only when this low reliability is highlighted by the salient displayed disclosures. These findings are in line with prior literature which finds that losses are an extreme level of earnings for which the perception of risk by investors is higher (Erickson et al., 2017). This high risk is especially emphasized by quantitative disclosures like the sensitivity analysis (treatment seven) and the reconciliation between carrying amounts (treatment eight). Thus, I find support for H3c.

Within **RQ1 (loss)** I raise the question of which type of additional disclosure leads to the highest level of perceived reliability and decision usefulness. Panel C of Table 16 indicates that a fair value loss reliability (mean rank=23.59) and decision usefulness (mean rank=23.20) are highest when the quantitative disclosure on the reconciliation between carrying amounts is presented salient. Reliability (mean rank=16.71) and decision usefulness (mean rank=15.42) are both lowest when the quantitative disclosure information on the sensitivity analysis is presented salient.

Concluding, RQ1 can be answered as follows after looking at the statistical results separately for fair value gain and loss: Independent of the fair value development, the current format mandated according to IFRS is the most decision-useful as the mean value is the highest (mean=7.05 as of Panel A, Table 15). However, when differentiating between gain and loss, the current format is least decision-useful with a fair value gain. Thus, the results indicate that decision usefulness of the current format depends on the development of the fair value. This result is further emphasized by the decision usefulness of reconciliation between carrying amounts (gain: treatment four; loss: treatment eight). While the salient presentation of the disclosure on the reconciliation between carrying amounts *increases* the decision usefulness the most with a fair value gain, it *decreases* the decision usefulness significantly with a fair value loss. Still, with a fair value loss, decision usefulness decreases even more when the disclosure on the sensitivity analysis is presented salient.

Panel A: Descriptive statistics for reliability and decision usefulness measures-mean [standard error]

	Presentation format	n	Mean
Reliability	Non-salient	21	5.86 [0.48]
	Salient	59	5.14 [0.25]
	Σ	80	5.33 [0.22]
Decision usefulness	Non-Salient	21	7.05 [0.58]
	Salient	59	5.64 [0.28]
	Σ	80	6.01 [0.26]

Panel B: Variance analysis for reliability and decision usefulness

		SS	df	MS	F	*p*
Reliability	ANOVA	8.063	1	8.063	2.07	0.154
	Levene's test		78		2.29	0.154
	Kolmogorov-Smirnov test		80		0.16	0.000
	One-way ANOVA					0.091
Decision usefulness	ANOVA	30.510	1	30.510	5.85	0.018
	Levene's test		78		2.24	0.037
	Kolmogorov-Smirnov test		80		0.13	0.002
	One-way ANOVA					0.039

Panel C: Salient vs. non-salient disclosure (non-parametric subgroup analysis)

	Treatments tested	n	*p*	Mean rank	Mean
Reliability	five/six	40	0.436	21.88/18.97	5.86/5.37
	five/seven	40	0.047	23.93/16.71	5.86/4.53
	five/eight	42	0.467	22.86/20.14	5.87/5.48
Decision usefulness	five/six	40	0.145	23.02/17.71	7.05/6.16
	five/seven	40	0.008	25.10/15.42	7.05/5.00
	five/eight	40	0.066	24.95/18.05	7.05/5.76

Table 16, Panel A presents participants' mean ratings of reliability and decision usefulness at the financial statement level with a fair value loss. Participants rated reliability and decision usefulness on a 12-point scale (0= not at all reliable/decision-useful; 11= highly reliable/decision-useful). Panel B presents the variance analysis of reliability and decision usefulness with and without additional disclosures with a fair value loss. Panel C presents the non-parametric subgroup analysis between treatments without and with additional disclosures and a fair value loss compared to the prior period.

Table 16: Effects of additional disclosures on reliability and decision usefulness with a fair value loss[54]

Hypothesis **H3d** predicts that the perceived reliability and decision usefulness for NPIs is higher when presenting additional fair value information saliently with a fair value gain, compared to a fair value loss. Panel A of Table 17 presents descriptive statistics on additional disclosures presented with a fair value gain or a fair value loss. Of the 168 participants that answered the manipulation check correctly, 125 received a financial statement with salient displayed related fair value information. Of these 125 participants, 66 received their information with a fair value gain ((treatment two (n=20), treatment three (n=23) and four (n=23)), while 59 received the

[54] Author's own illustration.

information with a fair value loss ((treatment six (n=20), treatment seven (n=23) and treatment eight (n=23)).

Table 17, Panel B indicates that the data is not distributed normally for either reliability or decision usefulness. Therefore, the null hypotheses on variance homogeneity for reliability (p=0.000) and decision usefulness (p=0.000) is rejected. Consequently, I use a one-way ANOVA on ranks to determine differences between the treatment groups. Hence, in line with my other hypotheses blocks, I also perform parametric tests (ANOVA) to ensure the robustness of my results. As predicted, significant differences exist in the reliability at the financial statement level between salient information presented with a fair value gain compared to a fair value loss. Specifically, as indicated in Panel B, the differences between the treatments are statistically significant for reliability (p=0.030) and decision usefulness (p=0.039).

The non-parametrical subgroup analysis in Panel C suggests that the reliability and decision usefulness is higher when additional disclosures are presented with a fair value gain, since all mean ranks are higher with a gain compared to a loss. The differences between means are significant between treatment three (gain: sensitivity analysis) and seven (loss: sensitivity analysis) for both reliability (p=0.003) and decision usefulness (p=0.007). As a result, especially with the presentation of the sensitivity analysis, the reliability and decision usefulness are significantly lower with a fair value loss compared to a gain. The results indicate that when the format of information is constant, like between treatment three and seven, the content matters to NPIs to judge the reliability and decision usefulness of accounting figures.

With **RQ2**, I raise the question of what causes the difficulties of NPIs to incorporate fair value disclosures into their decision-making process and distinguish between the format and the content as potential reasons. Panel C of Table 17 indicates that when the format is held constant, significant differences for the means of reliability pertain (p=0.003). This effect is the same for the decision usefulness (p=0.007). Thus, even though I determine that a format change affects reliability and decision usefulness, on examining gains and losses differently, I find that reliability and decision usefulness vary when the format is constant. Consequently, the results indicate that the difficulties of NPIs to incorporate fair value disclosures into their decision-making process are caused rather by the content than the format. The results further point out that the content of a fair value loss seems to cause the struggle to incorporate disclosure information for NPIs. The reliability (mean rank gain=26.52, mean rank loss=15.42) and decision usefulness (mean rank gain=26.11, mean rank loss=15.92) decrease due to the content of the disclosure information.

Panel A: Descriptive statistics for reliability and decision usefulness for additional disclosures-mean [standard error]

		n	Mean
Reliability	Gain	66	6.24 [0.24]
	Loss	59	5.14 [0.25]
Decision uefulness	Gain	66	6.42 [0.27]
	Loss	59	5.64 [0.28]

Panel B: Variance analysis for reliability and decision usefulness

		SS	df	MS	F	*p*
Reliability	ANOVA	38.164	1	38.164	10.271	0.002
	Levene's test		123		0.019	0.002
	Kolmogorov-Smirnov test		125		0.147	0.000
	One-way ANOVA					0.030
Decision usefulness	ANOVA	18.961	1	18.961	4.037	0.047
	Levene's test		123		0.058	0.047
	Kolmogorov-Smirnov test		125		0.131	0.000
	One-way ANOVA					0.039

Panel C: Gain vs. loss (non-parametric subgroup analysis)

	Treatments tested	n	*p*	Mean rank	Mean
Reliability	two/six	39	0.229	22.10/17.79	6.05/5.37
	three/seven	42	0.003	26.52/15.42	6.52/4.53
	four/eight	44	0.198	24.85/19.93	6.13/5.48
Decision usefulness	two/six	39	0.375	21.55/18.37	6.75/6.16
	three/seven	42	0.007	26.11/15.92	6.48/5.00
	four/eight	44	0.644	23.35/21.57	6.09/5.76

Table 17, Panel A presents participants' mean ratings of reliability and decision usefulness for additional disclosures at the financial statement level with a fair gain and value loss. Participants rated reliability and decision usefulness on a 12-point scale (0= not at all reliable/decision-useful; 11= highly reliable/decision-useful). Panel B presents the variance analysis of reliability and decision usefulness with additional disclosures either with a fair value gain or loss. Panel C presents the non-parametric subgroup analysis between treatments with salient disclosure with a fair value gain or loss.

Table 17: Effects of additional disclosure fair value development on reliability and decision usefulness[55]

Figure 12 summarizes the results on H3b, H3c, and H3d. Decision usefulness in the non-salient condition is higher with a fair value loss compared to a fair value gain. With the salient presentation of additional disclosure, decision usefulness increases with a fair value gain and decreases with a loss. The difference between the means, when salient information is presented with either a gain or loss, is significant.

[55] Author's own illustration.

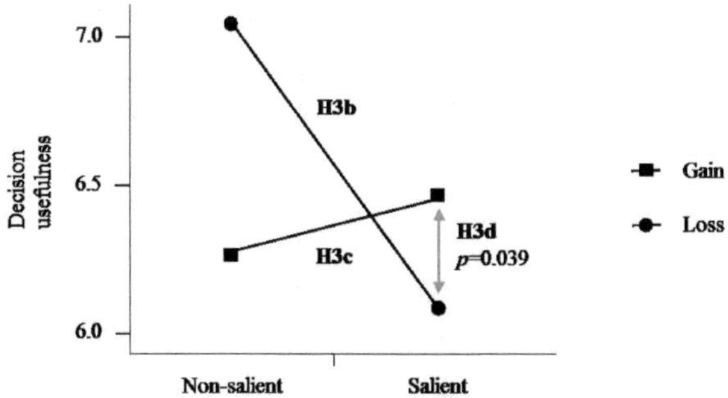

Figure 12 graphically depicts the mean results for participants' judgement on the decision usefulness of the financial statement information with a fair value gain (H3b) and a fair value loss (H3c). The participants indicate their judgements on a 12-point scale (0 = not at all decision-useful, 11= highly decision-useful).[56] Further, Figure 12 depicts the difference in decision usefulness with salient disclosures (H3d).

Figure 12: Mean results for H3b-H3d

This hypotheses block examined the relationship between gain and loss and salient vs. non-salient disclosure regarding perceived reliability and decision usefulness. As defined by the standard setter, information needs to be decision-useful for investors to make investment decisions. This is why the next and last hypotheses block deals with investment decisions of NPIs.

6.2.4 Hypotheses on investment decisions of NPIs

This hypotheses block evaluates the performance judgements of investors. Prior research finds that perceived reliability judgements mediate the P/E judgements of NPIs (Clor-Proell et al., 2014). Thus, the higher the reliability, the higher the P/E judgements. The P/E ratio can be an indicator for the future development of the firm, as higher P/E ratios may indicate higher firm growth in the future. Investors are more likely to purchase shares and thus make an investment decision when they expect a positive development of share prices in the future. Consequently, I predict in my hypotheses **H4a** that NPIs feel more able to make an investment decision if they rate the reliability and decision usefulness as high. I ascertain a highly significant positive correlation at the 1%-level between decision usefulness at the fair value level and the financial statement level. Therefore, NPIs that rate the fair value information or the financial statement as highly decision-useful are much more likely to invest into the firm. The descriptive statistics for H4a are presented in Panel A of Table 18. Panel B indicates that NPIs feel more able to make an investment decision with higher decision usefulness (p=0.000). My findings are in line

[56] Participant's rate decision usefulness of financial statements with non-salient disclosures higher with a fair value loss compared to a fair value gain. I conjecture these results could be driven by the fact that for other assets only the fair value loss is directly realized through the profit and loss statement but not the gain (e.g. due to OCI) (Hitz, 2007). In addition, the conservatism principle according to German Commercial Law, which the proxies in this experiment are familiar with, proposes a rather cautious treatment of gains compared to losses. Still, the results are puzzling as relative to a reference losses loom larger than gains according to Kahneman & Tversky (1979).

with earlier literature findings and predictions. Thus, I find support for H4a.

Panel A: Descriptive statistics for decision usefulness measures-mean [standard error]		
	n	Mean
Feel able to make investment decision	48	7.17 [0.15]
Feel not able to make investment decision	120	2.85 [0.13]
Σ	168	4.09 [0.18]

Panel B: Correlation between decision usefulness and investment decision					
		Spearman's rho		Pearson	
	n	ρ	*p*	r	*p*
Decision usefulness	168	0.360	0.000	0.354	0.000

Table 18, Panel A presents participants' investment decision ratings. Participants rated their ability to make an investment decision in a 12-point scale (0= don't feel able at all to make an investment decision; 11= feel totally able to make an investment decision). For purpose of presentation I present two groups: Feel able to make an investment decision (values 6-11) and Feel not able to make an investment decision (values 0-5). Panel B presents the non-parametric and parametric correlation between the extent, participants feel able to make an investment decision and their decision usefulness ratings.

Table 18: Correlation between decision usefulness and investment decision[57]

For **H4b,** I predict that NPIs will rather buy shares of a firm when the perceived decision usefulness is high compared to when it is low. Panel A of Table 19 presents the mean values of decision usefulness presented separately for the two possible share purchase decisions "yes" and "no". According to the findings of hypotheses block 1, I use the decision usefulness at the financial statement level for two reasons: first, it is the most aggregate measure of reliability and decision usefulness (fair value vs. financial statement) in this experiment, and second, the result of hypotheses block 1 show that reliability and decision usefulness at both the fair value and financial statement level are significantly positive correlated (cf. chapter 6.2.1). The mean values in Panel A indicate that the decision usefulness of the financial statement information is higher (mean=6.68) when participants make a positive share purchase decision, whereas when they decide to not purchase shares, the decision usefulness mean is lower (mean=6.14). Panel B of Table 19 shows that this difference in the mean values is not significant (p=0.265). As a result, there is no significant support for H4b and consequently this hypothesis has to be rejected.

[57] Author's own illustration.

Panel A: Descriptive statistics on decision usefulness and share purchase decision					
			n	Mean	
Share purchase	Yes		143	6.68 [0.47]	
	No		25	6.14 [0.18]	
	Σ		168	6.22 [0.17]	
Panel B: Correlation between decision usefulness and share purchase decision					
		Spearman's rho		Pearson	
	n	*p*	ρ	*p*	r
Decision usefulness	168	0.265	0.087	0.265	0.086

Panel A of Table 19 presents the descriptive statistics of the mean values of decision usefulness for the spare purchase decisions. Participants could decide if they either wanted to purchase shares of the firm ("yes" coded as one) or not ("no" coded as zero). Panel B presents the correlation between the share purchase and the decision usefulness of the financial statement information.

Table 19: Correlation between decision usefulness and share purchase[58]

After presenting the results for all hypotheses and research questions, the following chapter will provide results on my additional analysis and a path diagram with a summary of my results.

6.3 Additional analysis

The following chapter will provide information on additional analysis. Specifically, this analysis will provide insights on what additional information participants asked for to be better able to make an investment decision for real estate firms. Eventually, my additional analysis uses a path diagram to present the results on all hypotheses raised and tested throughout this thesis.

The participants of this experiment were asked if they felt being able to make an investment decision after receiving various information on the firm. Building up on that question, I further asked the participants if they would have needed additional information and if so, what type of information. 59 of the 88 participants in the gain treatment answered this question with a “yes” which marks 67%. When evaluating the answers, they can be grouped into three categories: real estate, shares, and disclosures. In the real estate category, the participants demand further information on the assets such as occupancy rate of the buildings, duration of the rental contracts, further information on the agent contracts, as well as the age structure of the buildings. Other information on the real estate industry the participants were interested in was the development of the real estate industry as well as the loss of predicted rental income for the valuation methods. Regarding shares, the participants demanded further information on the EPS as well as the development of the share prices. They further demanded more detailed disclosures

[58] Author’s own illustration.

especially on the investment properties of the firm (e.g., reasons for a change in the fair value of the assets and more details on the locations of the buildings).

Of the 80 participants that were in loss treatments, 56 demanded additional information for their investment decision. The information that these 70% of the participants demanded can be grouped into three categories: real estate, management report, and the management of the firm. In the category of real estate, they demanded additional information on the impairment of assets as well as on the future forecast for the assets. Further, they asked for information on the representative German rental index and details on the earnings due to rents. Several participants needed a management's report to feel more able to make an investment decision based on the provided data. The participants that received a treatment with a fair value loss compared to the prior period claimed that they would have needed information on the management of the firm as well as personal meetings with the management.

Consequently, I find that NPIs prefer to have more information on the key assets of the firm, which were real estate assets in my setting. It seems that they try to reproduce the valuation of the assets and thus demand further information on the real estate market as well as occupancy rates and durations of rental contracts. That the participants also demand more disclosures in the fair value gain treatment, which does not fit into the recent debate on disclosure overload. Participants in a treatment with a fair value loss only demanded meetings with the management and more information on the management itself. It seems that these participants want to ensure that the decrease in the fair value of assets is actually caused by the market, which is probably why they also asked for further information on the real estate market development and not on the management. It is in line with this argumentation that the participants of the loss group also demanded a management's report.

6.4 Summary of results

This chapter presents a summary of the results on all hypotheses. The statistical results of all hypotheses are depicted in Figure 13. The first step of my analysis is testing the basic assumption if higher reliability leads to higher decision usefulness as indicated by the standard setter. I could confirm this prediction as I discover significant positive correlation between the reliability and decision usefulness at both the fair value and financial statement level. Further, my research is among the first to distinguish between reliability and decision usefulness at the fair value and financial statement level. I determine that higher reliability at the fair value level also leads to higher decision usefulness at the financial statement level. Thus, if the reliability of a firm's key asset is evaluated positively, NPIs will also evaluate the overall reliability of the financial statement positively. Consequently, the reliability and decision usefulness of the key asset of a firm drives the disposition of the reliability of the financial statement overall. This further indicates that firms can positively influence the overall reliability and decision usefulness of the financial statement by contributing to a higher reliability of the firms' key asset measured at fair value. How firms can contribute to a higher reliability and decision usefulness and thus positively influence the investment decision process of NPIs is also investigated throughout this thesis.

The investment decision process is divided into three steps by the psychological framework around specific ways to enhance the information processing of NPIs by Maines and McDaniel (2000): information acquisition, evaluation, and weighting. I ascertain that with the salient presentation of disclosures, which I designate as additional disclosures in my work due to the presentation of the fair value disclosure information in an additional column in the balance sheet, that information acquisition is affected in a positive way. Consequently, information acquisition is more likely when additional disclosures are presented independent of the development of the fair value. When distinguishing between fair value gain and loss, I find that there is a significant difference in information acquisition that is caused by the development of the firm's key asset. I do not find support that NPIs are more likely to evaluate fair value information correctly if the related information is presented salient in the balance sheet independent of the fair value development. When differentiating between gain and loss, I discover support that NPIs are more likely to evaluate fair value information correctly if the related information is presented salient with a fair value gain compared to a fair value loss. Consequently, the correct evaluation of information strongly depends on the development of the fair value. In terms of information weighting, the results show that the weights NPIs place on investment properties are slightly higher, when related fair value information is presented saliently, but the differences remain insignificant. When distinguishing between gain and loss, I ascertain that when related fair value information is presented salient with a fair value gain, NPIs weight the fair value information higher compared to a fair value loss. Yet, this result is also not significant.

This work focuses on the reliability and decision usefulness of additional disclosures depending on the development of a firm's key asset measured at fair value. The results indicate that reliability and decision usefulness differ when information is presented salient compared to when it is not, independent of the development of the firm's key asset. Because previous work indicates that NPIs react differently to positive and negative development of earnings, I distinguish between the fair value gains and losses. With a fair value gain additional disclosures do not significantly increase reliability and decision usefulness in a positive way. In contrast, the presentation of additional disclosures decrease reliability and decision usefulness significantly with a fair value loss. The difference between the presentations of additional disclosures is significant between a fair value gain and loss. My results further indicate that the format currently mandated under IFRS is the format that leads to the lowest level of decision usefulness with a fair value gain but the one that leads to the highest level of decision usefulness with a fair value loss. Further, with a fair value gain, the highest level of decision usefulness can be achieved by presenting the reconciliation between carrying amounts (change value) as an additional disclosure. With a fair value loss on the other hand, the presentation of the sensitivity analysis (range value) as an additional disclosure leads to the lowest level of decision usefulness. The higher the perceived decision usefulness of accounting information by NPIs, the more they feel able to make an investment decision and consequently purchase shares of the firm. The additional analysis presents the results on the additional information participants would request to make the financial statement more decision-useful for them. Independent of the fair value development, the majority of the participants requested further disclosure information. The types of disclosure information requested differ with the development of the fair value. The results suggest that NPIs try to replicate the DCF and thereby verify the fair value of investment properties. Further, and with a fair value loss only, NPIs demanded meetings with the management which indicates that they want to ensure that the negative change in fair value of investment properties is driven by the market only and not the management.

Prior research indicates that especially NPIs have difficulties in incorporating fair value disclosures into their decision-making process. My research finds that NPIs face this struggle due to the content of the information and not the format. This is driven by the fact that the reliability and decision usefulness vary when the format of information is held constant. In terms of the disclosure overload debate, my research finds that the highest level of reliability and decision usefulness can be achieved with the presentation of the additional disclosure on the reconciliation between carrying amounts (range value).

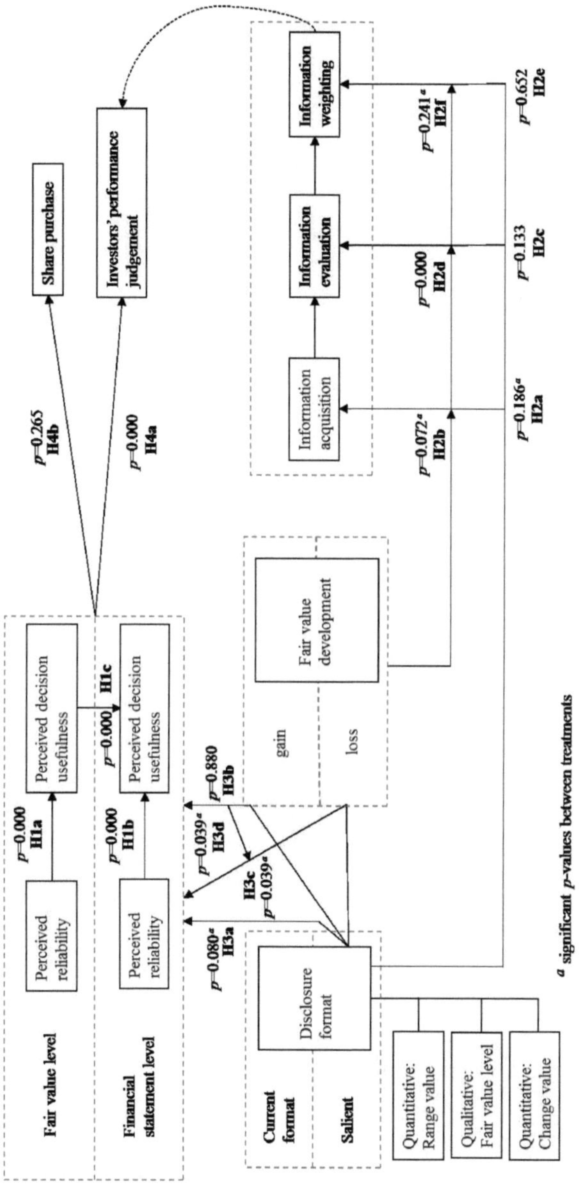

Figure 13: Result overview for all hypotheses[59]

[59] Author's own illustration.

Figure [illegible]

7 Discussion

In the following chapter, the results of my research will be discussed. I will first describe the results with regard to implications for future research in this field. I make contributions on two main knowledge debates: first, the one on the role of presentation formats on reliability and decision usefulness, and second, the one on the role of presentation formats on information processing. I have extended both knowledge debates by being the first to examine the effect of the fair value development (gain vs. loss) on both the reliability and decision usefulness as well as the processing of information. Following the implications for research, I will provide implications for companies and regulators. These fit well into the recent development of the extent of disclosures and the practical debate on disclosure overload that especially addresses disclosures of assets measured at fair value. Last, I will provide limitations to my research and close with an outlook for future research.

7.1 Implications for research

I contribute to the knowledge debate on presentation formats on reliability and decision usefulness. While the reliability and decision usefulness is a topic that was originally implicated by the standard setter (IASB, 2010), there has been extensive research on how changes to the format of the financial statement can enhance the ability of investors to use financial statement information. Yet, the effect of such changes to the presentation format has so far only been researched independently of the development of a firm's key asset. Thus, I examined in this thesis how format and fair value changes affect the reliability and decision usefulness of fair value-related information and financial statements for NPIs.

Further, I contribute to the understanding of reliability and decision usefulness, by Maines and McDaniel (2000) and Clor-Proell et al. (2014), by examining the correlation between the reliability and decision usefulness. I am the first to distinguish between the reliability and decision usefulness at the fair value level as well as the financial statement level. I find that reliability and decision usefulness at both levels are significantly positively correlated. As a result, if the reliability of an asset measured at fair value is high, NPIs will perceive the decision usefulness of this financial statement item as higher. Further, if the decision usefulness of this item is high, NPIs will automatically rate the overall decision usefulness of the financial statement higher. This interaction between reliability and decision usefulness helps to better understand the results of prior literature. These results are in line with the IASB, who propose that reliability is one of the main characteristics of decision-useful financial information.

I am the first to examine differences in the reliability and decision usefulness of additional disclosures with a fair value gain and loss. So far, research contributions on this filed of research focus on the effect of format changes on fair value gains only (Clor-Proell et al., 2014; Maines & McDaniel, 2000). Further, the proposed format changes of Maines and McDaniel (2000), Clor-Proell et al. (2014) as well as Lachmann et al. (2015) focus on the profit and loss statement (and OCI). I discover that the presentation format does have an impact on the reliability and decision usefulness of NPIs independent of the fair value development. Yet, the results indicate

T. Herrmann, *The Decision Usefulness of Additional Fair Value Disclosures*, Controlling und Rechnungslegung – Managerial and Financial Accounting,
https://doi.org/10.1007/978-3-658-24832-1_7

that there are strong differences between a positive development of the fair value (gain) and a negative development of the fair value (loss).

I determine that with a fair value gain, additional disclosures generally increase the reliability and decision usefulness, even though the effect is not significant. Since I distinguish between different types of additional disclosures, I ascertain that the decision usefulness is highest with a fair value gain, when the qualitative disclosure information on the fair value hierarchy is presented salient. The additional disclosure that also increases decision usefulness is the quantitative disclosure on the sensitivity analysis. With a fair value gain, it seems that investors especially value disclosures that help them assess the robustness of the gain itself. The disclosure that leads to the highest decision usefulness with a fair value gain helps the investors to understand how volatile the gain is and emphasizes that it might not be robust as the investment properties are classified at level 3 of the IFRS fair value hierarchy. Further, the disclosure on the sensitivity analysis also emphasizes the value fluctuation of the investment property. The fluctuation also includes a potential downside to the point value of the investment properties and consequently also emphasizes that the fair value gain might not be robust. Since investors evaluate financial statement information in order to make an investment decision, the robustness of gains is an important factor for them to consider.

When the disclosure information on the reconciliation between carrying amounts is presented, decision usefulness decreases compared to the current format. This could indicate that this disclosure might be too trivial for NPIs to add additional decision usefulness compared to the current format as the participants would theoretically be able to calculate the value themselves, which is not possible with the other disclosures. The fact that the participants in the experiment rated decision usefulness of the financial statement lower with the salient disclosure on reconciliation between carrying amounts could be driven by the fact that this rather trivial disclosure still represents a change to the current and thus known format for the participants. Consequently, the decision usefulness decreases due to the missing additional decision usefulness value of the disclosure along with the format change.

To sum up, it seems that with a fair value gain, NPIs only value salient disclosure information that helps them assess the nature and robustness of a fair value gain. If the disclosure does not fulfil this criterion, a format change to presenting (rather trivial) disclosure information salient even decreases the decision usefulness of NPIs. These results add to the discussion on disclosure overload by Beerbaum (2016) and Siegel (2018) as they point out that with a fair value gain only disclosures that emphasize the robustness of the asset value can emphasize the decision usefulness, which is the aim of the standard setter when mandating disclosures for assets and liabilities measured at fair value in the first place.

With a fair value loss, I find that additional disclosures generally decrease the reliability and decision usefulness significantly. Thus, the current format mandated under IFRS is perceived to be the most decision-useful by NPIs. Specifically, the reliability and decision usefulness are lowest when the quantitative disclosure on the sensitivity analysis is enclosed. It seems that with a fair value loss, the salient presentation of a disclosure highlights the uncertainty of the (remaining) asset value, thus decreasing the reliability of the value of the asset and thus the decision usefulness of the financial statement the most. Further, this disclosure bears uncertainty itself. It marks a possible but not certain value fluctuation of the asset. Therefore, besides highlighting the uncertainty of the asset, the disclosure adds some inherent uncertainty. This combination decreases the reliability the most for NPIs.

The other two disclosures, the qualitative disclosure on the fair value hierarchy and the reconciliation between carrying amounts, are perfectly certain. The reconciliation marks the difference between two-point values of the current and the past year. The disclosure highlights the uncertainty in the way that it emphasizes the extent to which the fair value can vary compared to the prior period. Yet, since the point values are fixed, the carrying amount is a fixed value as well. Due to the fact that the inputs to the fair value of investment properties are all classified at level 3, the classification of the asset with level 3 input parameters is certain.

To sum up, it seems that disclosures that emphasize the uncertainty of the asset measured at fair value but are not uncertain themselves decrease the reliability and decision usefulness less compared to disclosures that do not only highlight the uncertainty but bear uncertainty themselves. Again, these results contribute to the discussion on disclosure overload by Beerbaum (2016) and Siegel (2018). Since this study is the first to provide insights into the perception of disclosures of NPIs with a fair value loss (Clor-Proell et al., 2014), the results indicate that more research on the unique effect of disclosures along with a fair value loss is necessary to gain a deeper understanding of their effects on NPIs perception.

When investigating the differences in the decision usefulness of additional disclosures between gain and loss, the results show significant differences between the two. This indicates that disclosures that can increase the decision usefulness when presented with a fair value gain can decrease the decision usefulness with a fair value loss (e.g., the disclosure on the sensitivity analysis). As a result, it seems that while disclosures help investors to better assess the robustness of a fair value gain, the same disclosure only highlights the uncertainty of the asset with a fair value loss which leads to a decrease in the reliability of the fair value. This effect is even stronger when the disclosure that highlights the uncertainty bears uncertainty itself.

Taken together, my results indicate that NPIs have different information needs that are strongly linked to the development of the firm's key assets. The current format for fair values is curse and blessing at the same time in terms of reliability and decision usefulness. With a fair value loss, it is the most reliable and decision-useful format for NPIs, but with a fair value gain, it is one of the least reliable and decision-useful formats. Even though I discover that format changes affect the reliability and decision usefulness, I also find that with a constant format, reliability and decision usefulness vary. My results suggest that with a fair value loss, additional disclosures highlight the uncertainty of fair values and thus decrease reliability and decision usefulness. NPIs become aware of the low reliability of fair values only, when additional disclosure information is provided with a fair value loss. Consequently, and opposite to what was intended by the standard setter, disclosures decrease reliability and decision usefulness with a fair value loss. Finally, my results indicate to rather tailor disclosures to the development of a firm's key asset instead of pursuing a "one-fits-all approach".

Further, this thesis contributes to the understanding of the information processing of NPIs dependent of the fair value development. The model on information processing by Maines and McDaniel (2000) helps me to gain a deeper understanding of the different phases that determine the processing of investors and lead to their investment decision. The results of the experiment indicate significant differences between the information acquisition of salient information depending on the fair value development. Specifically, NPIs are more likely to acquire information when related fair value information is presented salient. This finding is in line with the argumentation of Hayn (1995) and Erickson et al. (2017) that losses are perceived as an extreme level of earnings and gains are not. Thus, the task to store and recall information is easier for NPIs when no extreme levels of earnings occur. This result holds for the correct evaluation of information as well. Consequently, the absence of extreme levels of earnings emphasizes the likelihood for NPIs to acquire and evaluate related fair value information correctly with a salient presentation format. Nevertheless, the results also point out that NPIs face difficulties to acquire information and evaluate them correctly with extreme levels of earnings (i.e. loss) and would need additional support. NPIs weight information more when fair value information is presented saliently with a fair value loss compared to a fair value gain. This indicates that NPIs strongly focus on a firm's key asset when the development of the fair value is negative. With a fair value gain, the results show that other financial statement positions, like liabilities due to banks and other accruals, are weighted higher by NPIs compared to a fair value loss. Hence, with a fair value gain, NPIs take other financial statement positions more strongly into account instead of focusing exclusively on the company's key asset.

Collectively, my research contributes to the extant accounting literature in at least five ways. First, I extend prior literature on format effects by examining the effect of a fair value loss on the reliability and decision usefulness. So far, research focus on fair value gains as they are deemed to be more prevalent than fair value losses (Clor-Proell et al., 2014; Maines & McDaniel, 2000). The reliability and decision usefulness differ significantly between a fair value gain and loss, which highlights the importance of my research. Second, I differ qualitative and quantitative types of disclosures. By doing so, I address the call of McDonough and Shakespeare (2015) to improve the understanding of fair value disclosures. While qualitative disclosures increase the decision usefulness the most with a fair value gain, quantitative disclosures decrease the decision usefulness the most with a fair value loss. I extend earlier literature by providing evidence that format changes affect reliability and decision usefulness when the content is held constant. When the content varies, I determine that format effects can no longer facilitate the information processing of investors. Third, I help to better understand the effect of the fair value development on the information processing of salient disclosure information and, thus, provide additional results on the widely used framework by Maines and McDaniel (2000). Fourth, I am the first to introduce an additional column in the balance sheet to display disclosure information on financial statement items salient. Finally, I am the first to differentiate between the reliability and decision usefulness at the fair value and financial statement level. I ascertain that the reliability of the asset measured at fair value also drives the reliability of the financial statement.

The results of the experiment also give some content-related implications for future research: First, future research could shed more light into the nature of different types of disclosures. The so far scarcely researched effect of disclosure information with a fair value loss indicates that the inherent uncertainty of a disclosure affects the decision usefulness of the corresponding asset and the financial statement. Through differing this uncertainty further by using different levels of inherent uncertainty, more light could be shed into the debate on decision usefulness of salient disclosures along with fair value losses. Second, the results on information weighting indicate that with a fair value gain, NPIs place greater weights on other financial statement items besides the firm's key asset. Even though theories by Hayn (1995) and Erickson et al. (2017) offer justification why this might be the case; this justification should be verified by evaluating NPIs risk perception along with their weighting. Thirdly, I find that the presentation format effects the perceived reliability and decision usefulness of NPIs. Yet, I isolate only one disclosure item and present it saliently. Future research could analyse if this effect holds when multiple disclosures are displayed salient.

Further, the results give some methodology-related implications for future research. The experiment indirectly observes the information processing of NPIs. Latest research contributions in this field introduce eye-tracking as a direct way to study how investors perceive and process information (Bozzolan et al., 2017). Therefore, future research could evaluate if my results remain when directly observing the information processing of NPIs. Another methodological implication could be to test the robustness of my results by using other methodologies to emphasize the information usage of NPIs. This could be, e.g., the categorization of information (Bloomfield et al., 2012) or the usage of search-facilitating technologies (Hodge et al., 2010).

7.2 Implications for company practice and regulation

Further, my research provides advice for practitioners, regulators, and standard setters, who have concerns that the additional disclosures are not incorporated by NPIs into their investment decision due to disclosure overload. I find that the same type of disclosure has a contrary effect on decision usefulness depending on the development of the fair value. I thus suggest regulators and standard setters to consider tailoring the disclosures to the development of the key asset, to address the aspect of disclosure overload. This could be arranged in a manner that with a fair value loss, qualitative, range, and change disclosures could be voluntary instead of mandatory, while qualitative and range value disclosures should remain mandatory with a fair value gain as they increase the decision usefulness with this development of the fair value. With a fair value gain, the disclosure on the reconciliation between carrying amounts (change value) decreases the decision usefulness and should therefore be voluntary with a fair value gain as well as a fair value loss.

The standard setter mandated disclosures on fair values to improve decision usefulness of financial statements for investors. For NPIs, this seems not to be the case when the development of the fair value is negative. The standard setter should therefore spend resources on alternative ways to make financial statements more useful for investors. One approach could be to think of alternative types of disclosures for assets when a fair value loss occurs. The qualitative information decreases decision usefulness the least compared to the current format, which could be a starting point for the standard setter. Moreover, my results indicate that with a fair value loss, NPIs want to ensure that the negative development of the asset is caused by the market and not the mismanagement of a firm. This could also be a starting point in a debate on new, decision-useful increasing disclosures for key assets measured at fair value.

In addition, I discover, as proposed by the IASB, that reliability is one of the main characteristics of decision-useful financial information. I shed more light into the illusive construct of decision usefulness, as I determine that it is significantly determined by the reliability of the firm's key asset. As a result, by aiming to provide decision-useful information on the key asset measured at fair value, firms should improve the decision usefulness of the financial statement. With a fair value gain, this can be achieved by presenting the different types of mandatory disclosures. With a fair value loss, firms now rely on new implications of the standard setter in the future to be able to make their financial statements more decision-useful and thus increase the likelihood of investors purchasing shares of the firm. These results are of special interest for firms with rounds of funding ahead. For these firms, it is especially important to provide decision-useful information as my results indicate that share purchase is more likely when the decision usefulness is high.

Nevertheless, up to now, different types of disclosures are mandatory according to IFRS. Hence, firms do not yet have a choice to waive fair value disclosures with a fair value loss to prevent decreasing the decision usefulness. This fact could emphasize a firm to engage in earnings management and try to avoid fair value losses. Therefore, it is important that the standard setter finds new ways to improve the decision usefulness with a fair value loss as earnings management is a major threat to decision-useful financial information.

7.3 Limitations and outlook

My study is subject to limitations that provide opportunity for future research. First, I examine the judgements of NPIs but do not explicitly measure their level of knowledge. Even though I retrieve information on participants' professional experience and ensure that they have sufficient accounting knowledge for the tasks at hand, I do not perform additional test to verify their exact level of knowledge. This exact level of knowledge could have an impact on my results on information processing as well as on the perceived reliability and decision usefulness because knowledgeable NPIs with high level of knowledge and a corresponding private investment experience could also proxy for professional investors. Yet, professional investors have significantly different information needs compared to NPIs. Future work might mitigate this issue by performing additional test on the knowledge level of NPIs.

Second, I make several assumptions for the design of this experiment to ensure a simplified decision context for NPIs. For instance, I set the gain and loss in this experiment at 5% of the average total assets. Consequently, I do not know if my results remain when gain and loss are less or more significant in the financial statement. Future work might examine different heights of gains and losses in this context. Besides, I do not examine a case where the fair value does not change compared to the prior year as a fair value is likely to vary. Nevertheless, future research could address this case and compare their findings for a (rather) constant or sparsely varying fair value, with a heavily varying fair value.

Finally, to simulate disclosure overload, I set a time limit for participants to evaluate the financial statement. I used a pre-test to evaluate a useful time limit to simulate disclosure overload but left enough time to the participants to process the provided information in order to be able to find out about their perceived reliability and decision usefulness. The set time limit is the average results of the individual time needs in the pre-test of my experiment. Yet, the weight of outliers might not be accounted for correctly with this calculation. Consequently, the use of differing time limits could lead to different results.

The impact of the introduction of a new financial statement format with the salient display of different fair value disclosure types varies with the development of a firm's key asset. The change to the presentation format can be useful with a fair value gain as it increases the decision usefulness of the financial statement when the presented disclosures are range values or qualitative information. The format change is not useful when the salient displayed information is a change value with a fair value gain. Thus, future research should follow up on the proposed changes to the financial statement for a fair value gain, especially when the displayed disclosures can be categorized as range value or qualitative disclosure. For NPIs, it seems that with a fair value gain, additional information should rather be presented in the profit and loss statement instead of in the balance sheet. This suggestion is driven by the fact that the results of this experiment are not highly significant for a fair value gain, while prior studies (Clor-Proell et al., 2014) find significant evidence that additional disclosures can increase the decision usefulness when they are presented in the profit and loss statement. With a fair value loss, the proposed format has a negative effect on the decision usefulness of financial statement data. This result is especially relevant for standard setters as the original aim behind the mandating of fair value disclosures can therefore not be fulfilled.

References

Abhayawansa, S., & Guthrie, J. (2016). Drivers and semantic properties of intellectual capital information in sell-side analysts' reports. *Journal of Accounting & Organizational Change, 12*(4), 434–471.

Agoglia, C. P., Doupnik, T. S., & Tsakumis, G. T. (2011). Principles-based versus rules-based accounting standards: The influence of standard precision and audit committee strength on financial reporting decisions. *The Accounting Review, 86*(3), 747–767.

Akerlof, G. A. (1970). The market for 'lemons': Quality uncertainty and the market mechanism. *Quaterly Journal of Economics, 84*(3), 488–500.

Alvey, J. E., Haigh, M. S., & List, J. A. (2007). Information Cascades: Evidence from a Field Experiment with Financial Market Professionals. *The Journal of Finance, 62*(1), 151–180.

American Accounting Association (1966). *A Statement of basic accounting theory.* Sarasota, FL.

Armstrong, C. S., Guay, W. R., & Weber, J. P. (2010). The role of information and financial reporting in corporate governance and debt contracting. *Journal of Accounting and Economics, 50*(2-3), 179–234.

Asay, H. S., Elliott, W. B., & Rennekamp, K. (2017). Disclosure readability and the sensitivity of investors' valuation judgments to outside information. *The Accounting Review, 92*(4), 1–25.

Balas, A., La Porta, R., Lopez-de-Silanes, F., & Shleifer, A. (2009). The divergence of legal procedures. *American Economic Journal: Economic Policy, 1*(2), 138–162.

Ball, R. (2006). International Financial Reporting Standards (IFRS): Pros and cons for investors. *Accounting and Business Research, 36*(Special Issue), 5–27.

Ball, R., Kothari, S.P., & Robin, A. (2000). The effect of international institutional factors on properties of accounting earnings. *Journal of Accounting and Economics, 29*(1), 1–51.

Ball, R., Robin, A., & Sadka, G. (2008). Is financial reporting shaped by equity markets or by debt markets? An international study of timeliness and conservatism. *Review of Accounting Studies, 13*(2-3), 168–205.

Ball, R., Robin, A., & Wu, J. S. (2003). Incentives versus standards: Properties of accounting income in four East Asian countries. *Journal of Accounting and Economics, 36*(1-3), 235–270.

Ballwieser, W., & Hachmeister, D. (2016). *Unternehmensbewertung: Prozess, Methoden und Probleme.* (5., überarbeitete Auflage). Lehrbuch.

Banker, R. D., Huang, R., & Natarajan, R. (2009). Incentive contracting and value relevance of earnings and cash flows. *Journal of Accounting Research, 47*(3), 647–678.

T. Herrmann, *The Decision Usefulness of Additional Fair Value Disclosures*, Controlling und Rechnungslegung – Managerial and Financial Accounting, https://doi.org/10.1007/978-3-658-24832-1

Barker, R., Hendry, J., Roberts, J., & Sanderson, P. (2012). Can company-fund manager meetings convey informational benefits? Exploring the rationalisation of equity investment decision making by UK fund managers. *Accounting, Organizations and Society*, *37*(4), 207–222.

Barker, R., & Imam, S. (2008). Analysts' perceptions of 'earnings quality'. *Accounting and Business Research*, *38*(4), 313–329.

Barker, R. G. (1998). The market for information—evidence from finance directors, analysts and fund managers. *Accounting and Business Research*, *29*(1), 3–20.

Barker, R. G. (1999). Survey and market-based evidence of industry-dependence in analysts' preferences between the dividend yield and price-earnings ratio valuation models. *Journal of Business Finance & Accounting*, *26*(3-4), 393–418.

Barth, M. (2006). Including estimates of the future in today's financial statements. *Accounting Horizons*, *20(3)*, 271-285.

Barth, M., Hodder, L., & Stubben, S. R. (2008). Fair value accounting for liabilities and own credit risk. *The Accounting Review*, *83*(3), 629–664.

Barth, M. E. (2014). Measurement in financial reporting: The need for concepts. *Accounting Horizons*, *28*(2), 331–352.

Barth, M. E., Landsman, W. R., Lang, M., & Williams, C. (2012). Are IFRS-based and US GAAP-based accounting amounts comparable? *Journal of Accounting & Economics*, *54*(1), 68–93.

Barth, M. E., Landsman, W. R., & Wahlen, J. M. (1995). Fair value accounting: Effects on banks' earnings volatility, regulatory capital, and value of contractual cash flows. *Journal of Banking & Finance*, *19*(3-4), 577–605.

Beach, L. R., & Mitchell, T. R. (1978). A Contingency Model for the Selection of Decision Strategies. *The Academy of Management Review*, *3*(3), 439–449.

Beaver, W. H. (1966). Financial ratios as predictors of failure. *Journal of Accounting Research*, *4*(3), 71–111.

Beerbaum, D. (2016). Disclosure overload - a literature review. *Working Paper, Aalto University*.

Belkaoui, A. (1991). *Handbook of cost accounting theory and techniques*. Westport, CT: Quorum Books.

Bens, D. A., Cheng, M., & Neamtiu, M. (2016). The impact of SEC disclosure monitoring on the uncertainty of fair value estimates. *The Accounting Review*, *91*(2), 349–375.

Benston, G. J., Bromwich, M., & Wagenhofer, A. (2006). Principles- versus rules-based accounting standards: The FASB's standard setting strategy. *Abacus*, *42*(2), 165–188.

Bettman, J. R. (1979). *An information processing theory of consumer choice*. Reading, MA: Addison-Wesley Publishing Company.

Beyer, A., Cohen, D. A., Lys, T. Z., & Walther, B. R. (2010). The financial reporting environment: Review of the recent literature. *Journal of Accounting and Economics, 50*(2-3), 296–343.

Bharath, S. T., & Shumway, T. (2008). Forecasting default with Merton distance to default model. *Review of Financial Studies, 21*(3), 1339–1369.

Bharath, S. T., Sunder, J., & Sunder, S. V. (2008). Accounting quality and debt contracting. *The Accounting Review, 83*(1), 1–28.

Bhat, G., & Ryan, S. G. (2015). The impact of risk modelling on the market perception of banks' estimated fair value gains and losses for financial instruments. *Accounting, Organizations and Society, 46*, 81–95.

Blacconiere, W. G., Frederickson, J. R., Johnson, M. F., & Lewis, M. F. (2011). Are voluntary disclosures that disavow the reliability of mandated fair value information informative or opportunistic? *Journal of Accounting and Economics, 52*(2-3), 235–251.

Black, F., & Scholes, M. (1973). The pricing of options and corporate liabilities. *Journal of Political Economy, 81*(3), 637.

Bloomfield, R., Hodge, F. D., Hopkins, P. E., & Rennekamp, K. (2012). Does enhanced disaggregation and cohesive classification of financial information help credit analysts identify firms' operating structures? *Working Paper, Cornell University.*

Bloomfield, R., Libby, R., & Nelson, M. W. (1996). Communication of confidence as a determinant of group judgment accuracy. *Organizational Behavior and Human Decision Processes, 68*(3), 287–300.

Bloomfield, R., Nelson, M. W., & Soltes, E. (2016). Gathering data for archival, field, survey, and experimental accounting research. *Journal of Accounting Research, 54*(2), 341–395.

Blumberg, B., Cooper, D. R., & Schindler, P. S. (2014). *Business research methods.* (4. European edition). London: McGraw-Hill Education.

Botosan, C. A. (2004). Discussion of a framework for the analysis of firm risk communication. *The International Journal of Accounting, 39*(3), 289–295.

Botosan, C. A., & Huffman, A. A. (2015). Decision-useful asset measurement from a business valuation perspective. *Accounting Horizons, 29*(4), 757–776.

Bozzolan, S., Joos, P., & Rubaltelli, E. (2017). How do analysts process managerial earnings forecasts? An eye-tracking study. *Working Paper, Luiss University.*

Braam, G., van Beest, F., & Boelens, S. (2009). Quality of financial reporting: Measuring qualitative characteristics. *Working Paper, Radboud University Nijmegen.*

Braun, G. P., Haynes, C. M., Lewis, T. D., & Taylor, M. H. (2015). Principles-based vs. rules-based accounting standards: The effects of auditee proposed accounting treatment and regulatory enforcement on auditor judgments and confidence. *Research in Accounting Regulation, 27*(1), 45–50.

Brockman, R., & Cicon, J. (2013). The information content of management earnings forecast: An analysis of hard versus soft information. *The Journal of Financial Research*, *36*(2), 147–173.

Brown, A. B. (2016). Institutional differences and international private debt markets: A test using mandatory IFRS adoption. *Journal of Accounting Research*, *54*(3), 679–723.

Brüggemann, U., Hitz, J.-M., & Sellhorn, T. (2013). Intended and unintended consequences of mandatory IFRS adoption: A review of extant evidence and suggestions for future research. *European Accounting Review*, *22*(1), 1–37.

Burgstahler, D. C., Hail, L., & Leuz, C. (2016). The importance of reporting incentives: Earnings management in european private and public firms. *The Accounting Review*, *81*(5), 983–1016.

Bushman, R., Engel, E., & Smith, A. (2006). An analysis of the relation between the stewardship and valuation roles of earnings. *Journal of Accounting Research*, *44*(1), 53–83.

Calder, B. J., Phillips, L. W., & Tybout, A. M. (1981). Designing research for application. *Journal of Consumer Research*, *8*(2), 197–207.

Campbell, D. T., & Stanley, J. S. (1966). *Experimental and quasi-experimental designs for reserach*. Chicago: Rand McNally College Publishing Company Chicago.

Campbell, J. H., Hilscher, J., & Szilagy, J. (2008). In search of distress risk. *The Journal of Finance*, *63*(6), 2899–2939.

Carrington, T., & Johed, G. (2007). The construction of top management as a good steward. *Accounting, Auditing & Accountability Journal*, *20*(5), 702–728.

Cascino, S., Clattworthy, M., Garcia Osma, B., Gassen, J., Imam, S., & Thomas, J. (2013). *The use of information by capital providers: Academic literature review*. Edinburgh: ICAS and EFRAG.

Cascino, S., Clatworthy, M., García Osma, B., Gassen, J., Imam, S., & Jeanjean, T. (2014). Who uses financial reports and for what purpose? Evidence from capital providers. *Accounting in Europe*, *11*(2), 185–209.

Chambost, I. (2008). Contribution à l'analyse de la formation du judgement des analystes financiers sell-side. *Dissertation, Conservatoire nationale des arts et métiers*.

Chan, C., Landry, S. P., & Troy, C. (2011). Examining external validity criticisms in the choice of students as subjects in accounting experiment studies. *Journal of Theoretical Accounting Research*, *7*(1), 53–78.

Charalambakis, E. C., & Garrett, I. (2016). On the prediction of financial distress in developed and emerging markets: Does the choice of accounting and market information matter? A comparison of UK and Indian Firms. *Review of Quantitative Finance and Accounting*, *47*(1), 1–28.

Chava, S., Kumar, P., & Warga, A. (2010). Managerial agency and bond covenants. *Review of Financial Studies*, *23*(3), 1120–1148.

Chen, K. C. W., & Lee, C.-W. J. (1993). Financial ratios and corporate endurance: A Case of the oil and gas industry. *Contemporary Accounting Research*, *9*(2), 667–694.

Chi, M. T.H., Feltovich, P. J., & Glaser, R. (1981). Categorization and Representation of Physics Problems by Experts and Novices. *Cognitive Science*, *5*(2), 121–152.

Chiyachantana, C. N., Jiang, C. X., Taechapiroontong, N., & Wood, R. A. (2004). The impact of regulation fair disclosure on information asymmetry and trading: An intraday analysis. *Financial Review*, *39*(4), 549–577.

Clor-Proell, S. M., Proell, C. A., & Warfield, T. D. (2014). The effects of presentation salience and measurement subjectivity on nonprofessional investors' fair value judgments. *Contemporary Accounting Research*, *31*(1), 45–66.

Clor-Proell, S. M., & Warfield, T. D. (2009). Financial statement presentation and nonprofessional investor's interpretation of fair value information. *Working Paper, Texas Christian University*.

Cohen, J., Krishnamoorthy, G., & Wright, A. (2004). The corporate governance mosaic and financial reporting quality. *Journal of Accounting Literature*, *23*, 87–152.

Cohen, J. R., Holder-Webb, L., & Zamora, V. L. (2015). Nonfinancial information preferences of professional investors. *Behavioral Research in Accounting*, *27*(2), 127–153.

Conlisk, J. (1996). Why bounded rationality? *Journal of Economic Literature*, *34*(2), 669–700.

Cook, T. D., & Campbell, D. T. (1979). *Quasi-experimentation: Design & analysis issues for field settings*. Boston, MA: Houghton Mifflin.

Crifo, P., Forget, V. D., & Teyssier, S. (2015). The price of environmental, social and governance practice disclosure: An experiment with professional private equity investors. *Journal of Corporate Finance*, *30*, 168–194.

Davis-Friday, P. Y., Folami, L. B., Liu, C.-S., & Mittelstaedt, H. F. (1999). The value relevance of financial statement recognition vs. disclosure: Evidence from SFAS No. 106. *The Accounting Review*, *74*(4), 403–423.

Dawes, R. M., & Corrigan, B. (1974). Linear models in decision making. *Psychological Bulletin*, *81*(2), 95–106.

Deloitte (2017a). Conceptual Framework - Comprehensive IASB Project. https://www.iasplus.com/en/projects/major/cf-iasb. Accessed 23.02.2017.

Deloitte (2017b). IAS 40 - Investment Property. https://www.iasplus.com/en/standards /ias/ias40. Accessed 23.01.2018.

Diamond, D. W., & Verrecchia, R. E. (1991). Disclosure, liquidity, and the cost of capital. *The Journal of Finance*, *46*(4), 1325.

Dietrich, R. J., Kachelmeier, S. J., Kleinmuntz, D. N., & Linsmeier, T. J. (2001). Market efficiency, bounded rationality, and supplemental business reporting disclosures. *Journal of Accounting Research*, *39*(2), 243–268.

Drymiotes, G., & Hemmer, T. (2013). On the stewardship and valuation implications of accrual accounting systems. *Journal of Accounting Research, 51*(2), 281–334.

Dunbar, A. E., & Weber, D. P. (2014). What influences accounting research? A citations-based analysis. *Issues in Accounting Education, 29*(1), 1–60.

Dutta, S., & Zhang, X.-J. (2002). Revenue recognition in a multiperiod agency setting. *Journal of Accounting Research, 40*(1), 67–83.

Einhorn, H. J., & Hogarth, R. M. (1981). Behavioral Decision Theory: Processes of Judgement and Choice. *Annual Review of Psychology, 32*, 53–88.

Elliott, B. W. (2006). Are investors influenced by pro forma emphasis and reconciliations in earnings announcements? *The Accounting Review*, *81*(1), 113–133.

Elliott, W. B., Hodge, F. D., & Jackson, K. E. (2008). The association between nonprofessional investors' information choices and their portfolio returns: The Importance of investing experience. *Contemporary Accounting Research*, *25*(2), 473–498.

Erickson, D., Hewitt, M., & Maines, L. A. (2017). Do investors perceive low risk when earnings are smooth relative to the volatility of operating cash flows? Discerning opportunity and incentive to report smooth earnings. *The Accounting Review*, *92*(3), 137–154.

European Central Bank (2012). Corporate indebtness in the Euro area. *Monthly Bulletin of the ECB*(2), 87–103.

Evans, J. S. B. T. (1984). Heuristic and analytic processes in reasoning. *British Journal of Psychology, 75*(4), 451–468.

Evans, M. E. (2016). Commitment and Cost of Equity Capital: An examination of timely balance sheet disclosure in earnings announcements. *Contemporary Accounting Research, 33*(3), 1136–1171.

EY (2012). *Applying IFRS: IFRS 13 Fair Value Measurement*. Hoboken, NJ: John Wiley & Sons, Inc.

EY (2013). *Applying IFRS in Real Estate: Fair value implications for the real estate sector and example disclosures for real estate entities*. Hoboken, NJ.

FASB (1980). *Statement of Financial Accounting Concepts No. 2: Qualitative characteristics of accounting information*. Norwalk, CT.

FASB (1997). *Statement of Financial Accounting Standards No. 130: Reporting comprehensive income*. Norwalk, CT.

FASB (2004). FASB Response to SEC Study on the Adoption of a Principles-Based Accounting System. https://www.dart.deloitte.com/resource/1/e23c495a-3f64-11e6-95db-0b85f5853c99. Accessed 27.03.2017.

FASB (2007). *The fair value option for financial assets and financial liabilities. Statement of financial accounting standards no. 159*. Norwalk, CT.

FASB (2010). *Original Pronouncements: Statement of Financial Accounting Standards No. 157: Fair Value Measurements*. Norwalk, CT.

FASB (2011). News Release 05/12/11 IASB and FASB issue common fair value measurement and disclosure requirements. http://www.fasb.org/cs/ContentServer?c=FASBContent_C&cid=1176158544944&d=&pagename=FASB%2FFASBContent_C%2FNewsPage. Accessed 20.01.2018.

FASB (2016). *Exposure Draft: Proposed Statement of Financial Accounting Concepts No. 8- Conceptual Framework for Financial Reporting-Chapter 7: Presentation*. Norwalk, CT.

FASB (2017). Comparability in international accounting standards: An overview. http://www.fasb.org/jsp/FASB/Page/SectionPage&cid=1176156245663. Accessed 24.10. 2017.

Ferreira, M. A., & Matos, P. (2008). The colors of investors' money: The role of institutional investors around the world. *Journal of Financial Economics*, *88*(3), 499–533.

Fest, M., Gürtler, M., & Heithecker, D. (2006). Einflussfaktoren von Immobilienpreisen bei Renditeobjekten. *Working Paper, Technische Universität Braunschweig*.

Fields, T. D., Lys, T. Z., & Vincent, L. (2001). Empirical research on accounting choice. *Journal of Accounting & Economics*, *31*(1-3), 255–307.

Fiske, S. T., & Taylor, S. E. (1991). *Social cognition*. New York, NY: MacGraw-Hill Education.

Floyd, E., & List, J. A. (2016). Using field experiments in accounting and finance. *Journal of Accounting Research*, *54*(2), 437–475.

Fréchette, G. R., & Schotter, A. (Eds.) (2015). *Handbook of experimental economic methodology*. New York, NY: Oxford Universiity Press.

Frederickson, J. R., & Miller, J. S. (2004). The effects of pro forma earnings disclosures on analysts' and nonprofessional investors' equity valuation judgments. *The Accounting Review*, *79*(3), 667–686.

Gagnon, E. (2010). *Qualitative Characteristics of Useful Financial Information. Statement of Financial Accounting Concepts No. 8. Conceptual Framework for Financial Reporting.* Norwalk, CT.

Gassen, J., & Schwedler, K. (2010). The decision usefulness of financial accounting measurement concepts: Evidence from an online survey of professional investors and their advisors. *European Accounting Review*, *19*(3), 495–509.

Gaynor, L. M., McDaniel, L., & Yohn, T. L. (2011). Fair value accounting for liabilities: The role of disclosures in unraveling the counterintuitive income statement effect from credit risk changes. *Accounting, Organizations & Society*, *36*(3), 125–134.

Geiger, M. A., & Epstein, M. J. (1994). Investor views of audit assurance: Recent evidence of the expectation gap. *Journal of Accountancy*, *177*(1), 60–66.

Gigerenzer, G. (1996). On narrow norms and vague heuristics: A reply to Kahneman and Tversky. *Psychological Review*, *103*(3), 592–596.

Gilovich, T., Griffin, D., & Kahneman, D. (Eds.) (2002). *Heuristics and Biases: The psychology of intuitive judgement*. Cambridge: Cambridge University Press.

Gjesdal, F. (1981). Accounting for stewardship. *Journal of Accounting Research, 19*(1), 208–231.

Glaum, M., & Friedrich, N. (2006). After the "bubble": Valuation of telecommunications companies by financial analysts. *Journal of International Financial Management and Accounting, 17*(2), 160–174.

Gold, A., Gronewold, U., & Pott, C. (2012). The ISA 700 auditor's report and the audit expectation gap - Do explanations matter? *International Journal of Auditing, 16*(3), 286–307.

Gopalakrishnan, V. (1994). The effect of recognition vs. disclosure on investor valuation: The case of pension accounting. *Review of Quantitative Finance and Accounting, 4*(4), 383–396.

Guay, W., Samuels, D., & Taylor, D. (2016). Guiding through the fog: Financial statement complexity and voluntary disclosure. *Journal of Accounting and Economics, 62*(2-3), 234–269.

Hans Böckler Stiftung (2014). *IAS 40: Als Finanzinvestition gehaltene Immobilien.*

Harper, R. M. J., Mister, W. G., & Strawser, J. R. (1987). The impact of new pension disclosure rules on perceptions of debt. *Journal of Accounting Research, 25*(2), 327–330.

Harrison, G. W., & List, J. A. (2004). Field experiments. *Journal of Economic Literature, 42*(4), 1009–1055.

Hayn, C. (1995). The information content of losses. *Journal of Accounting & Economics, 20*, 125–153.

Healy, P. M., & Wahlen, J. M. (1999). A review of the earnings management literature and its implications for standard setting. *Accounting Horizons, 13*(4), 365–383.

Heuser, P. J. (Ed.) (2012). *IFRS-Handbuch: Einzel- und Konzernabschluss.* (5. Auflage). Köln: O. Schmidt.

Higgins, E. T. (2002). How self-regulation creates distinct values: The case of promotion and prevention decision making. *Journal of Consumer Psychology, 12*(3), 177–191.

Highhouse, S. (1994). A verbal protocol analysis of choice under ambiguity. *Journal of Economic Psychology, 15*(4), 621–635.

Hilbert, M. (2012). Toward a synthesis of cognitive biases: How noisy information processing can bias human decision making. *Psychological Bulletin, 138*(2), 211–237.

Hirshleifer, D., Hou, K., Teoh, S. H., & Zhang, Y. (2004). Do investors overvalue firms with bloated balance sheets? *Journal of Accounting and Economics, 38*(2004), 297–331.

Hirshleifer, D., & Teoh, S. H. (2003). Limited attention, information disclosure, and financial reporting. *Journal of Accounting and Economics, 36*(1-3), 337–386.

Hirshleifer, D. A., Myers, James, N., Myers, L. A., & Teoh, S. H. (2008). Do individual investors cause post-earnings announcement drift? Direct evidence from personal trades. *The Accounting Review, 83*(6), 1521–1550.

Hirst, E. D., & Hopkins, P. E. (1998). Comprehensive income reporting and analysts' valuation judgments. *Journal of Accounting Research, 36*(3), 47–75.

Hirst, E. D., Koonce, L., & Miller, J. (1999). The joint effect of management's prior forecast accuracy and the form of its financial forecast on investor judgement. *Journal of Accounting Research,* 37(Supplement 1999), 101–124.

Hirst, E. D., Koonce, L., & Simko, P. L. (1995). Investor reactions to financial analysts' research reports. *Journal of Accounting Research, 33*(2), 335–351.

Hirst, E. D., Koonce, L., & Venkataraman, S. (2008). Management earnings forecasts: A review and framework. *Accounting Horizons, 22*(3), 315–338.

Hitz, J.-M. (2007). The decision usefulness of fair value accounting – A theoretical perspective. *European Accounting Review, 16*(2), 323–362.

Hodder, L., Koonce, L., & McAnally, M. L. (2001). SEC market risk disclosures: Implications for judgment and decision making. *Accounting Horizons, 15*(1), 49–70.

Hodge, F. D. (2003). Investors' perceptions of earnings quality, auditor independence, and the usefulness of audited financial information. *Accounting Horizons, 17*(supplement), 37–48.

Hodge, F. D., Hopkins, P. E., & Wood, D. A. (2010). The effects of financial statement information proximity and feedback on cash flow forecasts. *Contemporary Accounting Research, 27*(1), 101–133.

Hodge, F. D., Kennedy, J. J., & Maines, L. A. (2004). Does search-facilitating technology improve the transparency of financial reporting? *Accounting Review, 79*(3), 687–703.

Hogarth, R. M. (1989). *Judgement and choice: The psychology of decision.* (2. edition). A Wiley Interscience publication. Chichester u.a.: Wiley.

Holstrom, B. (1979). Moral hazard and observability. *The Bell Journal of Economics, 10*(1), 74–91.

Hopkins, P. E. (1996). The effect of financial statement classification of hybrid financial instruments on financial analysts' stock price judgements. *Journal of Accounting Research, 34*(supplement), 33–50.

Hou, T. C.-T., Hung, W., & Gao, S. S. (2014). Investors' reactions to analysts' forecast revisions and information uncertainty: Evidence of stock price drift. *Journal of Accounting, Auditing & Finance, 29*(3), 238–259.

IASB (2008a). *Exposure Draft on an improved conceptual Framework for financial reporting: The objective of financial reporting and qualitative characteristics of decision-useful financial reporting information.* London.

IASB (2008b). Frequently Asked Questions. http://www.ifrs.org/Current-Projects/IASB-Projects/Conceptual-Framework/EDMay08/Pages/Frequently-Asked-Questions.aspx.

IASB (2008c). International Accounting Standard 40: Investment Property: IAS 40.

IASB (2010). *The conceptual framework for financial reporting 2010.* London: IFRS.

IASB (2015). *Exposure draft: Conceptual framework for financial reporting.* International financial reporting standard, ED/2015/3. London: IFRS Foundation.

IFRS Foundation (2016). *Constitution.* London.

Imam, S., Barker, R., & Clubb, C. (2008). The use of valuation models by UK investment analysts. *European Accounting Review*, *17*(3), 503–535.

Israeli, D. (2015). Recognition versus disclosure: Evidence from fair value of investment property. *Review of Accounting Studies*, *20*(4), 1457–1503.

Jamal, K., & Tan, H.-T. (2010). Joint effects of principles-based versus rules-based standards and auditor type in constraining financial managers' aggressive. *The Accounting Review*, *85*(4), 1325–1346.

Johnson, E. J., & Payne, J. W. (1985). Effort and accuracy in choice. *Management Science*, *31*(4), 395–414.

Jorion, P., Liu, Z., & Shi, C. (2005). Informational effects of regulation FD: Evidence from rating agencies. *Journal of Financial Economics*, *76*(2), 309–330.

Kaburek, G. (2016). The case for principle-based accounting. http://www.ifrs.org /Features/Pages/The-case-for-principle-based-accounting-.aspx. Accessed 27.03.2017.

Kahneman, D. (1973). *Attention and effort.* Prentice Hall series in experimental psychology. Englewood Cliffs, NJ: Prentice Hall.

Kahneman, D. (2003). A perspective on judgment and choice: Mapping bounded rationality. *The American psychologist*, *58*(9), 697–720.

Kahneman, D., & Tversky, A. (1979). Prospect theory: An analysis of decision under risk. *Econometrica*, *47*(2), 263–292.

Kaplan, R. S., & Urwitz, G. (1979). Statistical models of bond ratings: A methodological inquiry. *Journal of Business*, *52*(2), 231–261.

Kelly, B., & Ljungqvist, A. (2012). Testing asymmetric-information asset pricing models. *Review of Financial Studies*, *25*(5), 1366–1413.

Kelton, A. S., & Murthy, U. S. (2016). The effects of information disaggregation and financial statement interactivity on judgments and decisions of nonprofessional investors. *Journal of Information Systems*, *30*(3), 99–118.

Kile, C., Pownall, G., & Waymire, G. (1998). How frequently do managers disclose prospective earnings information? *Journal of Financial Statement Analysis*, *3*(3), 5–16.

Kirk, R. E. (2013). *Experimental design: Procedures for the behavioral sciences.* (4. edition). Los Angeles, CA: SAGE.

Kleinmuntz, D. N., & Schkade, D. A. (1993). Information Displays and Decision Processes. *Psychological Science*, *4*(4), 221–227.

Kmenta, J., & Ramsey, J. B. (Eds.) (1980). *Evaluation of econometric models.* New York, NY: Academic Press.

Koehler, D. J., & Harvey, N. (Eds.) (2004). *Walking with the Scarecrow: The information-processing approach to decision research.* Blackwell handbook of judgement and decision making. Hoboken, NJ: Blackwell Publishing Ltd.

Kolev, K. (2009). Do investors perceive marking-to-model as marking-to-myth? Early evidence from FAS 157 disclosure. *Working Paper, Yale University.*

Kothari, S. P. (2001). Capital markets research in accounting. *Journal of Accounting & Economics, 31*(1-3), 105–231.

Kothari, S. P., Ramanna, K., & Skinner, D. J. (2010). Implications for GAAP from an analysis of positive research in accounting. *Journal of Accounting and Economics, 50* (2-3), 246–286.

Lachmann, M., Stefani, U., & Wöhrmann, A. (2015). Fair value accounting for liabilities: Presentation format of credit risk changes and individual information processing. *Accounting, Organizations & Society, 41*, 21–38.

Lachmann, M., Wöhrmann, A., & Wömpener, A. (2011). Acquisition and integration of fair value information on liabilities into investors' judgments. *Review of Accounting and Finance, 10*(4), 385–410.

Lambert, R. (1993). The use of accounting and security price measures of performance in managerial compensation contracts. *Journal of Accounting and Economics, 16*(1-3), 101–123.

Lambert, R. (2010). Implications for GAAP from an analysis of positive research in accounting. *Journal of Accounting and Economics, 50*(2-3), 287–295.

Lambert, R. A., Leuz, C., & Verrecchia, R. E. (2011). Information asymmetry, information precision, and the cost of capital. *Review of Finance, 16*(1), 1–29.

Lawrence, A. (2013). Individual investors and financial disclosure. *Journal of Accounting and Economics, 56*(1), 130–147.

Lawrence, A., Siriviriyakul, S., & Sloan, R. G. (2016). Who's the fairest of them all? Evidence from closed-end funds. *The Accounting Review, 91*(1), 207–227.

Lee, C. M.C. (1999). Accounting-based valuation: Impact on business practices and research. *Accounting Horizons, 13*(4), 413–425.

Lee, T. A., & Tweedie, D. P. (1975). Accounting information: An investigation of private shareholder usage. *Accounting and Business Research, 5*(20), 280–291.

Li, J. (2013). Accounting conservatism and debt contracts: Efficient liquidation and covenant renegotiation. *Contemporary Accounting Research, 30*(3), 1082–1098.

Libby, R., Bloomfield, R., & Nelson, M. W. (2002). Experimental research in financial accounting. *Accounting, Organizations & Society, 27*(8), 775–810.

Libby, R., & Brown, T. (2013). Financial statement disaggregation decisions and auditors' tolerance for misstatement. *The Accounting Review, 88*(2), 641–665.

Libby, T., Salterio, S. E., & Webb, A. (2004). The Balanced Scorecard: The Effects of Assurance and Process Accountability on Managerial Judgment. *The Accounting Review*, *79*(4), 1075–1094.

List, J. A. (2004). Neoclassical theory versus prospect theory: Evidence from the marketplace. *Econometrica*, *72*(2), 615–625.

Liu, H., Wang, L., Yao, M., Yang, H., & Wang, D. (2017). Self-other decision-making differences in loss aversion: A regulatory focus perspective. *Journal of Applied Social Psychology*, *47*(2), 90–98.

Maines, L. A., & McDaniel, L. (2000). Effects of comprehensive-income characteristics on nonprofessional investors' judgments: The role of financial-statement presentation format. *Accounting Review*, *75*(2), 179-207.

Maines, L. A., & Wahlen, J. M. (2006). The nature of accounting information reliability: Inferences from archival and experimantal research. *Accounting Horizons*, *20*(4), 399–425.

Malmendier, U., & Shanthikumar, D. (2007). Are small investors naive about incentives? *Journal of Financial Economics*, *85*(2), 457–489.

Manchiraju, H., Hamlen, S., Kross, W., & Suk, I. (2015). Fair value gains and losses in derivatives and CEO compensation. *Journal of Accounting, Auditing & Finance*, *31*(3), 311–338.

Markman, K. D., & Tetlock, P. E. (2000). Accountability and close-call counterfacts: The loser who nearly won and the winner who nearly lost. *Personaility and Social Psychology Bulletin*, *26*(10), 1213-1224.

Marton, J. (1998). Accounting and stock markets: A study of Swedish accounting for international investors and analysts. Unpublished dissertation. *Dissertation, University of Gothenburg, 1998.*

Mazza, C. R., Hunton, J. E., & McEwen, R. A. (2011). Fair value (U.S. GAAP) and entity-specific (IFRS) measurements for performance obligations: The potential mitigating effect of benchmarks on earnings management. *Journal of Behavioral Finance*, *12*(2), 68–77.

McDonough, R. P., & Shakespeare, C. M. (2015). Fair value measurement capabilities, disclosure, and the perceived reliability of fair value estimates: A discussion of Bhat and Ryan (2015). *Accounting, Organizations and Society*, *46*, 96–99.

McEwen, R. A., & Hunton, J. E. (1999). Is analyst forecast accuracy associated with accounting information use? *Accounting Horizons*, *13*(1), 1–16.

McEwen, R. A., Mazza, C. R., & Hunton, J. E. (2008). Effects of managerial discretion in fair value accounting regulation and motivational incentives to "go along" with management on analysts' expectations and judgments. *Journal of Behavioral Finance*, *9*(4), 240–251.

Michels, J. (2017). Disclosure versus recognition: Inferences from subsequent events. *Journal of Accounting Research*, *55*(1), 3–34.

Müller, M. A., Riedl, E. J., & Sellhorn, T. (2015). Recognition versus disclosure of fair values. *The Accounting Review*, *90*(6), 2411–2447.

Murphy, T., O'Connell, V., & Ó hÓgartaigh, C. (2013). Discourses surrounding the evolution of the IASB/FASB Conceptual Framework: What they reveal about the "living law" of accounting. *Accounting, Organizations and Society, 38*(1), 72–91.

Nelson, M. W., Elliott, J. A., & Tarpley, R. L. (2002). Evidence from auditors about managers' and auditors' earnings management decisions. *The Accounting Review, 77*(supplement), 175–202.

Nelson, M. W., & Tayler, W. B. (2007). Information Pursuit in Financial Statement Analysis: Effects of Choice, Effort, and Reconciliation. *Accounting Review, 82*(3), 731–758.

Newell, A., & Simon, H. A. (1972). *Human problem solving*. Englewood Cliffs, NJ: Prentice-Hall.

Niemeier, C. D. (2008). *Keynote adress on recent international initiatives 2008 Sarbanes-Oxley, SEC and PCAOB conference*. New York, NY.

Nisbett, R. E., Zuckier, H., & Lemley, R. E. (1981). The dilution effect: Nondiagnostic information weakens the implications of diagnostic information. *Cognitive Psychology, 13*(2), 248–277.

Nissim, D., & Penman, S. (2008). Principles for the application of fair value accounting. *White Paper (No. 2), Columbia University.*

O'Connell, V. (2007). Reflections on stewardship reporting. *Accounting Horizons, 21*(2), 215–227.

OECD (2016). List of OECD Member countries - Ratification of the Convention on the OECD. http://www.oecd.org/about/membersandpartners/list-oecd-member-countries.htm. Accessed 06.03.2017.

Olbert, L. (1994). Stock valuation methods of financial analysts in a thin stock market in Sweden, with comparisons to the United Kingdom and the United States. *International Journal of Accounting, 29*(2), 123–135.

Otuteye, E., & Siddiquee, M. (2015). Overcoming cognitive biases: A heuristic for making value investing decisions. *Journal of Behavioral Finance, 16*(2), 140–149.

Payne, J. W. (1976). Task complexity and contingent processing in decision making: An information search and protocol analysis. *Organizational Behavior and Human Performance, 16*(2), 366–387.

Payne, J. W. (1982). Contingent decision behavior. *Psychological Bulletin, 92*(2), 382–402.

Payne, J. W., Bettman, J. R., & Johnson, E. J. (1988). Adaptive strategy selection in decision making. *Journal of Experimental Psychology: Learning, Memory, and Cognition, 14*(3), 534–552.

Payne, J. W., Bettman, J. R., & Johnson, E. J. (1992). Behavioral decision research: A constructive processing perspective. *Annual Review of Psychology, 43*, 87–131.

Payne, J. W., Bettman, J. R., & Johnson, E. J. (1993). *The adaptive decision maker*. Cambridge, NY: Cambridge University Press.

Pellens, B., Fülbier, R. U., Gassen, J., & Sellhorn, T. (Eds.) (2014). *Internationale Rechnungslegung: IFRS 1 bis 13, IAS 1 bis 41, IFRIC-Interpretationen, Standardentwürfe Mit Beispielen, Aufgaben und Fallstudie.* (9. Auflage). Stuttgart: Schäffer-Poeschel Verlag.

Pellens, B., & Schmidt, A. (2014). *Verhalten und Präferenzen deutscher Aktionäre: Eine Befragung von privaten und institutionellen Anlegern zum Informationsverhalten, zur Dividendenpräferenz und zur Wahrnehmung von Stimmrechten.* Studien des Deutschen Aktieninstituts. Frankfurt am Main: Deutsches Aktieninstitut e.V.

Peytcheva, M., Wright, A. M., & Majoor, B. (2014). The Impact of principles-based versus rules-based accounting Standards on auditors' motivations and evidence demands. *Behavioral Research in Accounting, 26*(2), 51–72.

Pitt, H. L. (2001). *Public Statement by SEC Chairman: How to prevent future Enrons.* "Opinion editorial" for the Wall Street Journal.

Pitt, H. L. (2011). *Remarks before the AICPA Governing Council, SEC Speech.* U.S. Securities and Exchange Commission. Miami Beach, FL.

Psaros, J., & Trotman, K. T. (2004). The impact of the type of accounting standards on preparers' judgments. *Abacus, 40*(1), 76–93.

pwc (2006). Substance- A clash of perspectives? http://pwc.blogs.com/ifrs/2006/10/substance_a_cla.html. Accessed 30.03.2017.

Rapaport, A., Wallstein, T. S., Erev, I., & Cohen, B. L. (1990). Revision of opinion with verbally and numerically expressed uncertainties. *Acta Psychologica, 74*(1), 61–79.

Rashad Abdel-Khalik, A. (2010). Fair value accounting and stewardship. *Accounting Perspectives, 9*(4), 253–269.

Reimsbach, D., Hahn, R., & Gürtürk, A. (2017). Integrated reporting and assurance of sustainability information: An experimental study on professional investors' information processing. *European Accounting Review, 65*(4), 1–23.

RICS (2017). *RICS Valuation - Global Standards 2017: Incorporating the IVSC International Valuation Standards*. London.

Rosen, R. von (Ed.) (2009). *Verhalten und Präferenzen deutscher Aktionäre: Eine Befragung von privaten und institutionellen Anlegern zum Informationsverhalten, zur Dividendenpräferenz und zur Wahrnehmung von Stimmrechten.* (1. Aufl.). Studien des Deutschen Aktieninstituts, Heft Nr. 42. Frankfurt am Main: Deutsches Aktieninstitut e.V.

Rottke, N. B., & Thomas, M. (Eds.) (2011). *Immobilienwirtschaftslehre*. Köln: Immobilien Manager Verlag IMV; Auflage: 1.

Şabac, F., & Tian, J. (2015). On the stewardship value of soft managerial reports. *The Accounting Review, 90*(4), 1683–1706.

Saunders, M., Lewis, P., & Thronhill, A. (2016). *Research methods for business students.* (7. edition). Harlow, Essex: Pearson Education Limited.

Schick, A. G., & Gordon, L. A. (1999). Information overload: A temporal approach. *Accounting, Organizations & Society, 15*(3), 199–220.

Schipper, K. (2003). Principles-based accounting standards. *Accounting Horizons*, *17*(1), 61–72.

Schipper, K., & Vincent, L. (2003). Earnings quality. *Accounting Horizons*, *17*(supplement), 97–110.

SEC (2003). Study pursuant to Section 108(d) of the Sarbanes-Oxley Act of 2002 on the adoption by the United States financial reporting system of a principles-based accounting system. https://www.sec.gov/news/studies/principlesbasedstand.htm. Accessed 27.03. 2017.

SEC (2008). Sample letter sent to public companies on MD&A disclosure regarding the application of SFAS 157 (fair value measurement): Letter, 13 September 2008. https://www.sec.gov/divisions/corpfin/guidance/fairvalueltr0908.htm.

Shefrin, H., & Statman, M. (1985). The disposition to sell winners too early and ride losers too long: Theory and Evidence. *The Journal of Finance*, *40*(3), 777.

Shumway, T. (2001). Forecasting bankruptcy more accurately: A simple hazard model. *Journal of Business*, *74*(1), 101–124.

Siegel, M. A. (2018). *Disclosure Effectiveness.* Financial Accounting and Reporting Section Midyear Meeting. Austin, Texas.

Simon, H. A. (1955). A behavioral model of rational choice. *The Quarterly Journal of Economics*, *69*(1), 99–118.

Simon, H. A. (1956). Rational choice and the structure of the environment. *Psychological Review*, *63*(2), 129–138.

Simon, H. A. (1978). Rationality as process and as product of thought. *The American Economic Review*, *68*(2), 1–16.

Simon, H. A. (1979). *Models of thought*. New Haven, CT: Yale University Press.

Simon, H. A. (1981). *The sciences of the artificial.* (2. edition). Cambridge, MA: MIT Press.

Simon, H. A. (1990a). Invariants of human behavior. *Annual Review of Psychology*, *41*, 1–19.

Simon, H. A. (1990b). *Reason in human affairs.* (reprint). Stanford, Calif: Stanford University Press.

Simon, J. (2000). Europäische Standards für die Immobilienbewertung. *Grundstücksmarkt und Grundstückswert: GuG, Zeitschrift für Immobilienwirtschaft*, *10*(3), 134–141.

Sloman, S. A. (1996). The empirical case for two systems of reasoning. *Psychological Bulletin*, *119*(1), 3–22.

Slovic, P. (1972). From Shakespeare to Simon: Speculation -and some evidence- about man's ability to process information. *Oregon Research Institute Bulletin*, *12*(3), 1–29.

Slovic, P. (1995). The construction of preference. *American Psychologist*, *50*(5), 364–371.

Smith, V. L. (1982). Microeconomic systems as an experimental science. *The American Economic Review*, *72*(5), 923–955.

Socea, A.-D. (2012). Managerial decision-making and financial accounting information. *Procedia - Social and Behavioral Sciences, 58*(2012), 47–55.

Song, C. J., Thomas, W. B., & Han, Y. (2010). Value relevance of FAS No. 157 fair value hierarchy information and the impact of corporate governance mechanisms. *Accounting Review, 85*(4), 1375–1410.

Song, X. (2015). Value relevance of fair values-empirical evidence of the impact of market volatility. *Accounting Perspectives, 14*(2), 91–116.

Spivey, N. N. (1989). Construing constructivism: Reading research in the United States. *Poetics, Occasional Paper* No. 12, 169–192.

Sterling, R. R. (1967). A Statement of basic accounting theory: A review article. *Journal of Accounting Research, 5*(1), 95–112.

Stiglitz, J. E. (2000). The contribution of the economics of information to twentieth century economics. *Quaterly Journal of Economics, 115*(4), 1441–1478.

Tetlock, P. C. (2007). Giving content to investor sentiment: The role of media in the stock market. *Journal of Finance, 62*(3), 1139–1168.

Tversky, A., & Kahneman, D. (1973). *Judgement under uncertainty: Heuristics and biases*. Eugoene, Orgenon.

Ungson, G. R., & Braunstein, D. N. (Eds.) (1982). *Decision making: An interdisciplinary Inquiry*. The use of accounting information: Expert versus novice behavior. Massachusetts: Kent Publishing Company.

van der Meulen, S., Gaeremynck, A., & Willekens, M. (2007). Attribute differences between U.S. GAAP and IFRS earnings: An exploratory study. *The International Journal of Accounting, 42*(2), 123–142.

van Tendeloo, B., & Vanstraelen, A. (2005). Earnings management under German GAAP versus IFRS. *European Accounting Review, 14*(1), 155–180.

Vergoossen, R. G. A. (1993). The use and perceived importance of annual reports by investment analysts in the Netherlands. *European Accounting Review, 2*(2), 219–244.

Wagenhofer, A., & Ewert, R. (Eds.) (2007). *Externe Unternehmensrechnung: Bewertung von Immobilien*. Berlin, Heidelberg: Springer Berlin Heidelberg.

Wallsten, T. S., Budescu, D. V., Rapoport, A., Zwick, R., & Forsyth, B. (1986). Measuring the vague meanings of probability terms. *Journal of Experimental Psychology: General, 115*(4), 348–365.

Watts, R. L., & Zimmerman, J. L. (1978). Towards a positive theory of the determination of accounting standards. *The Accounting Review, 53*(1), 112–134.

Wickens, C. D., & Carswell, C. M. (1995). The proximity compatibility principle: Its psychological foundation and relevance to display design. *Human Factors: The Journal of the Human Factors and Ergonomics Society, 37*(3), 473–494.

Wieland, M. M. (2011). Identifying consensus analysts' earnings forecasts that correctly and incorrectly predict an earnings increase. *Journal of Business Finance & Accounting, 38* (5-6), 574–600.

Wright, M., Amess, K., Weir, C., & Girma, S. (2009). Private equity and corporate governance: Retrospect and prospect. *Corporate Governance: An International Review, 17*(3), 353–375.

Wu, J. S., & Zhang, I. X. (2009). The voluntary adoption of internationally recognized accounting standards and firm internal performance evaluation. *The Accounting Review, 84*(4), 1281–1309.

Zhong, N., Wang, S., & Yang, R. (2017). Does corporate governance enhance common interests of shareholders and primary stakeholders? *Journal of Business Ethics, 141*(2), 411–431.

Supporting information

T. Herrmann, *The Decision Usefulness of Additional Fair Value Disclosures*,
Controlling und Rechnungslegung – Managerial and Financial Accounting,
https://doi.org/10.1007/978-3-658-24832-1

Appendix S1 Overview of information classification of disclosures according to IFRS 13 and IAS 40

	Qualitative Information	Range Value	Change Value	Point Value
IFRS 13.93				
Fair value measurement at the end of reporting period				X
Level of fair value hierarchy	X			
Description of valuation techniques and inputs used in the measurement and any changes made to them including reasons for making such changes	X			
Quantitative information about significant unobservable inputs used in measurements		X		X
Total gains or losses for the period recognised in profit and loss and the items in profit and loss in which they were recognised				X
Amount of profit and loss attributable to the change in unrealised gains or losses and the items in profit and loss in which they were recognised				X
Total gains or losses for the period recognised in other comprehensive income and the items in profit and loss in which they were recognised				X
Purchases				X
Sales				X
Issues				X
Settlements				X
Amounts of transfers into or out of level 3 fair value hierarchy including reasons for transfers and policies for determining when transfers between levels are deemed to have occurred (Disclosed separately)		X		(X)
Description of valuation process	X			
Description of sensitivity of the fair value to changes in unobservable inputs	X	X		
(Facts why an asset is used in a manner that differs from its highest and best use)	X			
IAS 40.75				
Fair value or cost model	X			
Operating leases classified as investment property	X			

Criteria to distinguish investment properties from owner-occupied property and from property held for sale	X			
Methods and significant assumptions applied to determine fair value	X			
Extent to which fair value is based on a valuation by a qualified and independent assessor	X			
Rental income from investment properties during the period				X
Direct operating expenses for investment properties generating rental incomes				X
Direct operating expenses for investment properties not generating rental incomes				X
Cumulative change in fair value recognised in profit and loss (sale from a pool where cost model is applied to a pool where fair value is applied)			X	
Restrictions on the feasibility of investment property or the remittance of income and proceeds of disposal	X			
Contractual obligations to purchase, construct, or develop investment property or for repairs, maintenance or enhancements	X			
IAS 40.76				
Reconciliation between the carrying amounts of investment property at the beginning and the end of the period (...)			X	
Significant adjustments to an outside valuation	X		X	

Table 20: Classification of disclosures according to IFRS 13 and IAS 40[60]

[60] Author's own illustration according to IFRS 13 and IAS 40.

Appendix S2 Experiment: Introductory pages

Welcome!

Thank you very much for your contribution to this **scientific experiment**. By participating, you contribute in a **valuable way** to scientific research by helping to answer a research questions in the field of accounting. The participation in the experiment will take about 20 minutes. Your participation in this experiment is absolutely **anonymous**. The collected data will be used for scientific purposes only.

The experiment will proceed as follows:

1. On the following page of this document you will receive further information on the **procedure of the experiment** as well as your **participation number**.

2. In the course of the experiment you will be asked to open **envelope A, B and C** that contain further instructions and information as well as answering sheets.

With the participation in this experiment you will participate in a lottery to win one of three Amazon vouchers with a value of 20 EUR.

Thank you very much for your participation! If any questions occur throughout the experiment pleas raise your hand and we are happy to answer them for you.

General information on the experiment process

- Envelope **A** contains the **financial statement** of the fictional firm XY Crop. for the **current financial year** t=1, that contains as well information on the **previous year** t=0.
- Please assume that the XY Corp. accounts according to **IFRS**. If the standard allows different accounting **options** please assume that the firm chooses the same option in both years.
- You will have **10 minutes** to look at the financial statements of the XY Corp.. After the time is up you will receive different **questions** on the **financial statement information** as well as on the **performance** of the XY Corp. The financial statement **will not be available** to you when **you answer the questions**.
- Please consider the financial statement of the XY Corp. from an **investors' perspective.**
- At the bottom right of this page you can find **your individual participation number**. Please detach the number and fold it up. Keep the number until the end of the experiment to participate in the lottery on the Amazon vouchers.
- Please fill in the forms of the experiment **completely** and by **yourself**. By doing so, please do not use any assistive devices (e.g. internet). If you wish to make some **calculations**, you can use the provided calculator in the envelope. Further, you are welcome to take notes. I would like to ask you **not to communicate with other participants** throughout the experiment. This is important so each participant can make their own decisions without being influenced by other participants.
- Please follow the instructions provided by the supervisors of the experiment.

Please wait for further advice by the supervisors of the experiment now.

Do not open envelope A unless you're asked to do so.

00x

Appendix S3 Experiment: Envelope A

Information about the XY Corp.

The XY Corp. is a real estate company. The purpose of XY Corp. is to manage **commercial- and retail properties**. The objects are not held for trading and are located in one of Germany's seven biggest cities. The real estate portfolio consists of 20% commercial (t=1: kEUR 6.634) and 80% residential properties (t=1: kEUR 26.535). All contractual rents of XY Corp. are equivalent to market rents.

The objects of XY Corp. are accounted for at fair value. The corresponding positions in the financial statement are made according to the following fair value hierarchy.

The company's properties are recognized at fair value through profit and loss. The related declaration in the annual accounts corresponds to the following **fair value hierarchy:**

- Level 1: Input factors are quoted prices on active markets for identical assets or debts (**directly observable input factors**) that are accessible by the company on the day of assessment deadline.
- Level 2: Input factors are other than those characterized under level 1, including mentioned quoted market prices that are **directly or indirectly** observable for the asset or debt.
- Level 3: Input factors are **non-observable** input factors for the assets or debt.

The XY Corp. uses the full fair value approach to assess its properties. Thus, the depreciation or ascription is steadily **income statement-related on the profit and loss account**.

The XY Corp. **does not employ its own personnel**. For the company, the working personnel is remunerated within the frame of agency agreements.

Excerpt from the Financial Statement of XY Corp. (in kEUR)

Assets

	t=1 kEUR	t=0 kEUR	Disclosure	Reconciliation between carrying amounts from t=0 to t=1
Non-current Assets				
Investment Properties	33.169	31.312	D1	**1.857**
PP&E	1.351	1.382	D2	
	34.520	32.694		
Current Assets				
Inventories				
Work in Progress	522	513		
Receivables and Other Current Assets				
Trade Receivables	79	51	D3	
Other Current Assets	40	37		
	119	88		
Cash	1.087	1.329		
	1.728	1.930		
Total Assets	36.248	34.624		

Liabilities

	t=1	t=0	
	kEUR	kEUR	Disclosure
Equity			
Issued Share Capital	6.394	6.394	
Capital Reserve	2.089	1.430	
Accumulated other Reserves	6.599	5.923	
	15.082	13.747	
Provisions			
Other Provisions	2.216	1.820	
Liabilities			
Non-current Liabilities due to Banks	17.959	18.108	D4
Received Payments	548	536	
Trade Payables	120	117	
Other Liabilities	141	123	
	18.768	18.884	
Deferred Income	182	173	
Total Liabilities	36.248	34.624	

Profit and Loss

	t=1	t=0
	kEUR	**kEUR**
Income from Investment Properties	2.490	2.415
Expenses from Investment Property Management	633	762
Inventory Changes	9	3
Gains from the Fair Value Adjustments of Investment Properties	1.857	935
Amortization and Depreciation of Tangible Assets	31	35
Other Expenses	156	132
EBIT	**3.536**	**2.424**
Other Interests and Similar Income	13	19
Finance Expenses	899	936
EBT	**2.650**	**1.507**
Income Taxes	238	172
Profit of the Period	**2.412**	**1.335**

Excerpt from Disclosures

[...]

D Information on the statement of financial position of XY Corp.

D1. Investment properties

The investment properties are assessed at fair value. The fair values developed in the current period as follows:

All figures in kEUR	t=1	t=0
Value at the beginning of the period	31.312	30.377
Adjustment to fair value	1.857	935
Value at the end of the period	33.169	31.312

There were no disposals or additions during the financial year.

The fair value hierarchy for the valuation of investment properties is level 3 for the reporting dates in t=1 and t=0. The investment properties of XY Corp. were valued with the DCF method, which considers the future cash flows (especially from rents). The input factors are considered unobservable for the reporting dates t=1 and t=0, and therefore, they are classified as level 3 on the fair value hierarchy.

A review of the valuation was monitored by an independent third party and is conducted for every reporting date. The valuation method applied for the internal valuation of investment properties is in line with the valuation by a third party.

Sensitivity analysis:

In the case of a negative adaptation of the significant valuation parameters (rental growth 2% p.a. less than planned; increase of the discount interest rate by 0.1%, increase of the capitalization rate by 0.15%) a value of 31.676 kEUR for the real estate portfolio follows.

In the case of a positive adaptation of the significant valuation parameters (rental growth 2% p.a. more than planned; decrease of the discount interest rate by 0.1%; decrease of the capitalization rate by 0.15%) a value of 34.662 kEUR for the real estate portfolio follows.

The investment properties of XY Corp. serve as securities for the bank loans.

D2. Property, plant and equipment

This position includes classified properties as well as technical facilities, operating and business equipment in accordance with the IAS 16. The developments of the financial year correspond completely with the depreciation of the financial year.

The properties included in PP&E are essentially secured by a mortgage.

The PP&E are accounted for at acquisition and production costs less accumulated scheduled depreciations and accumulated impairment losses. The durability of the assets is estimated for the scheduled linear depreciations of 50 years. The durability of movable PP&E is four to ten years.

An audit regarding the impairment of PP&E is carried out if there are signs that indicate that the book value is stated higher than the recoverable amount. PPE are derecognized if there is a disposal as well as if future economic benefits are absent from further utilization or sale.

D3. Trade receivables

The trade receivables from rentals are interest-free. The allowances of receivables are formed based on their age pattern and/or depending on whether they involve current or former tenants.

D4. Liabilities due to banks

The corporation has loans taken from financial institutes to finance its real estate transactions. The majority of the liabilities due to banks have fixed interest rates or are secured by interest rate hedges 84% (previous year: approximately 88%). The average interest rate is approximately 5.0% (previous year: approximately 5.1%). The fixed interest loans have a maturity of over 5 years.

Appendix S4 Experiment: Envelope B

Questions (1/2)

Please answer the following **questions about the XY Corp**. As of now the financial statements of the firm are no longer available to you. Therefore please answer the questions by **recapitulating** the **financial statement information** you received earlier.

1.1)	**How do you assess the performance of the XY Corp. in t=1 compared t=0?**
	Please mark a number that appears plausible to you.

0 1 2 3 4 5 6 7 8 9 10 11

(poor performance) (very good performance)

1.2)	**To what extent did you consider the development of the following financial statement items of XY Corp. regarding your performance assessment of the firm?**
	Please mark a number that appears plausible to you.

	(not at all considered)											(intensively considered)
Property, Plant & Equipment	0	1	2	3	4	5	6	7	8	9	10	11
Investment Properties	0	1	2	3	4	5	6	7	8	9	10	11
Equity	0	1	2	3	4	5	6	7	8	9	10	11
Other Accruals	0	1	2	3	4	5	6	7	8	9	10	11
Liabilities due to banks	0	1	2	3	4	5	6	7	8	9	10	11

2.1)	Reliability means a high level of objectification and thus little subject input parameters. **How do you assess the reliability of the <u>fair value of investment properties</u>?**
	Please mark a number that appears plausible to you.

0 1 2 3 4 5 6 7 8 9 10 11

(not at all reliable) (very reliable)

2.2)	Reliability means a high level of objectification and thus little subject input parameters. **How do you assess the reliability of the <u>financial statements</u> of XY Corp. <u>overall</u>?**
	Please mark a number that appears plausible to you.

0 1 2 3 4 5 6 7 8 9 10 11

(not at all reliable) (very reliable)

2.3)	Decision-useful information enable investors to assess the height, timing and degree of uncertainty of future net cash-inflows as part of an investment decision in a firm. **How do you assess the decision usefulness of the <u>fair value of investment properties</u>?**
	Please mark a number that appears plausible to you.

0 1 2 3 4 5 6 7 8 9 10 11

(not at all decision useful) (very decision useful)

2.4)	Decision-useful information enable investors to assess the height, timing and degree of uncertainty of future net cash-inflows as part of an investment decision in a firm. **How do you assess the decision usefulness of the <u>financial statements</u> of XY Corp. <u>overall</u>?**
	Please mark a number that appears plausible to you.

0 1 2 3 4 5 6 7 8 9 10 11

(not at all decision-useful) (very decision-useful)

3.1)	**What is the value of investment properties in the financial statement of the XY Corp. in t=1?**
	Please mark one.

□ less than 25.000 kEUR □ more than 25.000 kEUR

3.2)	**According to the fair value hierarchy: Are the input parameters for the valuation of the investment properties of XY Corp. unobservable (level 3)?**
	Please mark one.

□ Yes □ No

3.3)	**Was there a change in the fair value of investment properties in t=1 compared to t=0?**
	Please mark one.

□ Yes □ No

3.4)	**Will there be a change in the fair value of investment properties in t=1 if there is an adjustment of the main valuation parameter?**
	Please mark one.

□ Yes □ No

3.5)	**How did the rental prices develop on the seven biggest cities sin Germany in t=1 compared to t=0?**
	Please mark a number that appears plausible to you.

-11 -10 -9 -8 -7 -6 -5 -4 -3 -2 -1 0 1 2 3 4 5 6 7 8 9 10 11

(Strongly decrease) (Highly increase)

4.1)	**You received several financial statement information on XY Corp.** **Do you feel able to make an investment decision on buying shares of the firm?**
	Please mark a number that appears plausible to you.

0 1 2 3 4 5 6 7 8 9 10 11

(Not at all) (Completely)

4.2)	**Do you want to purchase shares of the XY Corp.?**
	Please mark one.

□ Yes □ No

4.3)	**To what extent did you consider the following information when making an investment decision?**
	Please mark a number that appears plausible to you.

	(not at all considered)										(intensively considered)
Equity ratio	0	1	2	3	4	5	6	7	8	9	10	11
Liquidity	0	1	2	3	4	5	6	7	8	9	10	11
Change in the value of investment properties	0	1	2	3	4	5	6	7	8	9	10	11
Change in the liabilities	0	1	2	3	4	5	6	7	8	9	10	11
Change in the accruals	0	1	2	3	4	5	6	7	8	9	10	11

4.4)	**Are there other - not provided- financial statement information you would have needed to make an investment decision?**
	Please mark one.

□ Yes □ No

4.5)	**If you answered "yes" in question 4.4) please state which additional information you would have needed to make an investment decision.**
	Please state the missing information using **keywords.**

____

____

____

____

____

____

When you answered the questions above, please put these pages back into envelope B.

Please open envelope C after.

Appendix S5 Experiment: Envelope C

Questions (2/2)

Bringing this experiment to a close I would like to ask you to answer the following questions. The data is collected anonymously so that no conclusion to your person is possible.

1.1)	**How did the investment properties of the XY Corp. develop from t=0 to t=1?**
	Please mark one.

□ Increase □ Decrease

1.2)	**Which information was presented salient in the <u>balance sheet</u> of the XY Corp.?**
	Please mark <u>**one**</u> of the following.

□ None

□ Fair-Value-Hierarchy (Level Label)

□ Sensitivity analysis

□ Reconciliation between carrying amounts from t=0 to t=1

2.1) Please mark your gender.

□ Male

□ Female

2.2) Please state your year of birth. [ ]

2.3) Which is your highest University degree?

□ Bachelor □ Master □ Diplom □ MBA □ PhD

subject [ ]

2.4) How many <u>month</u> of professional experience in the field of business (audit, tax, financial accounting, and management control) do you have?

[ ]

2.5) Which service line do you work for?

□ Audit

□ Tax

□ Management Control

□ Consulting

□ Another service line called [ ]

2.6) Which of the following exams did you take successfully?

□ Tax consultancy exam

□ Certified Public Accountant (CPA) exam according to German law

□ Certified Public Accountant (CPA) exam according to U.S. law

□ Other [ ]

2.7) Do you have investment experience as a private investor (e.g. in the form of savings products, purchase of shares or stocks, investment in equity funds)? If so, how many <u>years</u> of investment experience do you have?

□ Yes, overall [ ] years of experience

□ No

Completion of the experiment

You now have completed the experiment successfully. Thank you very much for your participation.

Please remember to **keep your individual participation number** to take part in the lottery.

Remain calm until all participants of the experiment have completed their tasks. Please do not talk to co-workers about contents of the experiment since this could influence the behaviour of future participants in the experiment.

Please put these pages now back into envelope C.

Please put the calculator, the general instruction pages as well as envelopes A, B and C back into the big brown envelope. The big envelope will be picked up by the instructors of the experiment shortly.

Afterwards the folded up individual participation number will be collected by the instructors of the experiment. The lottery will take place immediately after that.

Thank you very much!

Appendix S6 Question overview

Question No.	Question	Response possibilities	Expected results	Background of the question	Hypo-theses
1.1	How do you assess the performance of XY Corp. In t=1 compared to t=0?	Mark a number on a scale from 0-11 0= poor performance 11= very good performance	Gain: Values of 6 or more; Loss: Values of 5 or less	Afferent question to 1.2	H2e and H2f
1.2	To what extent did you consider the development of the following financial statement items of XY Corp. regarding your performance assessment of the firm?	Mark a number on a scale from 0-11 for the following items, where 0= did not consider at all 11= intensively considered Property, Plant & Equipment Investment Properties Equity Other Accruals Liabilities due to Banks	Investors will place greater weights on the development of investment properties compared to other financial statement items when the related fair value information is presented salient With salient presentation investors will weigh the change in investment properties more with a gain compared to a loss.	The questions addresses the third part of information processing by (Maines & McDaniel, 2000).	H2e and H2f
2.1	How do you assess the reliability of the fair value of investment properties?	Mark a number on a scale from 0-11 0= not at all reliable 11= very reliable	Gain: Reliability of the fair value will be higher when additional fair value information is salient; Loss: Reliability of the fair value will be lower when additional fair value information is salient.	Does salient fair value information (i.e. as an additional disclosure) increase the reliability of the fair value itself? How is the variation among treatments? Is there a difference between gain and loss	H3a-d
2.2	How do you assess the reliability of the financial statements of XY Corp. overall?	Mark a number on a scale from 0-11 0= not at all reliable 11= very reliable	Higher values for treatments that received high scores with question 2.1. Gain: Reliability of the fair value will be higher when additional fair value information is salient; Loss: Reliability of the fair value will be lower when additional fair value information is salient.	Does higher reliability of the fair value lead to a higher reliability at the financial statement level? Does salient fair value information (i.e. as an additional disclosure) increase the reliability of the fair value itself? How is the variation among treatments? Is there a difference between gain and loss	H1c H3a-d
2.3	How do you assess the decision usefulness of the fair value of investment properties?	Mark a number on a scale from 0-11 0= not at all decision-useful 11= very decision-useful	Higher reliability at the fair value level leads to higher decision usefulness (as proposed by the standard setter)	Does higher reliability lead to higher decision usefulness at the fair value level? What are the differences between gain and loss (among treatments)?	H1a H3a-d

2.4	How do you assess the decision usefulness of the financial statements of XY Corp. overall?	Mark a number on a scale from 0-11 0= not at all decision-useful 11= very decision-useful	Higher reliability at the financial statement level leads to higher decision usefulness (as proposed by the standard setter)	Does higher reliability lead to higher decision usefulness at the financial statement level? What are the differences between gain and loss (among treatments)?	H1c H3a-d
3.1	What is the value of investment properties in the financial statement of the XY Corp. in t=1?	Mark either less than 25.000 kEUR more than 25.000 kEUR	More than 25.000 kEUR Information acquisition is more likely when fair value information is salient and with a fair value gain	Information acquisition is more likely with salient profit and loss information. Does this also apply to the balance sheet? So far only a gain compared to the prior period has been observed	H2a and H2b
3.2	According to the fair value hierarchy: Are the input parameters for the valuation of the investment properties of XY Corp. unobservable (level 3)?	Mark either yes no	Yes is the correct answer Information acquisition is more likely when fair value information is salient and with a fair value gain	Information acquisition is more likely with salient profit and loss information. Does this also apply to the balance sheet? So far only a gain compared to the prior period has been observed Information acquisition is more likely to occur when related fair value information is presented salient with a fair value gain compared to a fair value loss.	H2a and H2b
3.3	Was there a change in the fair value of investment properties in t=1 compared to t=0?	Mark either yes no	Yes is the correct answer Information acquisition is more likely when fair value information is salient and with a fair value gain	Information acquisition is more likely with salient profit and loss information. Does this also apply to the balance sheet? So far only a gain compared to the prior period has been observed. Information acquisition is more likely to occur when related fair value information is presented salient with a fair value gain compared to a fair value loss.	H2a and H2b
3.4	Will there be a change in the fair value of investment properties in t=1 if there is an adjustment of the main valuation parameter?	Mark either yes no	Yes is the correct answer Information evaluation is more likely if the information is acquired	Did information evaluation occur correctly? Information evaluation should be more likely to be correct with yes-answers for questions 3.2 and 3.3 as well as more than 25.000 kEUR for question	H2c and H2d

				3.1. Information evaluation is more likely to be correct with salient presentation of related fair value information and with a fair value gain compared to a fair value loss.	
3.5	How did the rental prices develop on the seven biggest cities in Germany in t=1 compared to t=0?	Mark a number on a scale from 0-11 -11= strongly decrease 0= no change 11= highly increase	Information evaluation is correct when: Increase(gain): 1 to 11 Decrease (loss) -1 to -11 0=wrong (gain& loss)	Did information evaluation occur correctly? Information evaluation should be more likely with yes-answers for questions 3.2 and 3.3 as well as more than 25.000 kEUR for question 3.1. Information evaluation is more likely to be correct with salient presentation of related fair value information and with a fair value gain compared to a fair value loss	H2c and H2d
4.1	You received several financial statement information on XY Corp.. Do you feel able to make an investment decision on buying shares of the firm?	Mark a number on a scale from 0-11 0= not at all 11= totally	When salient fair value information is provided NPIs should feel more able to make an investment decision compared to the current format mandated under IFRS	Investors need high decision-useful data to make an investment decision. Thus, if information is more decision-useful they should feel more able to make an investment decision.	H4a
4.2	Do you want to purchase shares of the XY Corp.?	Mark either yes no	Investors that perceive decision usefulness of the financial statement information higher are more likely to purchase shares.	If the decision usefulness is high, NPIs perceive financial statement information to be more reliable. According to the IASB decision-useful information is necessary to make an investment decision. Thus, if decision usefulness is high NPIs will rather buy shares of the XY Crop.	H4b

4.3	To what extent did you consider the following information when making an investment decision?	Mark a number on a scale from 0-11 for the following items, where 0= did not consider at all 11= intensively considered Equity ratio Liquidity Change in the value of investment properties Change in the liabilities Change in the accruals	The change in fair value of investment properties is very prominent in a real estate firm so consequently rational NPIs should consider this position for their investment decision. Further, the cash flow is generated by this financial statement position.	Indicated which item is especially relevant for NPIs when they make an investment decision for real estate firms. This adds explanatory power to the results of questions 4.1 and 4.2	Supporting information for H4a and H4b and additional analysis
4.4	Are there other - not provided- financial statement information you would have needed to make an investment decision?	Mark either yes no	Supporting information if NPIs feel that they cannot make an investment decision even though they rated the financial statement information as high decision-useful.		Additional analysis
4.5	If you answered "yes" in question 4.4 please state which additional information you would have needed to make an investment decision.	Open text			
5.1	How did the investment properties of the XY Corp. develop from t=0 to t=1?	Mark either increase decrease	Gain: increase Loss: decrease	Manipulation Check	N/A
5.2	Which information was presented salient in the balance sheet of the XY Corp.?	Please mark one of the following items: None Level label Sensitivity analysis Reconciliation between carrying amounts	Depending on the treatment of the participant there is only one correct answer	Manipulation Check	N/A

MIX
Papier aus verantwortungsvollen Quellen
Paper from responsible sources
FSC® C105338

If you have any concerns about our products, you can contact us on
ProductSafety@springernature.com

In case Publisher is established outside the EU, the EU authorized representative is:
Springer Nature Customer Service Center GmbH
Europaplatz 3, 69115 Heidelberg, Germany

Printed by Libri Plureos GmbH
in Hamburg, Germany